Alice Freeman Palmer

Faithfully Yours.
Alice Freeman Palmer.

Alice Freeman Palmer

The Evolution of a New Woman

RUTH BORDIN

Ann Arbor

THE UNIVERSITY OF MICHIGAN PRESS

92
Pl73b

Library of Congress Cataloging-in-Publication Data

Bordin, Ruth Birgitta Anderson, 1917–
    Alice Freeman Palmer : the evolution of a new woman / Ruth Bordin.
    p.   cm.
    Includes bibliographical references (p.) and index.
    ISBN 0-472-10392-X (alk. paper)
    1. Palmer, Alice Freeman, 1855–1902. 2. Wellesley College—
Presidents—Biography. 3. Women educators—United States—
Biography. I. Title.
LD7212.7 1882.B67 1993
378.744'7—dc20   92-46863
                                                                              CIP

Frontispiece photo of Alice Freeman Palmer courtesy of Wellesley College
Archives.

For the Wednesday lunchers, who each
in her way was a New Woman

Preface

The research for this biography of Alice Freeman Palmer began thirty-five years ago as I put together an exhibit for the Bentley Historical Library honoring the 1957 centennial of the inauguration of the teaching of history at the University of Michigan. Two women who trained in the pioneer history seminar of Charles Kendall Adams caught my attention, Alice Freeman and Lucy Salmon. I was startled to find women pursuing graduate training in history at that early date. I was also caught by the fact that both became distinguished educators with long careers. My interest in Palmer was rekindled thirty years later in the spring of 1987 by a symposium on "Changes in the Lives of Educated Women," sponsored by the Center for the Continuing Education for Women at the University of Michigan. At the symposium I particularized the wider picture of women and higher education in a brief paper on women's experience at the University of Michigan from 1870 to 1987. Palmer's wider influence on women's higher education attracted my attention once more.

Alice Freeman Palmer's career was distinguished and certainly not forgotten by scholars. She was a pioneer alumna of the first great American university to admit women; president of Wellesley College and a key figure on its board of trustees during two of its most crucial decades; the first dean at the University of Chicago; and leader, arbiter, and spokeswoman for women's place in higher education during much of her adult life. But her name was hardly a household word. Although she attracted her share of media attention during the last two decades of the nineteenth century, only specialists in the higher education of women or loyal Wellesley chauvinists and college history buffs are likely to remember her today.

Nonetheless the story of Alice Freeman Palmer's life, lived during a time when women rapidly invaded the professions, especially edu-

cation, when the financial independence of middle-class single females was gaining increasing acceptance, when to marry almost inevitably meant the end of a professional career, illustrates graphically
the many attempts to solve the problems that have concerned independent women down to the present day.

I have tried to convey in chapter headings the uncertain progress
of this evolving New Woman's life and her ambivalent quest for independence. Alice Freeman as president of Wellesley experienced
fulfillment. In contemplating marriage she faced a dilemma, temporarily resolved with the challenge of her position at Chicago, and she
eventually found a kind of resolution by accepting a dual life and a
dual role, a grand compromise that encompassed both fulfillment
and sacrifice.

Her problems a hundred years ago were not so different from
those of many late-twentieth-century women. Although she died
fifteen years before I was born, I found it almost too easy to identify
with Alice Freeman Palmer. Many of the issues she faced and the
compromises she accepted were close to the dilemmas that had
plagued my own life of seventy-five years. As I shared her story with
other academic women they too found resemblances to their own
victories and perplexities. A long look at a much earlier prototype
may not assist in solving those problems, but there is a certain reassur-
ance in the knowledge that the problems have been tackled before
and workable compromises achieved even in a less liberated age.

Because of the contributions she made and the way she lived her
life, Alice Freeman Palmer is important to historians of women, historians of education, and historians of professionalism. Nonetheless,
she has not been the subject of a full-length biography since her
husband's eulogistic memoir in 1908.[1] Despite a wealth of sources,
her life course has not been investigated exhaustively. Caroline Hazard edited a delightful exchange of courtship letters between Freeman and the man who became her husband.[2] Sketches of her appear
in studies dealing with women's higher education in the nineteenth
century.[3] Wellesley College's history has been done at twenty-year
intervals during this century, and Alice Freeman is never forgotten.[4]
The most extensive treatment of her work at Wellesley is in Patricia
Palmieri's doctoral dissertation.[5] Her Chicago career has been largely
ignored.[6] But all of this does not add up to adequate treatment of a
significant nineteenth-century educator.

Despite their profusion, sources posed some problems. Although Palmer left behind a rich cache of personal documents, this cache is restricted in scope and time. The only surviving diary is little more than a record book, useful but far from full or intimate. She wrote no autobiography. The vast bulk of her surviving correspondence is with George Herbert Palmer, the Harvard philosopher who became her husband in 1887. Therefore it covers only the period from the onset of their relationship in 1886 until her death. Her young adult years are adequately documented in her correspondence with Lucy Andrews, her college friend and confidant, but this correspondence ended when Lucy joined the Wellesley staff in 1884. Also a large, but insubstantial, file of letters to Eben Horsford relating to Wellesley College business has recently been deposited in the Wellesley Archives. Her presidency and her later influence on Wellesley through its board of trustees were of course recorded in the official minutes, but the dynamics of academic politics must be filled in from other sources, largely from her correspondence with George Palmer.

The published record left by Alice Freeman Palmer is negligible. Much of her influence in higher education was exerted in one-on-one encounters with other public figures and in the public speeches at which she excelled. Unfortunately her speeches were seldom, if ever, written, for she had that nineteenth-century gift of translating preparation and thought into an inspired spontaneity. She published very little in her lifetime. After her death, some of her writings were assembled by her husband to provide her with an oeuvre.[7]

Lack of published work by Palmer poses particular problems in getting at her ideas. In some ways her intimate life is more accessible than the intellectual framework that sustained her professional work. But of course one reason she did not publish was that a reasoned intellectual framework or ideology was not the way she got things done. She was a pragmatist and an improviser.

Where personal correspondence is available it is a very rich source. After Alice Freeman met George Palmer they saw each other very infrequently until a few months before their marriage, but they wrote confiding, detailed, comprehensive letters, sometimes more than once a day. Throughout their marriage they were frequently separated, and they wrote voluminously, often, and substantively to each other about their work. Thus in some ways Alice Palmer's tenure at the University of Chicago is the best-documented portion of her career. When she was absent from Chicago in Cambridge, she corresponded confidentially and fully with her Chicago colleagues William Rainey Harper, Marion Talbot, Laurence Laughlin, and Robert Herrick. Many of these letters have survived in the University of Chicago Archives and at Wellesley, and it is largely from these private sources, not used extensively before, that this biography has been constructed.

Much of the time I have felt uniquely privileged to participate on the highest level of intimacy in the living of Alice Freeman Palmer's life. I have been in her bedroom and at her table. More importantly, I have been privy to her frustrations with Pauline Durant, Wellesley's always vigilant and often difficult founding mother; I have followed step-by-step her decision to risk her career for marriage; I have watched her futile fight to convince her husband that a joint academic career at the University of Chicago would provide the most fulfilling path for their partnership. When the private sources are good, they are very good indeed. Using these sources I have recreated Alice Freeman Palmer's story. It is the story of a late-nineteenth-century professional woman who died too young to experience the changes the twentieth century brought, but whose life shows some of the problems and some of the solutions typical of both periods. She was born before the Civil War but in her lifelong struggle, often successful, to achieve independence from male control, she exemplifies the New Woman who had evolved by the century's end.

Many friends, colleagues, and archivists have contributed to this project. I owe a special debt to Wilma Slaight, Wellesley's archivist, for her help and support at every stage of this manuscript. I have also been substantially and cheerfully helped by archivists and librarians at the Bentley Historical Library, the Broome County Library, Bryn Mawr College, the University of Chicago, Carleton College, the Houghton Library, the Harvard University Archives, and the Schlesinger Library of Women's History. Two descendants of the Freeman and Palmer families, Stella Freeman Novy and Helen Palmer Avery, have also added several footnotes to the story.

A number of generous men and women, Barbara Sicherman, Christine Weideman, Kenneth Scheffel, Wilma Slaight, Edward Bordin, Marjorie Barritt, and Jean Campbell, as well as my editor and two anonymous readers, have read all or part of the manuscript and assisted in shaping it in useful ways. Kathryn Kearns helped with sources for the Freeman family history.

Diane Hatfield, Katharyn Pandora, Margaret Van Blaricom, and Carol Pintek have performed logistical services with skill, intelligence, and compassion. And Edward Bordin for over fifty years has been my understanding partner in resolving my own dilemma.

NOTES

1. George Herbert Palmer, *The Life of Alice Freeman Palmer* (Cambridge, Mass.: Riverside Press, 1908).
2. Caroline Hazard, ed., *An Academic Courtship: Letters of Alice Freeman Palmer and George Herbert Palmer* (Cambridge: Harvard University Press, 1940).
3. See especially Barbara Solomon, *In the Company of Educated Women: A History of Women and Higher Education in America* (New Haven: Yale University Press, 1985); and Helen Lefkowitz Horowitz, *Alma Mater: Design and Experience in the Women's Colleges from Their Nineteenth Century Beginnings to the 1930's* (New York: Alfred Knopf, 1984).
4. The most recent of these is Jean Glasscock, ed., *Wellesley College 1875–1975: A Century of Women* (Wellesley, Mass.: Wellesley College Press, 1975).
5. Patricia Palmieri, "In Adamless Eden: A Social Portrait of the Academic Community at Wellesley College, 1875–1920" (Ph.D. Diss., Harvard University, 1981).
6. Rosalind Rosenberg, *Beyond Separate Spheres: Intellectual Roots of Modern Feminism* (New Haven: Yale University Press, 1982), barely mentions her. Lynn D. Gordon, *Gender and Higher Education in the Progressive Era* (New Haven: Yale University Press, 1990) concentrates on Marion Talbot's career. George Palmer minimizes and distorts the Chicago period in his memoir.
7. Alice Freeman Palmer and George Herbert Palmer, *The Teacher: Essays and Addresses on Education* (Boston: Houghton Mifflin Co., 1908).

Contents

CHAPTER 1

The New Woman

At the turn of the century, Alice Freeman Palmer, middle-aged, respected, active, and knowledgeable, represented the very essence of what pundits, commentators, and even a few of her own sex had christened the New Woman. She was one of the new educated women whose professional training was on a par with that of her male colleagues. She had received her baccalaureate with honors from the University of Michigan in 1876 and done graduate work in history. She had earned her own living and been economically independent since she was nineteen, teaching and serving as principal in midwestern secondary schools before accepting a professorship at Wellesley College in 1879. She became Wellesley's first real, and clearly seminal, president on the death in 1881 of Henry Fowle Durant, Wellesley's founder, who personally guided the college during its first years. She resigned the presidency when she married but continued to be a major influence on Wellesley College for the rest of her life from the board of trustees.

Her role in higher education expanded, rather than contracted, with her marriage. She became a member of the Massachusetts State Board of Education at a time when teacher training was burgeoning all over the country, an influential supporter of the Annex in its struggle to become Radcliffe College, an advisor to Barnard, an almost perennial officer of Collegiate Alumnae, the rapidly growing and influential organization of college women that later became the American Association of University Women, and the commencement speaker at more graduation exercises than any other women of her era. She was chosen by William Rainey Harper when he opened the University of Chicago to be his first dean, and became his close advisor. She was independent, successful, useful, and one of the best-known women of her time. Although marriage limited her options,

2 / *Alice Freeman Palmer*

it did not result in her being completely submerged in her husband's world. Instead, as a married woman, she established her own identity. In important ways she had taken control of her own life from the time she was a child. She belonged to a new breed—the New Woman.

By 1900 the concept of the New Woman had almost replaced the cult of domesticity and the doctrine of spheres as well as its mid-nineteenth-century corollary, the Ideal of Real Womanhood, as the ideological totem around which women's position in society was viewed by the educated public.[1] Press and pulpit now used the idea of the New Woman as their point of departure when fulminating on the issue of women's proper place. The New Woman, with her younger sister the Gibson girl, had taken her place in American society.[2]

The phrase *New Woman* was coined originally by Henry James and intended by him to characterize American expatriates living in Europe: women of affluence and sensitivity, who despite or perhaps because of their wealth exhibited an independent spirit and were accustomed to acting on their own. The term New Woman always referred to women who exercised control over their own lives be it personal, social, or economic. However, when it came into general use in the United States for the first time, it was attached to the new American professional women emerging in increasing numbers in the last two decades of the nineteenth century.[3] Most of them were college educated. Often these women, like Alice Freeman Palmer and her University of Michigan classmates and friends Lucy Salmon, Angie Chapin, and Mary Marston, were trained at or teaching in the new women's colleges. Or like Eliza Mosher and Cora Benneson, two other early University of Michigan graduates, they pursued careers in medicine or law. They were professionally trained, career and role conscious, and usually self-supporting for a major part or all of their lives. They represented a new generation of American women, independent from male control and as likely to be assisting as receiving help from their families from whom they frequently lived apart. They organized their lives in patterns similar to those of single professional women today.

The New Woman departs from earlier nineteenth-century female innovators, especially social reformers, in her emphasis on taking responsibility for her own life and her independence from male control. As Nancy Cott has said, the New Woman "stood for self-development as contrasted to self-sacrifice or submergence in the family."[4] It is this emphasis on independence that makes her truly new. She is more than a good mother, a good wife, a good daughter. In fact, she need be none of those because she can stand independently.

The concept of the New Woman was not static. In the 1890s the emphasis was on economic independence and professionalism. In the first decades of the twentieth century the term New Woman was used to describe all innovators: reformers, athletes, scientists, Marxists, Bohemians, and aviators. The Jazz Age flapper defined the phalanx in the 1920s.[5] The flapper was more intent on sexual and personal freedom and taking charge of her life in terms of manners and morals, the right to drink or wear short skirts, for example, than a vocation. In this she more closely resembled James's original concept, which was concerned in most part with relatively superficial social conventions that set the behavior of upper-class American young women quite apart from their European counterparts, such as the lack of chaperones, absence of close parental supervision, and freer courtship patterns.[6] But common to all generations of the New Woman was an emphasis on independence from male control. For example, Daisy Miller, one of James's American heroines, asserted, "I've never allowed a gentleman to dictate to me or to interfere with anything I do."[7]

However the economic component of the independence waxed and waned. To the first generation of the New Woman, the one to which Alice Freeman Palmer belonged, professional and economic autonomy were paramount. Manners and morals took second place. While even the reformer grandmother of the New Woman had experimented with modifying social conventions, for example dress reform, the New Woman of the 1880s and 1890s found definition of her status not in the clothes she wore or in shocking social postures, but in financial independence and a career. It was in terms of her career, rather than manners and morals, that Alice Freeman Palmer identified herself. She conformed easily to the social mores of her time. There are occasional hints of the post–World War I New Woman in Alice Freeman Palmer, the freedom with which she accepted sexual attraction as a major factor in her relationship with George Palmer, for example. But the Victorian in her also carefully cherished earlier social codes. She could meet her lover clandestinely in a hotel room or the stateroom of a ship, but she did not invite discovery, as might the 1920s flapper, of these violations of accepted conventions.

Palmer's generation of New Women included the first generation of college-educated women. University-educated, professionally successful, aware of her expertise in her chosen field and eager to use it, Alice Freeman Palmer articulated a dominant voice in the burgeoning arena of higher education for women by the 1890s, and it was that voice which provided the core of her identity as a New Woman. She had trained for her job and expected to be, and was, paid a salary for the positions that she held.[8] Unlike activist women Frances Willard and Susan B. Anthony, for example, she was never (while single) dependent on the vagaries of lecture fees, voluntary collections, and freelance writing for her support. She saw her mission as educating women and guaranteeing their place as professional educators. At Wellesley she helped to perpetuate the secure base professional women faculty had established for themselves in the women's colleges, a beachhead they maintained until World War I and in some places until World War II. At the University of Chicago she attempted, with much less success, to create the same opportunities for women in coeducational universities.

It was Alice Freeman Palmer's recognized position as an educator that placed her among the ranks of the New Woman. To quote George Perry Morris, author and newspaper man:

> If President Bumsted of Atlanta University came north to seek counsel and sympathy, he found it in Mrs. Palmer. Presidents of colleges in foreign lands founded by American Christians turned instinctively to her for advice when they returned to this country in quest of teachers or funds. Donors to educational institutions for women in this country sought her opinion as to the form their gifts should take. Presidents of colleges for men often relied on her practical advice when facing administrative crises, and trusted her judgement in choosing candidates for executive and professorial positions.[9]

The tag New Woman was attached to her by her contemporaries, but with some reservations. President William Herbert Perry Faunce of Brown University described her as blending the ideals of the old and "of the new woman, the synthesis being a coalition and not a mere adhesion."[10] She was seen as proving "that an American woman with culture and spirit can be useful to state and society at large while obedient to the highest domestic ideals."[11]

Of course, what these men were praising was that she eventually married and seemed to preside happily over a home. Unlike her fellow college president, M. Carey Thomas of Bryn Mawr, Palmer was never rebellious about accepting the trappings of women's role. When she married, she had no qualms as did the suffragist Lucy Stone about losing her name. She reveled in being called Mrs. Palmer, although she carefully put the tokens of her academic respectability, Ph.D. and LL.D., after it. Like a true New Woman, however, she never easily relinquished her autonomy, and the painful negotiation that preceded her marriage and at the time of her acceptance of a position at Chicago was a careful exercise in compromise for both her and her husband, although he undoubtedly won the larger share of the bargain.

Although she wanted control over her own life, Alice Freeman Palmer's values were conservative. Palmer was in many ways not a feminist. The term, of course, was not used in her lifetime. During the last quarter of the twentieth century, feminism has been defined, redefined, and differentiated into half a dozen subgroups, one of which has been called "life-process feminism" by Joyce Antler, and defined as "the personal ways in which an individual struggles to achieve autonomy by confronting gender-defined issues at each stage of the life cycle."[12] If one accepts this definition as one aspect of the feminist tradition, Alice Freeman Palmer qualifies as a feminist, but only in part. Certainly her decision to pursue higher education, temporarily eschew marriage, and eventually marry into a partnership (where the negotiation of what marriage would mean to the living of her life and the pursuit of her goals) were gender-defined issues. They would not have arisen in the same way had she been a man. Nor would a man have settled for the same resolution of them.[13] A man would not have been forced to choose between marriage and the presidency of Wellesley, nor would he have had to compromise in accepting an administrative post at Chicago. Gender inevitably shaped her life.

She was very effective at promoting higher education for women. But she hung back, quite consciously, from espousing militant movements. The suffragists made attempts from time to time to engage her in their cause. She was likely to ridicule their efforts. "I have another invitation to be the Wendell Phillips of the woman suffrage movement... " she reported to George Palmer in 1887. "They think I could make a fortune. I suppose I ought to ask your advice before undertaking it, for it might interfere with the other three days of the week."[14] Not until late in her life did she publicly commit herself to the vote. She espoused temperance and peace, those mainstream movements of the late nineteenth century, but so did everyone else. She spent no time in the settlement house movement. Although sympathetic to the oppressed, she was not really a reformer, as her mother had been.[15] She was a professional, as were so many of the New Women, be they conservative or liberal in their politics.

Palmer's lack of ideology is perhaps partly explained by the fact that one reason young Alice Freeman followed the path she did was simple expedience. She both wanted and needed to earn her own living as did many of the first generation of college-educated women. Although she was bright, intellectually curious, and enjoyed academic challenges, she did not set out to change the world. First and foremost she needed financial independence. She chose to accomplish this in a way that she would enjoy. She performed a mildly venturesome act when she matriculated at the age of seventeen at the University of Michigan in 1872 and became the first member of her family to seek a baccalaureate, but her venturesomeness was within the parameters of acceptable female behavior for her era and class. At the same time, it was perfectly clear that her education was expected to provide economic rewards not only to her, but to her family.

Professionalism and careerism, not reform, provided the major themes of Alice Freeman Palmer's life. A life of service, but service exchanged for a salary, was the pattern she followed, a pattern also followed by many of her contemporaries. She earned money because she needed it. She enjoyed (most of the time) the career that brought her the salary that met her economic needs, but her private papers contain little talk, especially in the earlier years, about her professional contribution to a better society or to enhancing women's new role.

The earlier generation of activist women had been either single or married—marital status was not a condition of their participation in the public world of volunteerism or reform movements. Some of this generation, usually if they were either spinsters or widowed (for example, Susan B. Anthony and Frances Willard), made their livelihoods through the causes they espoused. Others received support from their husbands and families. The first generation of college-educated professional women were supported in a different way, by being paid a salary for practicing their professions. They were slow to marry and almost never married during the active phase of their professional careers, not because men were afraid of their accomplishments or found educated women undesirable as mates, nor because the women themselves cherished their independence too dearly to find marriage unattractive. They sacrificed their emotional independence gladly enough in close, demanding relationships with other women that did not bar them from earning their own livings. And Alice Freeman, while she found the repeated proposals she received a nuisance at times, never discouraged the men whose company she enjoyed from making offers of marriage. Postponement of marriage was largely an economic decision because of the overriding social dictum that middle-class married women did not work for money.

She became an independent professional woman, at least in part, because it was imperative she achieve economic autonomy and financially assist her family which suddenly found itself in straightened circumstances. However a seventeen-year-old female did not leave the rural Susquehanna Valley in 1872 to be one of the first women students at the University of Michigan without a considerable drive to control her own life and prove her own worth. And it was not long before she had translated practical economic need into a strongly felt mission to further women's right to higher education and to careers in higher education on an equal basis with men.

She also wanted marriage and a home and probably children. At the height of her career, when she was president of Wellesley College, she fell in love. She then faced a new dilemma. Should she sacrifice her career or fight to preserve it? She fought, lost her career in some ways, but preserved her position in the world of higher education. Hers is the story of the evolution of a New Woman in the closing decades of the nineteenth century, an evolution represented in her triumphs and her disappointments, her successes and her failures in asserting control over her own life.

There are many subthemes to Alice Freeman Palmer's story and all of them complement the general story of the New Woman: the importance of networking among early professional women, the inevitable part that the old concept of "womanliness" played in the career of even the successful nineteenth-century New Woman, the role of the Midwest in the creation of the eastern women's colleges, and Palmer's failed attempt to secure a firm and lasting equality of opportunity for women in the coeducational university.

One of these subthemes documents in some detail the role of the Midwest, especially the old Northwest, in the professionalization of women educators and development of the eastern women's colleges. Innovation in women's higher education began in the old Northwest. When the new eastern women's colleges, Vassar, Wellesley, Smith, and later Mount Holyoke as it moved to collegiate status, and Radcliffe as it progressed from Harvard Annex to affiliate status, had to find faculty to teach the young women eager to enroll in the new collegiate programs. Men, trained in the East, were of course available and used at Radcliffe, Vassar, and Smith, but Wellesley was committed to a female faculty. No eastern colleges, except a few struggling institutions that were little more than ladies' seminaries, provided collegiate training for women until 1872 when Cornell opened its doors a tiny crack. But by 1872 the University of Michigan had women students in three departments. Also, Oberlin and Antioch had been awarding baccalaureate degrees to women since 1837, and those degrees represented solid training. It was to the old Northwest that the new women's colleges looked in large measure for faculty and staff. A recent study laments the dearth of research on the migration of eastern-educated women to other parts of the country.[16] Actually much of the migration was the other way. At least in terms of professional training one can say that the New Woman migrated from west to east as well as the other way around.

In December of 1925, the *Wellesley Alumnae Magazine* catalogues in a brief article, "Michigan Women at Wellesley," eighteen Michigan-trained women who taught at Wellesley in the nineteenth century.[17] The Michigan contribution to Wellesley's seminal decades was by far the largest academic influence on the college. Mary Sheldon Barnes in history, Katharine Coman in economics, Olive Mary Marston and Angie Chapin in Greek, Anna Bardwell Gelston in mathematics, and Lucy Andrews in ethics were only part of the roster. There were few places other than Michigan from which to recruit. Although most of the new state universities west of the Alleghenies reluctantly permitted women to join their student bodies, they had yet to establish their academic credentials. Michigan was the oldest of the transmountain institutions and traced its roots to a Detroit academy established in 1817, twenty years before Michigan achieved statehood. By the 1870s it was a full-scale university, the largest in the land, with a faculty whose scholarship was nationally recognized and with standards as high as any American university. No wonder it was a primary source of women to staff the faculties of the new women's colleges.

Another aspect of Palmer's career as a professional educator is even more remarkable. After her marriage she commuted to the University of Chicago for three years, from 1892 to 1895, serving as dean and close advisor to President William Rainey Harper, helping to build a great new graduate university in the Midwest that would provide equal opportunity for women as faculty, staff, and students. Here again the Midwest pioneered, providing the New Woman with opportunities that would not open to her in the great eastern universities for three-quarters of a century. And this work of a New Woman at Chicago had lasting effects, especially on research. Rosalind Rosenberg sees the new academic women, especially at Chicago, many of them there at least indirectly because of Palmer, as vanguards in abolishing male and female stereotypes. By 1920 a generation of research centered in Chicago had destroyed the myth of the rational man and irrational woman.[18]

Alice Freeman Palmer's career in higher education took place during a period of enormous expansion in college enrollments as well as significant expansion in the scope of education, especially training for the professions. For the first time women were instrumentally active in the direction these new developments took, and in the initial stages Palmer played a key role. Women not only influenced old scholarly fields, they also developed new ones, like sanitary science (later public health) and social work. Palmer, especially at Chicago, helped set the stage. She was a leading actor in higher education during a period of flux not to be duplicated until after World War II. This was also an era when the goals of higher education, especially undergraduate education, were being articulated as the "well-rounded" person who had been prepared for the challenges of modern life. It was the pattern of campus life that Palmer and Marion Talbot attempted to establish at Chicago and spread from there to other coeducational institutions that best embraced this goal.

Alice Freeman Palmer's biography is also the story of a marriage, of changing gender roles that the New Woman both faced and helped to bring about. It is the story of one woman's dilemma and one woman's solution, or perhaps one couple's solution. This too makes her a pioneer among the New Women. Many of Alice Freeman's generation of educated professional women who chose active, challenging careers did not marry. Alice Freeman eventually made a husband and home her life choice, but in such a way that she preserved her professional stature and prestige. Her position as the dominant voice in women's higher education was not thereby challenged. In this she foreshadowed the second generation of the New Woman like Crystal Eastman or Lucy Sprague Mitchell, who came of age in the first decade of the twentieth century. The second generation often married but, as Eastman said, was not "satisfied with love, marriage and a purely domestic career. But she wants husband, home, and children, too. How to reconcile these two desires in real life, that is the question."[19]

Alice Freeman Palmer's story also had a purely personal side. Along with the professionalism and independence that distinguished the New Woman and made Alice Freeman Palmer one of them, she brought a magic, a charisma, that transformed a simple human relationship into high excitement for those who knew her. Lucy Sprague Mitchell, a prominent educator who was one of her primary disciples, wrote that "to me, she seemed—and still seems—one of the great people in the world. . . . Her zest for life, her capacity to listen as wholeheartedly as she talked, her versatility, her light touch even in executive matters in which she was a master, made her literally unique."[20] Lyman Abbott, Boston clergyman, critic, and an older contemporary of Freeman Palmer concurred. He wrote that from their first meeting she fascinated him. She seemed to him "like an opal, you can be sure to find a wonderful life in it, but with what changing colours it will glow when you next look at it, you cannot tell."[21]

As anthropologist and educator Catherine Bateson has pointed out, everyone crafts her own life, but the innovative life is harder to live than one that unfolds through preexisting paths worn smooth by generations of use.[22] Alice Freeman Palmer chose some well-worn paths and made many new ones for herself. The problems she faced and the solutions she found were sometimes out of the past and sometimes foreshadowed those arrived at by women in the twentieth century. Her life is a vivid case study in the evolution of the New Woman.

NOTES

1. For a recent commentary summarizing how historians have viewed the ideology of spheres over the last generation, see Linda K. Kerber, "Separate Spheres, Female Worlds, Woman's Place: the Rhetoric of Women's History," *Journal of American History* 75 (June 1988): 9–39. For a discussion of the ideal of the Real Woman, see Frances B. Cogan, *The All-American Girl: The Ideal of Real Womanhood* (Athens: University of Georgia Press, 1989). See Carroll Smith-Rosenberg, *Disorderly Conduct: Visions of Gender in Victorian America* (New York: Oxford University Press, 1985), p. 176–77, for a comprehensive discussion of the concept of the New Woman. Patricia Marks, *Bicycles, Bangs, and Bloomers: The New Woman in the Popular Press* (Lexington, University Press of Kentucky, 1990), is the most recent study of both English and American New Women. Marks sees the term itself as derogatory, which was not always true. Martha Banta, in *Imaging American Women: Idea and Ideals in Cultural History* (New York: Columbia University Press, 1987), devotes her first chapter to a valuable, well-illustrated discussion of the American Girl and the New Woman. See also Elaine Showalter, *Sexual Anarchy: Gender and Culture at the Fin de Siècle* (New York: Viking, 1990), chap. 3; Tiziana F. Rota "Between 'True Women' and 'New Women': Mount Holyoke Students, 1837–1908" (Ph.D. diss., University of Massachusetts, 1983); Anna Firor Scott, "What Then, Is This New Woman?" *Journal of American History* 65 (December 1978): 679–703. In England the invention in 1894 of the term New Woman is attributed to the feminist novelist, Sarah Grand. See Lucy Bland, "Marriage Laid Bare," in Jane Lewis, *Labour and Love: Women's Experience of Home and Family, 1850–1940* (Oxford: Basil Blackwell, 1986); Gail Cunningham, *The New Woman and the Victorian Novel* (London: Macmillan Press, 1978), chap. 2; and the introduction to *The New Woman and her Sisters: Feminism and the Theater,* ed. Vivien Gardner and Susan Rutherford (Ann Arbor: University of Michigan Press, 1992).

2. The term was in popular, lay use by the end of the century. For example, Jennie Muzzey Covert, a pioneer coed at the University of Wisconsin described herself as "an incipient 'new woman'" when reminiscing of her 1870s college career. (Jennie Muzzey Covert, "At the Dawn of Coeducation," *Wisconsin Alumni Magazine,* March 1901, 243.)

3. The same pattern and use of the term occurred in England at about the same time. See Jane Rendall, ed., *Equal or Different: Women's Politics, 1800–1914* (Oxford: Basil Blackwell, 1987), 143.

4. Nancy F. Cott, *The Grounding of Modern Feminism* (New Haven: Yale University Press, 1987), 39.

5. Estelle B. Freedman has surveyed the literature on the New Woman of the 1920s. See "The New Woman: Changing Views of Women in the 1920s," *Journal of American History* 61 (September 1974): 372–93. See also James R. McGovern, "The American Woman's Pre–World War I Freedom in Manners and Morals," and Kenneth A. Vellis, "Prosperity's Child: Some Thoughts on the Flapper," in *Women's Experience in America: An Historical*

Anthology, ed. Esther Katz and Anita Rapone (New Brunswick: Transaction Books, 1980), 345–88; Dorothy Brown, *Setting a Course: American Women in the 1920s* (Boston: Twayne, 1987); a recent literary study of the 1920s New Woman is Sarah Beebe Fryer, *Fitzgerald's New Women: Harbingers of Change* (Ann Arbor, Mich.: UMI Research Press, 1988); see also Marks, *Bicycles, Bangs, and Bloomers,* chap. 6.

6. See Henry James, *Daisy Miller* (London: Martin Secker, 1915).

7. Ibid., 72.

8. The literature on professionalism in American culture is extensive. The most useful is Burton Bledstein, *The Culture of Professionalism: The Middle Class and the Development of Higher Education in America* (New York: W. W. Norton, 1976). See also Magali Sarfatti Larson, *The Rise of Professionalism: A Sociological Analysis* (Berkeley: University of California Press, 1977); Rudolph C. Blitz, "Women in the Professions, 1870–1970," *Monthly Labor Review,* May 1974, p. 34–39; Penina Migdal Glazer and Miriam Slater, *Unequal Colleagues: The Entrance of Women into the Professions, 1890–1940* (New Brunswick, N.J.: Rutgers University Press, 1987); John H. Ehrenreich, *The Altruistic Profession: A History of Social Work and Social Policy in the United States* (Ithaca: Cornell University Press, 1985), chap. 2; Gloria Moldow, *Women Doctors in Gilded Age Washington: Race, Gender, and Professionalization* (Urbana, Ill.: University of Illinois Press, 1987), 162–68.

9. *American Monthly Review of Reviews,* February 1903, 170.

10. Ibid., 171.

11. Ibid.

12. Joyce Antler, "Was She a Good Mother: Some Thoughts On a New Issue for Feminist Biography," in Barbara Harris and Jo Ann McNamara, eds., *Women and the Structure of Society: Selected Research From the Fifth Berkshire Conference on the History of Women* (Durham, N.C.: Duke University Press, 1984), 53. I find Naomi Black's definition of feminism most congenial, "advocacy of the Rights of Women (based on the theory of the equality of the sexes)," in *Social Feminism* (Ithaca: Cornell University Press, 1989), 19.

13. One historian of higher education saw Palmer reflect the ambivalence toward the domesticity ideal that was institutionalized at Wellesley, in that as president she attempted to combine strong academic programs with the cultivation of the ideal of true womanhood. Frankfort saw this dichotomy become a personal crisis over the issue of marriage. Roberta Wein [Frankfort], "Women's Colleges and Domesticity," *History of Education Quarterly* (Spring 1974): 31–47; Frankfort, *Collegiate Women: Domesticity and Career in Turn of the Century America.* (New York: New York University Press, 1977), chaps. 2–3.

14. Alice Freeman to George Herbert Palmer, January 9, 1887. Typescripts of correspondence between Alice Freeman Palmer and George Herbert Palmer, Wellesley College Archives. Hereafter cited as Wellesley Typescripts. Originals of these letters are to be found in the George Herbert Palmer Papers, Houghton Library, Harvard University.

15. Alice Freeman Palmer's resistance to reform causes was not necessarily typical of professional women. See Robyn Muncy, *Creating a Female Dominion*

in American Reform, 1890–1935 (New York: Oxford University Press, 1991), Introduction.

16. Sally Schwager, "Educating Women in America," *Signs* 12 (Winter 1987): 336.

17. "Michigan Women at Wellesley," *Wellesley Alumnae Magazine* December 1925.

18. Rosalind Rosenberg, "The Academic Prism: The New View of American Women," in *Women of America: A History*, ed. Carol Berkin and Mary Beth Norton (Boston: Houghton Mifflin Co., 1979), 319–35; and Rosenberg, *Beyond Separate Spheres: Intellectual Roots of Modern Feminism* (New Haven: Yale University Press, 1982), chap. 2.

19. Crystal Eastman as quoted in *The New Woman: Feminism in Greenwich Village, 1910–1920*, June Sochen, (New York: Quadrangle Books, 1972), 124.

20. Lucy Sprague Mitchell, *Two Lives: The Story of Wesley Clair Mitchell and Myself* (New York: Simon Schuster, 1953), 73.

21. Lyman Abbott, *Silhouettes of My Contemporaries* (London: George Allen and Unwin, 1922), 60–61.

22. Catherine Bateson, *Composing a Life* (New York: Atlantic Monthly Press, 1989), 1–2.

CHAPTER 2

Genesis

Alice Elvira Freeman was born February 21, 1855, at Colesville, Broome County, New York. Colesville was a tiny community, not really a village, but simply a collection of farms in the Susquehanna River valley, not far from the Pennsylvania border. Binghamton was the nearest town of any size. The area was then, as it is today, beautiful, wooded, hilly, fertile country with the winding Susquehanna River providing, in the nineteenth century, both an avenue of travel and a source of ever-changing pastoral beauty. Vistas were both intimate and distant. Rain, fog, and sun, the varying light of morning, midday, and evening, the gradual but dramatic change of seasons, all added to the rich visual panorama the valley provided. Lumbering was the original industry. Oxen hauled the logs to mills that used waterpower to saw them. Some mills continued to exist into the late nineteenth century, but by the time Alice was born, much of the timber was gone, and dairy farming was the major occupation of the valley's people.

Alice's paternal grandfather, James Freeman, had been part of the first wave of New England migration that peopled west central New York late in the eighteenth century. Soon after the Revolutionary War he walked from Connecticut to take up land along the Susquehanna. The elder James Freeman was to marry a Knox, daughter of James Knox, a Scotsman and member of George Washington's Lifeguard who left his family's lands near Stockbridge, Connecticut, about the same time as Freeman. Both families became substantial landowners in the valley.[1]

Alice drew her physical characteristics from her father, James Warren Freeman. He was a large man, tall, red-headed, and the red lights in Alice's abundant dark hair were her father's legacy. Her

15

Alice Freeman at age five. (Courtesy of
Wellesley College Archives.)

husband also credited James with bestowing on Alice what he called
her "moral beauty."[2]

Alice's mother, Elizabeth Josephine, was descended from Roswell
Higley, another Revolutionary War veteran and early settler who
acquired land in the Occanum area near Windsor.[3] She was one of
five daughters, all reported beautiful, of Samuel Higley, a Colesville
farmer, and Elvira Frost, a school teacher. From her mother's family,
Alice acquired her dark hair and eyes. Her mother, like her father,
was amply proportioned, and Alice was tall, nearly five feet ten when
she graduated from college, but she was of slender build and weighed
a mere hundred and eight pounds.[4]

Alice's mother was only seventeen when Alice was born. James
Freeman was thirteen years her senior, twenty-nine at the time of his
marriage, and Alice later saw herself and her mother growing up

together. Certainly Alice was given heavy responsibilities as a small child. By the time she was five she had acquired a brother, Fred, and two sisters, Ella Louise and Roxie Estelle, usually called Stella. Her husband reports that from early childhood she carried her share of household tasks. As the eldest daughter she was busy gathering eggs, making beds, dressing the three younger children, and drying dishes long before she started school.[5]

Not only did mother and child share farm and household tasks, they also shared a concern with public questions. Elizabeth Freeman taught briefly before her marriage, but her generation of educated middle-class women most often turned to reform causes rather than careers to expand women's sphere. She was an ardent worker in the temperance cause throughout her life, campaigned with equal zeal for protective legislation for women and children, and was the moving force behind the establishment of a hospital for women and children in Saginaw, Michigan, her residence during the latter half of her life.[6] Causes were important to Elizabeth Freeman, and even when she was ill, she continued her many public concerns. But during these early years Alice and her mother learned and worked together, almost like sisters, as the precocious, eldest child assumed more and more responsibilities. This closeness to her mother was to affect Alice's life in more than one way. Her activist mother may have provided a model for Alice as educator and advocate. Perhaps more importantly, Alice's insistence on the training that would make her financially independent and able to support herself was inspired in part by her mother's vulnerability to the vagaries of the family's fortunes.

Elizabeth Freeman does not come through clearly as a person in Alice's surviving correspondence. I would hardly have guessed at the breadth of her interests had I not discovered them through other sources. She is someone Alice asks for a length of fabric or a bit of lace to remodel an old garment rather than as a confidant or source of support. Alice's interactions with her siblings, Stella, Ella, Fred, and with her father, are much more substantive. Later Alice often treated her mother's myriad demands as a confounded nuisance, although she always gave her the support she needed. She emulated her mother in many ways, but she also refused to identify with her completely. Her father could also annoy her, but she adored him despite his faults. Her feelings toward her mother were much more ambivalent. However, her mother had provided a model, a woman whose interests went far beyond the domestic sphere and who tried to make a difference in the public world. However, it was James Freeman whom Alice preferred as a friend and companion throughout her life rather than her mother. It was her father who in 1884 accompanied her to Europe the first time. After she left home it was the hours with her father that she most cherished on visits to the family. It was her father's interest in further education, in science, and in helping people in a personal, hands-on way that shaped the direction of her life rather than her mother's devotion to changing the world through reform causes. Alice took, as everyone does, from both her parents in shaping her own identity. But it was her father, despite his failures, who called forth her deepest love.

Alice influenced her siblings, but, as the eldest child, they seem to have had a relatively minor influence on her except to add to her cares and responsibilities. The older of her sisters was to a major extent dependent on her all of Alice's life. Her younger sister died as a young adult. Her brother was always a cherished companion and friend, someone she enjoyed, and she willingly helped to finance his education, but he was not someone she looked to for advice or support.

The Freemans, Knoxes, Higleys, and Frosts provided Alice with a sturdy, stable, and hardworking set of forebears. Nineteenth-century county histories show them as prosperous lumbering and farming families, but not taking political leadership in the county. They did not become county officials or justices of the peace. Although all of these families had substantial landholdings, the young Freemans, while owning their own farm, seem not to have inherited money.[7] The family was not poor, although Alice's husband, George Palmer, liked to think of them that way. One of Alice's nieces was certain that James Freeman was "one of the wealthier members of the community."[8] In terms of his original land holdings this may well have been true. However, the James Freemans, like farm families generally, appear to have had few cash reserves, and in 1877, they lost their land and all their other property because of James Freeman's unwise investments of 1873 in a speculative mining venture which left him with a large burden of debt.[9] The rented house in Windsor where they lived during Alice's school days was a comfortable, tasteful ten-room Greek revival dwelling on Windsor's main street, but not markedly different from a number of other residences in the town. They were clearly middle class, but the family fortunes were highly volatile.

According to Alice Freeman, hers was a happy childhood. She loved the countryside and found sustenance in the quiet pleasures close contact with the earth provided: changing seasons, growing things, preserving the land's abundant bounty. As her husband wrote, "She knew the farmyard, the country road, the breeding cattle, the upturned soil."[10] Although she never again lived on a working farm, she always gloried in rural pursuits and the Susquehanna River valley was always home. Throughout her life Alice Freeman was the competent farm girl who could bottle the surplus crab apples, make jam from the uneaten peaches, or remodel and refashion a still-usable dress. Much of her early adult life was lived in institutional settings or in boarding houses at the University of Michigan, or in Wellesley's College Hall, and she seems to have eaten what was put in front of her without protest or much comment. Her University of Michigan student letters are remarkably free of the age-old student complaint about the food. But she was always quick to organize a celebratory feast in college rooms and never missed a church oyster supper. After her marriage servants helped her in her Cambridge house and the Botsford farm. She rarely participated directly in housekeeping chores except on visits to her parents where she would wallpaper a room, put up produce for the winter, or dig up a flower-bed. On the rare occasions she performed them, however, everyday tasks gave her great satisfaction. And her childhood experiences had left her with practical common sense and useful knowledge of the household arts that she used professionally in institutional management through her life.

But there was another side to Alice, perhaps fostered by her parents or perhaps the result of her own talents and inclinations. Alice taught herself to read at three, and this in a household which, although literate and well informed, was certainly not a place of learning. From an early age she loved to read aloud, and like many of her generation, she continued to enjoy that favorite Victorian pastime for the rest of her life. Her husband, among others, commented on her beautiful voice and suggested that her devotion to reading to friends and family developed her skills in public speaking.[11]

Other than that she loved books and reading and was also a competent assistant with farm chores and household tasks, we know little of Alice as a child on the Susquehanna farm. A daguerreotype made when she was five shows a solemn, alert, thoughtful moppet, with masses of dark curly hair and enormous dark eyes. But already she was developing a public persona. The woman who later was much admired for her eloquent extemporaneous addresses was foreshadowed by the child attending a village festival who awoke from her nap, stood on a table, recited a poem with fervor, and when the audience applauded, in sheer delight at her own success, clapped her hands along with them.[12]

She had a will of her own and a quick temper. Tantrums where she threw herself down and kicked her heels against the floor were not unknown. But she early learned to couple her determination with self-control. George Palmer included in his memoir of Alice an anecdote that was obviously a much-cherished family story. The Freemans, still on the farm, were at evening prayers. A june bug came through the open window and settled in Alice's thick hair. She kept quiet and attentive until the prayer was over and the family rose from its knees. Only then she burst out, "I wanted to scream, but I couldn't upset you and God!"[13]

All of this was family lore, affectionately recorded by George Herbert Palmer, but what really made this young woman tick we can only guess. Her competence was obvious. Everyone loved her, as testified to a hundred times over the years. She was always her father's favorite. Her students adored her, her colleagues were devoted. Men found her engaging. Her temper and determination remained with her throughout her life, but seldom out of control. She managed her feelings well. She was always optimistic, flexible, and could see the best way out of a tough situation. She faced, with aplomb and serenity, what to others would have seemed insurmountable frustrations: the interruption of her college years, the relinquishment of the presidency of Wellesley on her marriage, her bouts with tuberculosis and her family's penchant for poor health and financial crises. No doubt these frustrations inspired on occasion both anger and despair. But these emotions were always followed by determination to solve the problem in the most satisfying, efficient way possible. She never wasted time complaining; instead she managed. Otherwise God and those near to her might have been upset.

The family's financial affairs were complicated by James Freeman's decision in 1861, when Alice was six, to study medicine. He began by attaching himself to the physician in the next town as an apprentice, but the next year he entered the Albany Medical School, a proprietary school founded in the 1830s with some state assistance and from which he graduated in 1864. Freeman was following a common pattern in medical education. Medical schools replaced apprenticeship as the dominant form of training in the second quarter of the nineteenth century. By 1860 there were forty-seven such degree-granting institutions, sixteen of them in the Northeast. Most states treated an M.D. diploma as equivalent to a license.[14] Although requiring residence in Albany, the periods of instruction for James Freeman were fairly brief. Two four-month terms almost universally led to a degree.[15] However, during her husband's absences, Elizabeth Freeman not only cared for her four young children, but supported the family and her husband's schooling by managing the farm.[16]

What sent James Freeman off searching for a new career in 1861? No doubt he was a restless man. This was not the last major change in life patterns that he asked of his family. When he returned from Albany, the family moved to nearby Windsor, one of the oldest towns in the valley. Ten years later he shifted his scene of operations to Otego, New York, and only a few years after that to Saginaw, Michigan. He found it hard to take root. However, his decision to train for a career in medicine coincided with the outbreak of the Civil War. Did he see himself in the army as a surgeon? He was thirty-three in 1861 and never used his newly acquired medical skills serving in the Union armies, but many his age and older did. Or had he decided that farming in the Susquehanna Valley would not provide his growing family with an adequate living and that medicine was a way to improve his fortunes? George Palmer implies that one of James Freeman's motives could have been to earn a better living, and reports that the family's income increased after he became a physician.[17] This may have been true in the long run. Perhaps he wanted another intellectual challenge, for in the last analysis, a country doctor in the mid-nineteenth century could not expect great prosperity. Medicine was neither the high-prestige or high-income profession that it became in the twentieth century.

Assessing developmental influences is at best a tricky business. The pitfalls of extrapolation are many. Evidence that Alice felt her father's departure as a traumatic experience would have to be secondhand either in a letter from her parents or contributed by Alice

Alice Freeman as a young girl. (Courtesy of
Wellesley College Archives.)

long after the fact in the form of reminiscence. No such letter or memoir is available. But given the lifelong relationship between Alice and her parents, it seems likely that this bright, sensitive, five-year-old felt her father's absence, which she only partly understood, as a deep deprivation and a dire threat to her security. Twice Alice was to lose her father as protector and guardian. His departure for medical school was the first time. The second was when his speculative ventures, during her last two years at college, left him bankrupt and broken and in acute need of rescue by her. We know she responded constructively and courageously in the second instance. She took charge of her own life, made heroic efforts to assist her family, and made it possible for her father eventually to rehabilitate himself. We know almost nothing about her experience of abandonment when she was five or the effect of his departure on her mother, but that trauma also may have contributed to her decision to pursue a career.[18]

Alice began attending the nearby rural district school when the family still lived on the farm. Before she was five, she was saying her lessons to a young woman who was paid two dollars a week to teach all grades and who boarded with the families of her pupils. Alice continued to attend that school until the Freemans left the farm when James Freeman completed medical school in 1864, and they moved to Windsor where Dr. Freeman set up his first practice.

The town of Windsor like the rest of the valley had been settled in the last decade of the eighteenth century, but the village itself, situated on the river, had a population of only 339 in 1860. However, it boasted three churches and an academy.[19] And it was at Windsor Academy, a private school founded in 1837, that Alice matriculated in the fall of 1865 when she was ten years old. Windsor Academy was quite unlike Troy, Ipswich, and Utica, the eastern women's seminaries, with their large proportion of boarders. Instead it provided an educational setting that more closely resembled the public union schools being organized during the same period in the newer states west of the Alleghenies. Most of its pupils lived in the community and it was coeducational. Alice lived at home, her school accepted both male and female students, and offered both sexes the same curriculum. Despite spending much of her professional career in a women's college, all of Alice Freeman's education was obtained in a coeducational setting, and she strongly believed that coeducation supplied the mode in which both men and women were best prepared for real life.

In 1860 Windsor Academy had two teachers and fifty-nine students, thirty-six of whom were in the classical curriculum.[20] Its physical plant was valued at slightly less than $4,000, compared to Utica Female Seminary's generous $23,000, and its annual expenditures (less than $600) were among the lowest of any of the state's academies.[21] However, the principal since 1857 had been Joseph Eastman, a Dartmouth graduate who had attended both Harvard College and Andover Theological Seminary.[22] He was concurrently pastor of the Presbyterian church that the Freemans attended and where James was an elder. The other teacher had been trained at Monmouth College, Princeton, and Yale.

George Palmer called Windsor Academy "a school of superior rank," but he also consistently denigrated the quality of Alice's education and seemed to have had serious doubts about its adequacy.[23] When Windsor Academy's new building was dedicated in 1900 Alice herself said:

Many of us got our start to the life of today in the old Academy. Most of us formed our hopes, our ideals, twenty years or more back, in the old school; there was something more than mere friendship formed—we formed our ideals that were to change and make our life. Words do not properly express the thanks we owe the teachers who taught us—not mathematics, French, Latin and Greek, for we have forgotten a great deal of it; but who taught us truthfulness, to be honest and upright, and who enthused us with that feeling which went with us as we went out to other scenes and to other duties, which made us men and women.[24]

Although Windsor Academy was small and struggling, its teachers were relatively well trained, and it offered a classical preparatory curriculum including Latin, Greek, and mathematics. However, Alice's preparation was not sufficient to satisfactorily fulfill the entrance requirements of the University of Michigan when she matriculated there in 1872, and she had to make up some of the work. Hers was certainly not the best possible secondary education.

Perhaps the critical factor is not whether Windsor Academy provided Alice Freeman with adequate training. More important was that it was close at hand and that she was there at all. In 1870 only 2

Ella, Alice, and Estelle Freeman. Alice was about twelve years old when this photo was taken. (Courtesy of Wellesley College Archives.)

percent of American seventeen-year-olds were graduates of secondary schools. And although more girls than boys were enrolled, secondary education was beyond the scope of most young people, male
or female.[25] Graduation from Windsor Academy inducted Alice
Freeman into a small elite group of educated women.

Alice was a leader at the academy. She won the prizes for elocution
and composition. She led the Windsor delegation to regional oratorical contests. She excelled at her studies. She made the very most she
could of her seven years within its doors. Church, school, and family
were by necessity the center of her life during the Windsor years, for
little Windsor could provide nothing else. But clearly Alice saw herself as a leader and acted as one in that circumscribed community.

Alice's opportunities for exploring the world outside her immediate environs were few. But during the winter of her sixteenth year,
Anna Dickinson, popular Civil War orator and lyceum lecturer, spoke
in Binghamton, and Alice persuaded her father to take her there by
sleigh. It was the first time she had ever heard a woman speak, and
she was deeply moved.[26] No doubt this experience emphasized for
her the new opportunities opening for women. That same winter she
took upon herself a community service quite beyond what would be
usual in a young girl. Her church was poorly lit, and she decided to
remedy the situation herself. During her last year at the academy she
went without a coat and purchased, out of the meager sum she was
saving for college, a chandelier for the sanctuary.[27]

Young Alice Freeman took her religious beliefs very seriously.
During her last year at Windsor Academy, she joined the Presbyterian church.[28] Alice's religious life for the next decade was not untyp-
ical of young mid-nineteenth-century women. She saw conversion
and the conscious pledging of oneself to a personal savior as well as
formal membership in a church as necessary to leading a Christian
life. She also associated Christian practice with good works and governed her daily behavior and her relationships with others by what
she saw as Christian principles. In 1876, in a typical letter to her most
intimate friend, she wrote:

> You know some of the things I have to do for my friends before
> this earthly life of mine is over, and that may not be long as the
> great mystery of sin and sorrow and disappointment is everywhere
> about me. You are asking Heaven and earth, Lucy, why the curse

is upon us. . . . My little one, we must not expect that the cup of sorrow will not be pressed to our pale lips, if He drank it to the bitter dregs for His friends. . . . I feel that my Father has given me and gives me all the time something so infinitely great and good— Himself—and such a beautifully strong hope for the "city that hath foundations" (isn't that a wonderful expression?) that I cannot help longing and trying to give some of it to hopeless hearts. . . . "[29]

There are many such early letters in Alice Freeman's papers. They show how real was her faith in the Christian Trinity, how unquestioning her acceptance of biblical truth, how truly she believed in a life after death.

At this point in her life religious faith was an emotional commitment as well as something society expected of her. She was to continue this approach to religion through her college years when she taught Sunday school and was a leader in the Student Christian Association, and it continued into her teaching career at Wellesley. Although her religious faith became less rigid with the years, in many ways this combination of conformity and commitment continued to be her approach to religion through her life. Alice Freeman was both a sincere believer and a secularizer. She loved this world as she loved her religion. Eventually she was able to further her goals in tandem. But Alice Freeman as a young woman was not a nonconformist or religious liberal. Nor was she attracted, as were some of the women leaders of her generation, to new byways in religious experience and thought such as Swedenborgianism, spiritualism, or later, Christian Science. Only her determined quest for higher education set her apart from the mainstream of her peers as a young woman.

While she attended Windsor Academy, Alice was involved in her first romantic attachment. A young man, Thomas D. Barclay, came to the academy to teach in 1866 hoping to earn enough to repay some of his college debts and finance the remainder of his theological studies. Barclay was a Monmouth College graduate who had also attended Union College and Princeton Theological Seminary, which meant that he was probably a Presbyterian like the Freemans. He remained on the Windsor faculty for four years, and Alice, as star pupil, of course attracted his attention. Although she was only fourteen, he fell in love with her, as many men were to do later, and persuaded her to consent to an engagement.[30] Her mother had married when not much older, and committing herself to an older man would not have seemed strange to her. She was following a family pattern.

In 1870 Barclay returned to school to complete his ministerial training at Yale Divinity School. As he looked forward to his first pastorate, he urged Alice to marry him and join him in his work. But on February 16, 1871, Alice wrote in her journal that she broke the engagement. Although she added that it was terminated by mutual consent, she probably meant that the break was amicable.[31] Barclay soon married a minister's daughter. However, he seemed not to have quite forgotten his early love, for he named his first daughter Alice. And Alice in turn had been deeply influenced by Barclay. Not only had he been an inspiring teacher, he had lent her books and encouraged her intellectual curiosity. He was the first young college graduate she had known intimately, and he unleashed educational ambitions in Alice that resulted in his losing her. Both her diary and George Palmer imply that Alice broke the engagement not because her affections had changed, but because she was determined to attend college.

The possibility of a college education had probably not occurred to her until she met Barclay. Most likely she had known no woman who harbored that ambition. Her family could hardly be expected to encourage her. Even her sympathetic father who amiably transported her fifteen miles to Binghamton so that she could hear Anna Dickinson was distressed that she should want to pursue so expensive and demanding a course.

Nonetheless her father had unwittingly contributed to her decision. Alice had always been very close to her father. When she was a small child she no doubt followed him around the farm, attempting to help with the chores. She accompanied him on his round of house calls, holding his horse while he made his professional visits, after he began the practice of medicine.[32] She must also have identified deeply with his desire for professional education and absorbed some of his enthusiasm for learning a new body of knowledge.

One can also speculate that her father's long absences from home attending medical school influenced Alice Freeman in another way. She was witness to her young mother, already burdened with four small children, having to cope with a man's responsibilities and become an economic mainstay of the family in terms of managing the farm. This may unconsciously have motivated Alice to prepare herself for the possibility that she too might have to earn her own living. More than one woman who either sought or fostered higher education in the nineteenth century saw education as necessary professional training.[33]

The father of Mary Lyon was a pious farmer who died when she was seven, leaving Lyon's mother to run the farm and support the family.[34] Lyon, the founder of Mount Holyoke, early recognized how necessary and useful vocational training was for women. And from the time her mother remarried, when she was thirteen, Lyon had to support herself.[35] Zilpah Grant, the first head of Ipswich Academy and an early colleague of Lyon, lost her father at two. Her mother also had to run the farm.[36] Mary Woolley, president of Mount Holyoke, did not lose her father, but she was in high school when his career as a Congregational minister was traumatically interrupted by deep conflict with his congregation over social issues, and the family's livelihood cut off.[37] Vida Scudder, a distinguished Wellesley professor, was the daughter of a Congregational missionary in India who drowned when she was a small baby, and her mother was forced to return to her family.[38] Katharine Lee Bates, another early Wellesley professor, was born just one month before her father, a Congregational minister, died, leaving his widow with five little children to support.[39]

Alice Freeman Palmer, as a prominent late-nineteenth-century educator, always honored service as the primary goal of women's education, but also saw college training as "life insurance for a girl," a pledge that she can "earn a living for herself and others in case of need."[40] Just because women's proper sphere was thought to be home and family did not mean that in the nineteenth century women were spared assuming responsibility for family support.

For whatever reasons Alice Freeman chose to go to college, her decision was not accepted by her family without some reservations. Her parents had practical grounds for opposing her plans. Although James Freeman seems initially to have been successful in his new calling and acquired a large practice, fees were small and much of a physician's work was done for those who could not pay. He also may have been an inept, albeit ambitious, businessman. The family, possibly better off than it had been on the farm, was still pressed for ready cash. It seemed likely funds could be found to educate only one child, and by nineteenth-century tradition and practice that should be the son.[41] However, Alice was adamant. She would acquire a college education if it took until she was fifty. If her family would consent to help her, she promised not to marry until she had provided the wherewithal to put her brother through college and given her sisters whatever education they wished.[42]

One may easily overestimate how radical on the part of a young woman a decision to go to college was in the 1870s. For an upper-class girl, an immigrant's daughter, or a member of the urban working class, higher education was a radical and usually impossible course. For a daughter of the professional, economically insecure middle classes, it was unusual, but did not necessarily represent a large measure of rebelliousness. More women than men had the secondary educations that prepared them for further training. Although the old colonial men's colleges were closed to them, normal schools, state universities, and church-related colleges were almost all coeducational. The opportunities were really not as limited for middle-class women as has sometimes been suggested.

Alice Freeman through all of her life was a conservative person, and this was especially true in her youth. She did not demand a college education because of a burning zeal for women's rights. Her motivations were only two: a real intellectual curiosity and love of learning, and her practical desire for the "life insurance" policy that she wrote about later and, as time went on, was going to need desperately for herself. She wanted independence and a way to support herself if necessary, and the easiest and most socially acceptable route to that goal was secondary school teaching. By the late 1870s good secondary school posts increasingly required some exposure to higher education. Because for many years she was to have no choice but to earn her own living, she was fortunate to be able to obtain the best education available.

Perhaps a further goal motivated Freeman to seek a college education. As we shall see later, she was always interested less in ideas than in people. By going to college, she could expand her horizons beyond the little community she had already thoroughly explored. Her father had gone off to Albany, not exactly a metropolis, but he must have brought home tales of people he had known whom Alice would never meet if she did not leave home. Thomas Barclay had also experienced other places, other personalities, other ways beyond the isolation of the Susquehanna. Alice yearned for broader horizons, new friends, a wider view of the world.

NOTES

1. Marjorie B. Hinman and Bernard Osborn, *Historical Essays of Windsor, Township and Village* (Windsor, N.Y.: Broome County, 1976), 10, 54; H. P. Smith, *A History of Broome County, New York* (Syracuse: D. Mason and Co., 1885), 327, 330.

2. George Herbert Palmer, *The Life of Alice Freeman Palmer* (Boston: Houghton Mifflin Co., 1908) 20. Cited hereafter as Palmer, *Life*. Some Freeman genealogy is evident in Palmer's biography yet made even more explicit in the joint diary, written on facing pages by Alice and George after their marriage. The diary was also retrospective: year by year and month by month, each recorded on facing pages the events of their lives before they met. (Alice Freeman Palmer Papers, Wellesley College Archives.) This volume is cited hereafter as Diary.

3. Hinman and Osborn, *Historical Essays*, 10–11.

4. *The Chronicle* 7 (June 30, 1876). *The Chronicle* was a student publication of the University of Michigan.

5. Palmer, *Life*, chap. 2.

6. Ibid., 20.

7. Ibid., 21.

8. Mrs. Frederick Novy to Wilma Slaight, archivist, September 8, 1980. Wellesley College Archives.

9. *Windsor Times*, August 20, 30, September 13, 1873; January 8, 1874.

10. Palmer, *Life*, 18.

11. Ibid., 25.

12. Ibid.

13. Ibid., 32–33.

14. William G. Rothstein, *American Physicians in the Nineteenth Century* (Baltimore: Johns Hopkins University Press, 1972), 85, 93, 97; Colin B. Burke, *American Collegiate Populations: A Test of the Traditional View* (New York: New York University Press, 1982), 323.

15. Kenneth Ludmere, *Learning to Heal: The Development of American Medical Education* (New York: Basic Books, 1985), 15.

16. Diary, 1861–64.

17. Palmer, *Life*, 41–42.

18. Some trauma or catastrophe appears common among activist women of the late nineteenth century. Using as her database the hundreds of biographical sketches in *Notable American Women, Women of the Century,* and the first *Women's Who's Who,* Barbara Kuhn Campbell has meticulously documented the unstable, catastrophe-prone family situations during the childhoods of prominent turn of the century American women. *The "Liberated"*

Woman of 1914: Prominent Women in the Progressive Era, (Ann Arbor, Mich.: UMI Research Press, 1979) chap. 1.

19. *Historical and Statistical Gazetteer of New York State* (Syracuse: R. P. Smith Co., 1860), 130.

20. Ibid.

21. Ibid.

22. *Historical and Statistical Record of the State University of the State of New York* (Albany: Weed, Parsons, and Co., 1885) 729; Diary, 1865; Palmer, *Life,* 34–35.

23. Palmer, *Life,* 34.

24. *Windsor Echo,* 15 (1900): 67.

25. Mabel Newcomer, *A Century of Higher Education For Women* (New York: Harper Bros., 1959), 35; Burke, *American Collegiate Populations,* 215.

26. Palmer, *Life,* 43.

27. Ibid., 38, 42.

28. Ibid., 38.

29. Alice Freeman to Lucy Andrews, November 19, 1876. Alice Freeman Palmer Papers, Wellesley College Archives. Hereafter references to Freeman's correspondence is to Alice Freeman Palmer Papers, Wellesley College Archives, unless otherwise noted.

30. Alice's engagement is discussed in Palmer, *Life,* 34–41; and Diary, 1869.

31. Diary, February 16, 1871.

32. Palmer, *Life,* 28.

33. David Allmendinger in his study of Mount Holyoke students observed that economic necessity led young women to prepare to earn their own livings. "Mount Holyoke Students Encounter the Need For Life Planning, 1837–1850," *History of Education Quarterly* 19 (Spring 1979): 27–46. Studies showing the economic compulsions driving nineteenth-century women into paid work are summarized in Schwager, "Educating Women," 351–55.

34. Elizabeth Green, *Mary Lyon and Mount Holyoke: Opening the Gates* (Hanover, N.H.: University Press of New England, 1979), 10.

35. Ibid.

36. Ibid., 38.

37. Anna Mary Wells, *Miss Marks and Miss Woolley* (Boston: Houghton Mifflin Co., 1978), 20.

38. Vida Scudder, *On Journey* (New York: Dutton, 1937), 15.

39. Dorothy Burgess, *Dream and Deed: The Story of Katharine Lee Bates* (Norman: University of Oklahoma Press, 1952), 13–14.

40. Alice Freeman Palmer, *Why Go to College* (New York: Thomas Y. Crowell and Co., 1897), 3–4.

41. Palmer, *Life,* 42.

42. Ibid.

CHAPTER 3

Commitment

In June of 1872 Alice Freeman, accompanied by her father, traveled from Binghamton, New York, to Ann Arbor, Michigan. Their route took them across Canada from Niagara Falls to Windsor, Ontario, and they changed trains in Detroit. Alice made this trip several times over the next four years. The journey was long, tedious, and she had to spend a night on the train, which arrived in Detroit in the morning. But she usually traveled by drawing room, purchased a berth for the night, provided herself with an ample hamper of lunch from home, and enjoyed the journey.[1] This first trip with her father combined the excitement of academic exploration and new geographical vistas. She had never before ventured beyond the Susquehanna River valley.

Alice and James Freeman spent commencement week in Ann Arbor. Their purpose was to secure Alice's admission to the University of Michigan, but their visit also allowed them to assess the institution and the town where Alice was to spend most of the next four years. In the 1870s, Michigan's graduation festivities lasted several days, and candidates for admission the next fall were examined along with the festivities which included baccalaureate services, receptions, class day exercises, and commencement proper. The Freemans seem to have remained in Ann Arbor for the full program. Madelon Stockwell, the first woman admitted to the University of Michigan, only two years before, gave one of the commencement orations, as would Alice four years later.[2]

In the late 1860s and early 1870s when Alice Freeman's decision to go to college was taking solid form, higher education for women was on the threshold of revolutionary expansion. The number of women seeking college training increased dramatically, and, both as cause and result of that increase, society's attitudes toward educated women changed markedly. When Alice Freeman set off for Michigan in 1872, attending college, according to historian Barbara Solomon, was still "an unusual and complicated choice for native white women."[3] However, it was not truly a radical choice, and by 1900 these female collegians were completely accepted. At the turn of the century blacks and the foreign-born found the road to college difficult to travel.

The women who chose to pursue higher education in the early 1870s had, in fact, a wide choice of institutions, ranging from women's colleges and academies (as classical preparatory schools were called) to coeducational universities and teachers' colleges.[4] The best of the women's academies, such as Troy, Mount Holyoke, and Catharine Beecher's schools, foreshadowed the women's colleges, the first of which was Vassar, founded in 1865. The first coeducational institution, Oberlin, had admitted women in 1837, followed by a few other small denominational colleges, for example Hillsdale and Antioch in the 1840s and 1850s. By 1870, eight state universities, all in the West, admitted women and enrolled about 200 female students, and about forty private colleges were coeducational and trained some 600 women. However, many college women, about 2,200 in all, were enrolled in the growing roster of women's colleges.[5] In 1870, according to census figures, over 11,000 women were enrolled in some kind of higher education, mostly in classical academies and teacher training institutions. Women were 21 percent of all students. However, actual numbers were small. Only 0.7 percent of American women eighteen to twenty-one years of age attended college.[6] By 1900, nearly 3 percent of college-age women were receiving training beyond high school, and women made up 40 percent of the total students in tertiary institutions.[7]

Why did increasing numbers of women aspire to college education in the last decades of the nineteenth century? In part, no doubt, because the colleges were there. The middle decades of the nineteenth century were a period of rapid college building in the United States, rivaled only by post–World War II expansion. State colleges and universities proliferated west of the Alleghenies and in the South. Part of this pattern of new institution building was stimulated by the Morill Act, which passed Congress in 1863 and offered federal land grants to states that provided agricultural education. But the number of church-related colleges also increased rapidly at mid-century. In the Midwest the new immigrant denominations, a half-dozen Lutheran synods reflecting national origins and two Dutch Reform bodies founded their own colleges, imitating the patterns earlier established by the Anglo-protestant denominations. Not all of these institutions admitted women, but most of the immigrant denominational colleges did, and the new teachers' colleges, usually funded at least in part by the states, invariably accepted women. Although the many new Catholic colleges were closed to women, Catholic women's academies multiplied.[8] Hardly anyone in the settled parts of the country lived more than a few miles from some college or other.

Another factor directly encouraged the education of women. Employment opportunities were growing. By 1870 one woman in eight over ten years of age was employed.[9] Most of their jobs were as servant girls or factory hands, but women had also preempted the teaching profession. The few men who continued to be schoolmasters in the post–Civil War period were largely in administrative posts or taught briefly to earn money to continue their professional educations. Women became the teachers, and, as secondary schools increased in numbers, the demand for educated women increased proportionately.[10]

From the beginning, women's higher education was intended as professional education. The early academies saw themselves as training teachers. For example, Alfred Academy, and later University, in western New York which was coeducational from its beginnings, defined its primary mission as training teachers, and at mid-century 150 teachers were graduated there annually.[11] The first colleges admitting women and the women attending those colleges saw teacher training as their function. Even fiction emphasized that American "girls" going to college were after professional training and the means of earning a living.[12] The same thing was true in England. Queen's College and Bedford College, opening in the late 1840s, were intended to upgrade the training of governesses. The North London Collegiate School for Girls and Cheltenham Ladies College, both dating from the 1850s, trained teachers for the middle schools.[13] Women also became teachers in Germany. They were hired in Berlin for the first time in 1863. By 1880 women totaled 461 out of 1,490 public elementary school teachers, and in the late 1860s and 1870s institutions for training them proliferated.[14] Higher education for women had professional roots on both sides of the Atlantic. Women went to college to prepare for a profession as well as to indulge their desire for knowledge.[15]

At the same time, the young woman who aspired to college faced considerable social pressure to stay home. A college education was not viewed as a broad highway to social prestige and upward mobility, although for Alice Freeman it eventually led to both. Nor was higher education seen as preparing women for homemaking and parenthood, although seminaries sometimes framed their purposes in domestic rhetoric. Instead conventional wisdom decreed that homemaking could best be taught by female relatives, and parents were likely to see the overeducated female as unsuited for marriage or at least unmarriageable. And if parents, who paid most of the bills, did not see it that way, pundits did.

Although earlier in the century women's ability to learn had been seriously questioned, the educability of women had been proved several times over by 1870. Women had been exposed to academic pursuits and had done as well as or better than men. But the arguments questioning the wisdom of educating women were not so easily put down. In the post–Civil War period women's increasing presence in institutions of higher learning only seemed to intensify the public attack. At least part of the male establishment felt genuinely threatened by women's accomplishments in their sphere. Darwinian theory taught that woman's sphere was biologically determined and lent the weight of apparent scientific proof to women's prescribed domestic role.[16] But the most belabored argument by 1870 was that women's limited energy would be used up in study and leave them unfit for their real destiny as childbearers. The best-developed and best-known formulation of these ideas appeared in Edward H. Clarke's *Sex in Education* (1873).[17]

Whether college women found these ideas personally threatening is not easily verified. Some writers have assumed that they did.[18] But I find no evidence that Alice or her Michigan friends read Clarke or were aware of him. Not once in Freeman's correspondence is Clarke's book mentioned. Some women students probably cared little for marriage and children, but others did. Certainly Alice's desirability as a marriage partner seems not to have been diminished one whit by her pursuit of higher studies. Perhaps Clarke's argument should have run that education would make women less eager for marriage rather than decrease their capacity for it. But Alice's family accepted the imperative that she be able to earn her own living as a corollary to her receiving college training, and they seem not to have been unduly concerned about whether she would not marry or be unfitted by college for marital responsibilities. In fact, had she married any earlier than she did, they would have been very apprehensive about their own financial future. They agreed to the bargain she proposed, that if they educated her, she would educate her younger siblings, and this meant at least the postponement of marriage.

Once college became a possibility Alice had to decide where to go. She seems to have made that decision some time in the spring of 1872 before the June trip to Ann Arbor. According to her husband she saw herself as having few choices.[19] Elmira, founded in 1855 and legally a college, was close at hand, but its resources were so meager that its offerings in 1872 were not much beyond the preparatory school level. Mount Holyoke was little more than a ladies' seminary. Vassar, the first true women's college, had opened seven years before, and was duly considered by Alice. She may actually have been ready to enroll at Vassar when a male Windsor classmate told her that its entrance requirements were lower than for the eastern men's colleges.[20] Alice could never have accepted something she thought second rate. In any case, more than that must have gone into her decision. Vassar, according to its catalog, aimed "to accomplish for young women what colleges of the first class accomplish for young men, that is to furnish them the means of thorough, well-proportioned, and liberal education, *but one adapted to their wants in life*." (italics mine).[21] Could Alice have rebelled at the idea that gender would shape her education in any way?

In any case she seems not to have trusted education designed solely for women. Perhaps her tutor and ex-fiance, Thomas Barclay, urged that Michigan was her best opportunity since the eastern men's colleges were closed to her. Or her determination to obtain the same education as her male confreres may have been fostered by her previous experience with coeducation. All her life Alice Freeman believed that her choice of a coeducational institution was fortunate. Her husband reported that she was convinced coeducation replaced "giddiness and sentimentality" with good sense and companionship. The choice of adjectives may well have been his rather than hers. But he believed she could not have built Wellesley so strongly "if she had not been trained in the company of young men."[22] Ironically, one of the major builders of America's women's colleges was both enriched by and a firm supporter of coeducation. Certainly Michigan provided useful patterns for her later work at the University of Chicago.

Alice seems not to have considered Cornell, the only private university admitting women, or Oberlin, Antioch, or other coeducational denominational colleges. She looked to the new state universities, of which Michigan was the oldest and largest. Certainly it offered high-quality training. Michigan was among the most prestigious universities in the country. By the 1870s there were disciplines, such as history, in which it excelled Harvard and Yale.[23] And it was less expensive than many of its competitors.

In 1872 the University of Michigan, which opened its doors in Ann Arbor in 1841, had three flourishing colleges, literature and science, medicine, and law. Twelve hundred students, over half in its professional schools, made it the largest university in the country.[24] Its library had recently been increased by 10,000 volumes through the purchase of the collection of a Heidelberg scholar, and like Harvard its 40,000 volumes were being catalogued on cards.[25] Its zoological collection by 1876 contained a quarter million specimens, over half of which were added during Alice's tenure at the university.[26] Its student constituency was national in scope. Over half its undergraduates came from out of state, many from nearby midwestern states, but students from five foreign countries and thirty states were at Michigan in the winter of 1872–73.[27] Michigan was cosmopolitan and eclectic.

The state of Michigan's first constitution included an article on education modeled on the Prussian system of schools with a great university at its head. Public funds had been allocated for support of a university from the beginning of statehood. Henry Philip Tappan, the university's first president, was a great admirer of German scholarship and the German university system and established innovative patterns that were to characterize Michigan's next thirty years. His willingness to experiment attracted young scholars with new ideas to the faculty. For example, Andrew Dickson White, later founding president of Cornell, found it an easy choice to forgo a Yale professorship for which he had trained in Europe to begin his academic career at Michigan.[28] In fact the man who much later was to become Alice's husband, George Herbert Palmer, a distinguished Harvard

Alice Freeman when she arrived at the University of Michigan in 1872. (Courtesy of Wellesley College Archives.)

classicist and philosopher, had hoped for an offer from Michigan in 1870. He saw Michigan as a "fresh field" where the religious aberration of his first wife (she was a Swedenborgian) would be less embarrassing and where he could develop freely his scholarly ideas and experiment with his teaching.[29]

When the Freemans arrived in Ann Arbor, Michigan's fourth president, James Burrill Angell, had just completed his first academic year on campus. Angell had been lured from the University of Vermont because he found in Michigan an institution "shaped under broader and more generous views of university life than most of the eastern colleges."[30] Angell was also attracted because Michigan "had in its faculties at the time of my arrival men of marked ability."[31] Angell, in turn, attracted new faculty, seven in the fall of 1872 alone.[32] And Angell gave his full support to the university's new commitment to coeducation, initiated just the year before he arrived.

The university was strengthened in many ways under Angell's presidency which lasted until 1909. Women found a secure place (as students, not faculty) in all its colleges, including medicine and law.[33] Angell also deliberately buttressed Michigan's already strong commitments, which dated from the Tappan era, to the basic sciences. In the early 1870s while Alice Freeman was still a student, Charles Kendall Adams introduced the seminar method of teaching history, her major field of interest, another example of the innovative, venturesome atmosphere Angell encouraged on campus.

Alice and her father were ushered on that June morning in 1872 into Angell's office, for Angell served as registrar, dean of the Literary College, and professor of international law as well as president. Angell met the Freemans in the law building. University Hall, a much grander edifice linking the original classroom and dormitory buildings erected in 1840, a building that typified the dynamic expansion of the university, was under construction next door. Angell described Alice as he remembered her from that first encounter as "a simple modest girl of seventeen . . . a child of much promise, possessed [of] a bright alert mind, of great energy, of quick sympathies and an instinctive desire to be helpful to others."[34] Angell was immediately smitten by that charismatic personality, and he was to remain her adoring friend and fervent supporter for the rest of her life.

In order to be admitted to the university, Alice had to pass examinations administered by the faculty. Nineteenth-century colleges di-

The University of Michigan in 1872. University Hall is still incomplete. The Law Building is on the left. (Courtesy of Bentley Historical Library.)

rected their own entrance examinations. College Boards were not available until 1903.[35] Alice met formidable obstacles. Unfortunately, she received heavy conditions in Greek and mathematics, and the examiners decided further preparation was in order.[36] But Angell himself took responsibility for overriding the examiners and for admitting her "on a trial of six weeks," a confidence Angell found "fully justified."[37] Alice erased the conditions but not without great effort. She studied all summer with a Windsor classmate, George Smith, who was preparing for Amherst.[38] She stayed in Ann Arbor through her vacations the first year. She hired tutors in Greek and in algebra. The other subjects she made up by herself while carrying freshman work.[39]

When Alice Freeman came for her entrance examinations she had her father for support. When she returned to Ann Arbor in the fall to begin her freshman year, she was alone, separated from her family for the first time. At least she had seen Ann Arbor before, and had taken part in a form of freshman orientation that spring. And she had potential women friends. There were eleven women among the seventy-five students in the freshman literary class. She had seen and probably met Madelon Stockwell the previous spring and noted the honors she received. But what sustained this tall, slender, black-eyed girl was her desire for new horizons. She was probably the first resident of Windsor to journey so far west in quest of a college degree. She had studied all summer; she was prepared to work hard.

Alice Freeman arrived at the little Ann Arbor, Michigan, Central Railroad station at midday. Her room, directly across State Street from the campus square, must have been engaged during her June visit, for she wrote home that her landlady was expecting her and had dinner waiting.[40] She both boarded and roomed at the same place and had a front parlor to herself that first year, although Lucy Andrews, later to become her best friend and roommate, lived upstairs.[41] She described her room as pleasant, "nicely furnished, with everything one could want, even to bookshelves."[42] The new First Congregational Church was being built on one side of her rooming house. On the other side a school for little children held sway. The location was convenient but hardly quiet. Undoubtedly she was tired and a little frightened. But I suspect the black eyes shone, and that she was eager to begin her new life as a student.

Of necessity Freeman plunged into academic work. Classes were large and classrooms crowded. Eleven hundred students were taught by only thirty-three professors. Mass education already was well on its way in the United States, quite in contrast to European elitist institutions. For example, in the 1870s the University of Marburg in Germany had only 430 students and sixty-two professors.[43] Also Michigan had many rules. It had not completely moved from its small college beginnings. Class attendance was compulsory. Expulsion was automatic after ten unexcused absences.[44]

The freshman classical curriculum, in which Alice was enrolled, required Latin, Greek, and mathematics plus a written English exercise each week. Botany was added the second semester. There were no electives for first year students in 1872–73.[45] Latin, Greek, mathematics, and English essays were continued in the first semester of the sophomore year, but second semester course offerings broadened considerably. Rhetoric and English literature were added, and history could be substituted for mathematics, an option Alice chose. In the junior year history could be elected to replace Greek, while physics and chemistry were each taught for a semester, French and speech were required in the fall semester, and either astronomy or French were part of the spring work. In the senior year all work was elective.

Harvard, under its new president Charles Eliot, introduced the elective system in 1871. From the early 1870s Michigan allowed electives, but students continued to agitate during that decade for more curricular freedom and made considerable progress during the years Alice was in Ann Arbor. In addition to required courses, Alice studied political economy, United States and English constitutional history, English literature, philosophy, Italian, and Greek tragedy. Among her professors were President Angell, Henry Simmons Frieze, Charles Kendall Adams, and Moses Coit Tyler, all distinguished scholars with national reputations. She was also enrolled in the seminaries (seminars) offered for students preparing to teach.[46]

In his memoir George Palmer does not credit Alice Freeman with being a scholar. He evaluates her "scholarly work as not quite solid."[47] He attributes this to poor preparation and the strain of overwork. No doubt Alice Freeman was overextended. In her freshman year she not only had to master the regular curriculum but make up her deficiencies in Greek and mathematics. She was forced to drop out for over half of her junior year to earn money teaching, and made up junior courses during her senior year. But she did this expeditiously. She studied at home during the summer, passed her junior physics course by early November, the fall of her senior year, and was ready to be examined in French and English literature just after Thanksgiving. As an upper classwoman she sometimes got up at six in the morning to write her history essay, but only because she had attended an extracurricular lecture the evening before.[48]

Despite George Palmer's negative evaluation, Alice's undergraduate scholarship hardly seems deficient. She turned in a stellar performance at the oral freshman Latin examination, astounding Henry Frieze, who had been in Europe on leave that year and did not know her, with her ability to translate Horace's satires.[49] One of her male classmates reported that their class had "read more Greek and done more work in Math. [*sic*] than any preceding class."[50] Much as Palmer admired and loved Alice he did feel the need, on occasion, to downgrade her, especially her family background and her scholarship. President Angell, in contrast, always praised her academic excellence. And the record bears him out. No grades, only pass-fail, appeared on academic transcripts in the 1870s. But unless Alice Freeman had been among the highest ranking scholars in her class, she would never have been chosen by the faculty as one of the commencement orators. Alice spent her life not as an academician and scholar, but as an educator and a doer. Although she wrote no technical treatises and her only book was a collection of poems published posthumously,[51] her letters as an adult attest to her ability to use the English language with high skill. But it is fair to say that despite her academic competence, her intellectual interests were secondary. She did not find her challenges in the world of ideas but in her relationships with people. Undoubtedly had she felt a call to academic scholarly activities she would have performed with the same excellence and flair she brought to the administrative, promotional, and instructional activities that did engage her.

The campus experience of the first generation of Michigan women has been described by Olive San Louie Anderson, a student contemporary of Alice Freeman, in her autobiographical novel, *An American Girl and Her Four Years in a Boys' College*.[52] The picture Anderson painted is one of harassment, discrimination, and a large degree of unwelcome. Landladies refused to rent to women students, church members did not speak to them. As Anderson saw it, the price women paid for entering a male preserve was high. Anderson's description of the University of Michigan has been used frequently by scholars to attest to the hostility early women students faced at Michigan. However, the picture presented by Alice Freeman's letters and diary is quite different. Alice described a nurturant concerned faculty, friendly male students, and a rich, rewarding church life.

A letter to her family at the beginning of her junior year showed her integration into and delight with campus life. She reported that she and her friend Lucy had a pleasant journey and were met in Detroit by two of their male classmates who escorted them to Ann Arbor. Everyone, including her minister, George Duffield,

was so glad to see us back that it really made me quite glad to be here myself. And my boys! [her Sunday school class] and all the rest! . . . Prof. D'Ooge [of classics] came down to the Mission yesterday to see me and expressed himself very much delighted with my return.[53]

Perhaps Alice's experience, as exemplified in that letter and several others, can be explained by her sunny disposition. President Angell described her character as "a bright, beautiful, optimistic type," a "radiant center of life."[54] Alice Freeman's personality no doubt had much to do with how she viewed her college years, and inevitably she translated every experience into high adventure; however, the period of antagonism, if there really was any, toward women students at Michigan was very brief, and women were fully integrated into most phases of university life by 1872. Over one hundred women were on campus by fall 1875, Alice's last year.[55] When Madelon Stockwell joined the Michigan student body five years before, she was treated at first as a curiosity, but she was soon accepted. Two years later she was one of her class's commencement orators, and she married a classmate in a ceremony performed by one of their professors. Angell was a major force in the acceptance of women. He believed women belonged in the university. He did not believe Edward Clarke's assertion that study was bad for women's health. Instead he argued that "the regularity of the life and the deep interest that it awakens and maintains, are manifestly conducive to mental and physical health."[56]

Alice Freeman enjoyed her years at Michigan. She formed many close friendships with both men and women and participated fully in the life of the college and the community. She certainly was not harassed. Her relationship to the faculty was close, almost familial. Benjamin Cocker, professor of philosophy, also visited her Sunday school class, Angell watched over her like a guardian angel, and Charles Kendall Adams, who presided in her history seminar, invited her to Christmas dinner with his family.[57] Alice Freeman's women friends also enjoyed their college years and explored their new universe with high excitement. It is true that only venturesome girls would take on a "boys' college," but once there, they seemed even to have enjoyed "the boys," and "the boys" certainly to have enjoyed them.

Helen Horowitz in her study, *Campus Life*, saw women's position in coeducational universities somewhat differently than I found it experienced by Alice Freeman.[58] Horowitz reported that college men at Cornell and Michigan put "women into the established groove of the pauper scholar and ostracized them accordingly."[59] Horowitz's analysis of the nineteenth-century campus showed two groups of students: a wealthy elite who tended to fight the authority of the faculty and who clearly controlled undergraduate college life, and a relatively impoverished group of docile future ministers, lawyers, doctors, and teachers who attended college for formal training in the professions.[60] And Horowitz puts women, when they appeared on male campuses in the 1870s, with the latter. Men were forced to sit beside women in class, but college life continued to be completely dominated by men.[61]

Again this assessment fails to match Alice's experience. It is true that Alice, like other women, did not come to the university to be "finished," but rather to prepare herself for a profession that would permit her to earn her living and help support her family. Nor did she experience college life through the social fraternity. Fraternities were of course closed to women, and in any case Alice had deep moral reservations about the fraternity system. She worried about the spiritual life of fraternity members, writing Lucy Andrews, "Let us pray for the noble young men, who are going down unless the arm 'mighty to save' is quickly thrown around them."[62] But fraternities did not dominate the Michigan campus in the 1870s. There were no residential fraternity houses until 1879, and the J-Hop (junior dance), the most important early-twentieth-century social occasion of the college year and firmly under fraternity control by 1890, was still an all-campus event attended by everyone in the 1870s.

The Student Lecture Association, dating from 1854 and run by a student board, was the major contributor to student social and intellectual life in the 1870s, and women and men sat side by side at its lectures by such luminaries as the poet James T. Fields, E. L. Godkin, editor of the *Nation,* the actress Mrs. Siddons, and the feminist Mary Livermore.[63] The columns of student publications such as *The Chronicle* and the *Oracle* were open to women. Alice wrote a substantial essay championing the elective system for the *Oracle* in 1874.[64] Women were prominent members of the Student Christian Association, the largest campus club. It was at its meetings that Alice first met her classmates, Eliza Mosher and Lucy Salmon, both of whom were also to make substantial contributions to the position of women in academic life.

In fact women were more closely integrated into the student power structure and campus life during their first two decades at Michigan than they were at the turn of the century, when fraternities were more clearly in control of college activities. By 1900 student publications largely excluded women as did the Student Union, the largest organization on campus. When the union's new building opened after World War I, women were denied use of the front door until the 1950s. The pioneer women who opened the classrooms and college societies in the 1870s were treated much more as companions, colleagues, and equals than their nieces and daughters who followed a generation later.

Michigan's early acceptance of women was not unique. Much the same pattern of acceptance followed by rejection occurred at the University of Wisconsin. Women were initially ostracized, then accepted, especially after the arrival of John Bascom as president in 1874. But the atmosphere changed again in the 1890s when women, whose numbers on campuses greatly increased, began to be seen as ornaments of college social life and "had to fight for the right to be intellectual beings." By 1900 Wisconsin women were the recipients of grossly prejudiced behavior by professors, as they were by then in the Michigan Medical School.[65] M. Carey Thomas saw herself as treated well by the men at Cornell when she began her studies there in 1875 and saw herself as a "complete convert to 'Coed'."[66] However by the fall of 1877 when she was struggling to be accepted for graduate work at Johns Hopkins she saw it as "very hard for a lady in a mixed university."[67]

In Alice's letters and diaries we see firsthand how one woman and her friends experienced coeducation at Michigan in the 1870s. These women were not cut off. They had many male friends. They were independent, as Alice herself was later to write: "The girl who goes to the University of Michigan today, just as when I entered there in 1872, finds her own boarding place . . . ; makes the business arrangements for her winter's fuel and its storage; finds her washerwoman or laundry; she chooses her own society, clubs, and church. The advice she gets comes from another girl student. . . . Strong is the comradeship among these ambitious girls."[68]

They were "University girls," as they called themselves with pride, the center of the universe, curiosities perhaps but desirable curiosities. As students they were treated as equals, sharing organizations, honors, and lifestyle. Angell and most of the faculty obviously enjoyed their presence. Why else would they have invited them to holiday dinners, found them jobs when they needed them, listened to their swains' appeals for assistance in their unrequited suits? Women on the Michigan campus in the 1870s may have been seen as exotic, but they were certainly equal, given equal consideration, equal respect, and equal accolades. Only later were women forced into circumscribed niches that have since been ascribed to the whole period. Women always seem to do well when they first invade a previously male preserve, when traditional prejudices seem temporarily set aside. For example, women in the New Deal found their best opportunities in newly organized and innovative agencies. When those agencies became part of the establishment, women were pushed aside.[69]

The initial acceptance of women may also have been nurtured by the winds of reform and change buffeting academia in the 1870s. Students were in the vanguard of this reform. Michigan's class of 1876 to which Alice Freeman belonged saw itself as a reforming legion that permanently changed campus life at the University of Michigan.[70] They agitated successfully for the elective system, for which Alice campaigned. They championed a better-trained faculty, and they abandoned obnoxious student customs.

Student behavior was a problem at campuses across the country in the 1870s. Michigan was no worse, and was probably better, than a dozen eastern institutions. When Michigan classes gathered on campus in the fall of 1872, however, the first chapel convocation was absolute bedlam, juvenile and disgusting. Freshmen and sophomores engaged in the traditional interclass fight. When the freshmen entered the law lecture room used for chapel, the sophomores tried to throw them over the bannister and down the steps. Hymn books, rotten eggs, and tomatoes were all used as weapons. Puerile sport, such as holding a man's head under the campus pump, was common. Hazing continued through the fall and then stopped, at least on campus. Whether they deserved it or not, the class of 1876 took the credit.[71] Hazing was to reappear a hundred times over the next century, but the excesses of nineteenth-century university life were temporarily halted.

President Angell contributed to the more adult campus atmosphere. He transformed chapel into a civilized occasion both by force of personality and by making it voluntary,[72] and *The Chronicle* intoned that hazing "after one or two dying throes, lies dead." The practice had to be stopped before doing "serious injury to the University."[73]

It was not dead, only temporarily unconscious, but its incidence markedly decreased. Perhaps the presence of women on campus had an effect. There were eighty-eight women on campus in 1872.[74] That was a large enough group to be a visible presence. Perhaps the elegance of new University Hall, dedicated in the fall of 1873, also contributed. At long last there was a real chapel, built for the purpose, seating 550 students, with four doors, one for each class, to keep students properly stratified, as well as a second floor auditorium seating over 2,000 people, ample provision for rainy commencements, winter concerts, and important events of the Lecture Association.[75] Recreation rooms for society meetings and social events also helped provide enough space so that students had no need to spill into the streets. For one reason or another, the excesses of male undergraduate life were modified.

In the 1870s higher education was not thought to improve young women's matrimonial prospects, and as late as 1904–8 only 52 percent of Michigan women graduates married.[76] Alice herself married late, as was typical of those college women who did marry, but she was literally plagued by suitors during her college years. According to her diary four fellow students proposed to her in November and December of 1874.[77] And this was not atypical. One of her classmates reported five social engagements with gentlemen in a single week.[78] The late age and infrequency of marriage by nineteenth-century college women may well reflect the pressing financial obligations that often sent them to college in the first place. Proposals were a constant during Alice Freeman's college years.

Charles Wooldridge, a member of the 1875 class, an editor of *The Oracle,* and Alice's erstwhile mathematics tutor, was a student from Iowa who lived around the corner. She complained that Wooldridge, "whom I clearly disliked, had offered himself at regular intervals since spring 1873."[79] He introduced her to the opera which she enjoyed "exceedingly." But she ended up with a "nervous headache" and felt it unwise "to indulge in such exciting pleasures often."[80] No matter. Wooldridge was not acceptable to her. He deeply embarrassed Alice by appealing to President Angell, Dr. Benjamin F. Cocker, Methodist clergyman turned professor of philosophy, and others for assistance in pressing his suit.[81] Alice wrote her friend Lucy when Wooldridge bombarded her with fervent letters after she left Ann Arbor temporarily to teach. "Why is it that I seem to be doomed to this thing. . . . It is such a passionate letter, and I know he must be terribly in earnest to talk so and I tremble for the effect it will have on him just now. Do be kind to him."[82] Olive San Louie Anderson may have been describing Alice as a student when she wrote: "At first glance you would say she had not a single element of beauty. Her hair was red, and her nose had a decided inclination to turn up; she had freckles and light eyebrows, and yet no person became acquainted with [her] who did not think her beautiful, and before her college life was over, more than half a dozen boys had fallen hopelessly in love with her."[83]

Alice Freeman, the Michigan student, liked pretty clothes, and chose and wore them in Ann Arbor with the same careful attention to style and color she was to give her wardrobe the rest of her life. There was little money for luxury during her college years, and most of her new clothes were presents. Her friend Lucy gave her little tokens of ribbons and gloves. A new dress was her Christmas gift from her family in 1874.[84] For her first evening at the opera she "wore my blue suit, which with my blue and white hat and white gloves makes a pretty outfit for such an occasion."[85] And at another engagement, "I wore my blue merino suit that evening at Mr. Markham's with the 'boiled out' tie and the bow the same shade, that Ella [her sister] made for me, on the back of my hair."[86]

However, it was Alice's personality that contributed most to her presence on campus. She captivated everyone she met, from President Angell to her women classmates. No disappointment defeated her. As Angell said, "her genial outgoing spirit seemed to carry with her an atmosphere of cheerfulness and joy."[87] In a letter to her friend Lucy, Alice advised her that "the best thing you can do . . . is to be just as happy as you can in any way that you can. . . . Shun everything that hurts you and be good to yourself always and everywhere."[88] On another occasion she wrote her mother that she believed God helps those who help themselves and confessed, "I have come to several places . . . where I could only see one step ahead; but as soon as I have taken that, another has been opened to me."[89]

She occupied a special place among her fellow students. Mary Caswell, a cousin of President Angell's wife Sarah, first met Alice in 1876 at the president's commencement reception. She wrote many years later:

I can see her now as she stood by the piano, surrounded by fellow students who were taking their leave before they went out in the world. Perhaps the real reception was, after all, there. Miss Freeman was then a slender young girl, not beautiful or even striking in appearance, but as she stood talking with her fellow students, it was easy to see her preeminence among them; that in taking their leave of her, they were parting from a person whose attraction and power they had felt in a helpful and inspiring way.[90]

Optimism, openness, and faith in herself and others nourished the flame that attracted others to her, women as well as men.

Until she married, Alice Freeman's formal religious affiliation was always with the Presbyterian church. She joined the Windsor congregation at fourteen, and in January of 1873 transferred her membership by letter to the First Presbyterian Church of Ann Arbor. Again in 1875 when she interrupted her Ann Arbor years to teach in Illinois, she attended the Presbyterian church in Ottawa as a matter of course. Sundays were busy, two services with sermons, a prayer meeting, and a Bible class.[91] She taught Sunday school on Sunday afternoons, recruited by an upperclassman who took her strolling after Sunday afternoon dinner in the local cemetery, a favorite student haunt.[92] Sunday schools relied heavily for staff on young people, especially women, who volunteered. Her class was composed largely of German working-class boys whom she found bright and interesting.[93] One wonders if she taught her Sunday school boys English, because Sunday schools in the 1870s were designed to serve the educational as well as the religious needs of the urban poor, especially new immigrants. She left this class in the hands of a friend, Hattie, when she temporarily left Ann Arbor to teach in 1875.[94] But her "boys" kept in touch with her by letter.[95]

The Sunday school relationship was important to both teacher and pupils. During her college years it represented her social contribution to the community. Alice experienced no prejudice as a woman in local churches. She reported in the fall of 1874 that "everyone [at church] was so glad to see us [the women students] back that it made me quite glad," and they welcomed her return to the Mission Sunday school.[96]

However, Alice's religious life in Ann Arbor centered on the Student Christian Association, a nondenominational group with broad student membership and support that met in the early evening twice a week and held daily prayer meetings in December.[97] Like most institutions of higher learning, the nineteenth-century University of Michigan had a distinctly religious, if nonsectarian, atmosphere. Its earliest professors had been clergymen. Chapel was required until Angell made it voluntary in 1872, and attendance at Sunday church services was expected. Founded as the first college Young Men's Christian Association (YMCA) in the country, the Student Christian Association advocated the admission of women to the university and admitted women to membership as soon as they arrived on campus, hence the more inclusive name.[98] Its members came from all the university's colleges (or departments as they were then called), and it was easily the most active organization on campus.

When Alice was forced to leave the campus to earn money by teaching, she seems to have missed the Student Christian Association more than any other college activity. Her friend Lucy Andrews had been raised in the Sandwich Islands (now Hawaii) where the missionary influence was still dominant, and it was to Lucy that Alice poured out her disappointment at not being in Ann Arbor for a long planned day of prayer. "You must tell me all about [it]. I have hoped and prayed so much for it."[99] In the 1870s, for most middle-class Americans, ideals and goals were framed within the ethos of Protestant evangelical Christianity. Alice Freeman did what she did as a Christian. As a young woman, she felt Christ looking over her shoulder as she helped her family, worked in a mission Sunday school, or assisted in the conversion of a classmate. However Alice was never a zealot. She was not above admitting that she felt glad when Sunday services were over one dreary, rainy day in Otego, New York, during summer vacation in 1875.[100] When missionaries visiting the campus urged her to join their work in Turkey when she graduated, she seems not to have taken their recruitment effort very seriously, adding wryly: "I don't believe I'm wanted very badly anywhere."[101]

The most persistent worry that plagued Alice's college years was financial. Support from home seems to have been uncertain and erratic. She was frequently short of funds, had bills in arrears, and felt it necessary to impress on her parents in her letters the frugalities she assiduously practiced. In the 1870s Michigan was not the most expensive place to acquire a college degree, but it was not cheap. One historian has estimated that $1,400, or $350 a year, would see a student through to a bachelor's degree in contrast to nearly $1,000 a year needed to attend Yale.[102] One of Alice's male classmates who kept careful records bears out this estimate. He spent $321.75 for the 1872–73 academic year.[103] Admission fees were $25.00 for nonresidents, annual fees $10.00, room and board with private families $3.00 to $5.00 a week.[104]

These were modest enough charges; nonetheless, they represented a considerable outlay, clearly straining the resources of a middle-class family. Michigan offered no scholarships from 1866 to the 1890s, nor were there any student loan funds.[105] Alice's needs may well have taken most of the Freeman cash income. The number of physicians in the United States had increased much more rapidly than population in the 1860s, intensifying competition. Only well-educated urban specialists were particularly prosperous, and even in New York City a young physician earned only about $400.00 a year.[106] James Freeman practiced in a small country town where many of his fees would be paid in kind by local farmers.

Many Michigan students delayed their educations, teaching school while they accumulated the cash to support their Ann Arbor years. The Freemans must have been relatively prosperous in the summer of 1872, for they were able to send Alice directly to the University of Michigan on graduation from Windsor Academy. James Freeman had kept his farm when he entered practice and expected lumber from woodlands on that property to supplement his medical fees. Flooding of the Susquehanna in the spring of 1874 swept away the timber Freeman had accumulated on its banks and destroyed that source of income.[107] During the fall of 1874 money became increasingly tight, and by Christmas Alice had decided she must leave school and teach for awhile.[108] Her father closed his Windsor consulting rooms that winter and moved the family and his practice to Otego, New York,[109] a larger community that he no doubt thought would offer a more reliable income. But money troubles continued to plague him, and his health also began to deteriorate.[110]

The Panic of 1873 compounded James Freeman's difficulties. It precipitated the deepest depression the United States had yet experienced, and the market for lumber and agricultural products fell so low that many mortgages were foreclosed. Freeman's financial woes, part of a national catastrophe, were compounded by his mining speculations. Had he not suffered personal losses, he would still have faced drastic loss of income from the general downturn in the agricultural economy. The American economy in the nineteenth century was expanding and rich in opportunities, but also highly volatile. Entrepreneurs frequently acquired and lost more than one fortune.

A letter home during Alice's senior year reported that she had only $16.00 and needed much more to pay her obligations. Her wood bill alone was $12.00 (the winter had been very cold) and she needed new shoes, having only cloth summer ones, and books had been more expensive than usual.[111] Obviously her previous year's teaching had not left her with sufficient reserves to support herself, or perhaps more likely she had used her savings to assist her family. She tutored a young man in Greek, which took most of Saturday, and coached another young man in Virgil during her vacation.[112] She forwent spending the holiday with friends to earn this money.[113] She promised her family that if they could help her through this year she would "push my own canoe afterwards."[114] The evolving New Woman was beginning to take charge of her life.

Her brother Fred, not quite two years younger than Alice, had now finished secondary school, and it was his earnings that provided part of her support during her last year. As she wrote to her mother from Ann Arbor during the summer of 1875, she wished Fred too could go to school, but her "wishing is not good for much as long as I do nothing but spend money."[115] She promised that Fred would get his chance, and she did eventually help him through medical school.

The state of the Freeman family exchequer convinced Alice before the end of the first semester of her junior year to leave school temporarily to teach. President Angell assisted her in finding a position as principal of the high school in Ottawa, Illinois, and she did not inform her family of her decision until her plans were complete. The salary was more than adequate, $700 for five months.[116] It was not uncommon for Michigan students to leave the campus for several months to teach school and make up the work by examination.[117] Four of her friends, all men, saw her off at the Michigan Central station after Christmas. She received some help with her missed work from classmates, especially Lucy Andrews, who sent her class notes, corrected exercises, and kept her informed of reading assignments, but of course she had no way to recoup the lectures and class work.[118] She returned to Ann Arbor for commencement in late June of 1875 and resumed her campus residence the following September.[119]

Other than worrying about making up her college work and missing her friends, Alice found her new role as teacher stimulating and rewarding. The family where she boarded lived comfortably and welcomed her as another daughter. Their piano and library were "always at my service." The superintendent called for her and escorted her to school, introducing her en route to the president of the bank and

> all the important people. . . . We at last reached the high school and then in an inquisitive, criticizing way, three hundred young people looked over "the new teacher." I sat up in front pretending to listen to them expounding the mysteries of algebra while I examined the faces before me and smiled to myself as I wondered what they were thinking of me, for it does seem absurd. . . . They look as old as I do.[120]

She was not yet twenty.

Her schedule was arduous and her responsibilities heavy. She rose at six A.M. because early morning was the only time she could find for her eight daily preparations. Except for the dinner hour she was busy with classes from 9:00 to 4:30. She stayed after school to do paperwork. Saturday afternoons she criticized essays. Her evenings were always interrupted by callers.[121] She had no previous teaching experience except her Sunday school classes and tutoring, and her classes were overflowing with sixty students the rule. But by February she could write, "I think I am getting along pretty well. I am certainly beginning to enjoy it a good deal."[122] But Ann Arbor was never long from her mind. She wrote her friend Lucy:

> Tell me about this semester's work. I suppose the chemistry is all in lectures so I can do nothing with that myself. Are you reading any book in connection with the class? If so, please give me the title. . . . What are you reading in Plato? And is it very difficult?[123]

And a month later:

> This has been such a busy week, and next week is going to be still harder, and then, a rest of a week, when I shall try to write you a whole letter, without struggling away from reports and examinations to do it!![124]

At Ottawa everyone, as usual, loved her. "It really seemed pleasant to get back to school [after spring vacation] and see so many bright young faces smiling a good morning—to have dozens of young people crowd around me to tell me 'how glad they were to have school begin again'.... You see there is some pleasure as well as work and care in this kind of living."[125] And when she attended the lyceum and an oyster supper, she was "made the center around which any number of people revolved—'a University Girl!!', you know. But that's nothing new."[126]

At times the daunting workload was too much, even for the resilient Alice. "I am too tired to write.... Such a busy week," but she went on to closely fill four pages that overflowed into the margins.[127] And she denied being "blue or sick or dreadfully overworked," just very busy "with a superabundance of things I might do if there were plenty of time and strength."[128] Her spring vacation was taken up with grading essays and helping with the senior play. She complained, that it was "Oh, Miss Freeman! We can't do a thing without you...from Mr. Schrieb [the superintendent] to the youngest scholar...but chum you know how everyone thinks I've nothing to do but help them."[129]

She had agreed to teach only twenty weeks, but when the end of the school year approached, the school board told her how pleased they were with her work, and she wrote her mother that they "begged me to reconsider...telling me I must stay.... They say I know enough now and can finish my studies by myself. As if they knew!"[130] Unfortunately most of her family's letters to Alice have not survived, so we do not know how her mother replied to this letter. Even if her hard-pressed parents were apprehensive about supporting Alice through a last year at the university, she was not about to modify her goals. She was determined to have her degree in hand before she ventured further into the world of work.

Aside from her persistent money troubles Alice Freeman's only serious worry during her college years seems to have been an occasional bout of ill health. Consumption plagued the Freeman family. James Freeman's health was frequently uncertain, and Alice's younger sister Stella was to die of tuberculosis at nineteen. Alice's health first began to trouble her while she was teaching at Ottawa.[131] When she returned home in the summer she continued not to feel well, was sleepless, and found the unseasonably cold, rainy weather difficult.[132] But her health did not improve when she returned to the university. She wrote home in November:

> I have coughed a good deal this fall. There has not been a time since the week after I came when I have not had a cold, have had three heavy ones, with all the care I could take. I know I never was so susceptible to colds before.... Don't send a prescription for I haven't any money.[133]

Money and health problems were to continue to plague the Freemans.

As the academic year drew to a close, the class of 1876 was increasingly concerned with commencement, post–college plans, and the inevitable partings. That same spring the great exposition celebrating the 100th birthday of the Republic opened in Philadelphia's Fairmount Park. The class of '76 thought of itself as the "Centennial Class," with special obligations to a maturing American society, obligations it had already begun to fulfill through its contributions to reforming campus life, especially ending hazing and prodding curricular reform.

In March, commencement speakers for all three of Michigan's colleges were announced. Three women were among them, Alice and Annie Warden Ekin for the Literary College, and Eliza Mosher in medicine. All of the chosen, men and women, were Alice's "good friends."[134] Although *The Chronicle* reported that everyone was satisfied with the faculty's selection that year, a *Chronicle* editorial complained that other universities get addressed by men like Ralph Waldo Emerson while Michigan got "declamations" from boys and girls.[135] But undergraduate grousing was unlikely to diminish the enthusiasm of the elect. In April, Alice selected the topic for her address, "The Relation of Science and Poetry." She later changed the word "relation" to "conflict," but no copy of the paper has survived, so we have no way of assessing the merit of her argument. However, the class prophecy attested to her fiery and fluent way with words:

> If you would feel in all its force Dean Swift's heart cutting satire,
> Then a very easy remedy, just rouse Miss Freeman's ire.[136]

Except for two who had died, all the women who entered with the class in the fall of 1872 graduated, although attrition had been nearly

50 percent among the men. Women did not take higher education lightly in the 1870s. A third of the graduating class was from Michigan, sixteen from New York, and another sixteen from nearby states. Eight had come to Ann Arbor from foreign countries.[137] The weather was splendid and the exercises festive, including a class concert, a student carnival, and dancing at the Class Day reception.[138] Whether Alice's family was able to be there we do not know.

Alice was to return to Ann Arbor many times over the years both for ceremony and study, and for two years before the decade was out she was again to be a resident of Michigan. However no later experience or environment was to rival Alice Freeman's undergraduate years at Michigan in shaping her life. Not only had her intellectual horizons been immeasurably expanded, her relationship to her family had changed from one of dependence to autonomous control of her own destiny and was soon to include a large measure of dependence by her family on her for financial and emotional sustenance. But most importantly, a Michigan network had been forged.

The Michigan network was composed of a core of able, independent, achieving women whose paths were to be much intertwined in the next decades and who provided both collegiality and emotional support for these pioneering women as they moved out into the wider world of work and career. But the network also included male students and faculty who contributed to the support system forged at Michigan. The Michigan influence was to affect Alice Freeman for a very long time.

NOTES

1. Alice Freeman to "Dear Ones at Home," September 27, 1874.
2. Commencement program in Edward D. Barry Scrapbook, Bentley Historical Library, University of Michigan.
3. Solomon, *Educated Women*, 77. Solomon's study of women's education is definitive and indispensable. Newcomer, *Higher Education*, blazed the trail a generation earlier, as did Thomas Woody, *A History of Women's Education in the United States*, 2 vols. (New York: Science Press, 1929), in the 1920s.
4. Although the public high school was common in the West by 1870, much secondary education was still offered through private or semiprivate academies, frequently known as seminaries. Colleges and universities offered baccalaureate degrees. Seminaries and academies, like other secondary schools, did not.
5. Newcomer, *Higher Education*, 13–90.

6. Newcomer, *Higher Education*, 46; Solomon, *Educated Women*, 63–64; Burke, *American Collegiate Populations*, 215.

7. Newcomer, *Higher Education*, 46; Solomon, *Educated Women*, 63–64; Burke, *American Collegiate Populations*, 215.

8. Solomon, *Educated Women*, 49–50.

9. Ibid., 45.

10. See Michael B. Katz, *Reconstructing American Education* (Cambridge: Harvard University Press, 1987), chap. 1.

11. Kathryn M. Kerns, "'Farmers' Daughters': The Education of Women at Alfred Academy and University Before the Civil War," *History of Higher Education Annual* 6 (1986): 11–28.

12. For example, see Olive Anderson, *An American Girl and Her Four Years in a Boys' College* (New York: Appleton and Co., 1878), 8.

13. Joan Burstyn, *Victorian Education and the Ideal of Womanhood* (London: Croom Helm, 1980), 23–24; and Martha Vicinus, *Independent Women: Work and Community for Single Women, 1850–1920* (Chicago: University of Chicago Press, 1985), chap. 4.

14. James G. Albisetti, *Schooling German Girls and Women: Secondary and Higher Education in the Nineteenth Century* (Princeton: Princeton University Press, 1988), 67.

15. Jurgen Herbst, *And Sadly Teach: Teacher Education and Professionalism in American Culture* (Madison: University of Wisconsin Press, 1989), is the most comprehensive account of the professionalization of teacher training in the United States. See also Bledstein, *Culture of Professionalism*.

16. See Barbara J. Harris, *Beyond Her Sphere: Women and the Professions in American History* (Westport, Conn.: Greenwood Press, 1978), 57–59; Rosenberg, *Beyond Separate Spheres*, 5–12.

17. Edward H. Clarke, *Sex in Education: A Fair Chance for the Girls* (Boston: Osgood, 1873).

18. See Dorothy G. McGuigan, *A Dangerous Experiment: One Hundred Years of Women at the University of Michigan*, (Ann Arbor, Mich.: University of Michigan Center for Continuing Education of Women, 1970), chap. 8.

19. Palmer, *Life*, 43.

20. Unidentified clipping, Alice Freeman Palmer Papers, Bentley Historical Library, University of Michigan.

21. *Vassar College Catalog*, 1865–66, p. 16, as quoted in Newcomer, *Higher Education*, 55. M. Carey Thomas also believed Vassar inferior to Cornell.

22. Palmer, *Life*, 51, 53.

23. Ruth Bordin, *Andrew Dickson White: Teacher of History*, Bulletin no. 8 (Ann Arbor: Michigan Historical Collections, 1958).

24. Secondary sources on the history of the University of Michigan include: Howard H. Peckham, *The Making of the University of Michigan* (Ann Arbor: University of Michigan Press, 1967); Ruth Bordin, *The University of Michigan: A Pictorial History* (Ann Arbor: University of Michigan Press, 1967); Wilfred B. Shaw, ed., *The University of Michigan: An Encyclopedic Survey* (Ann Arbor: University of Michigan, 1941–1958) 4 vols.; the extensive and well-

processed archives of the University of Michigan are housed in the Bentley Historical Library.

25. Peckham, *University of Michigan*, 67.

26. *The Chronicle*, 7 (March 18, 1876): 126.

27. *The Chronicle*, 4 (January 25, 1873): 91.

28. Bordin, *Andrew Dickson White*, 8–10.

29. George Herbert Palmer to Ellen Wellman Palmer, August 4, 1870. Alice Freeman Palmer Papers, Wellesley College Archives.

30. James Burrill Angell, *The Reminiscences of James Burrill Angell* (New York: Longmans, Green, and Co., 1912), 227. See Laurence R. Vesey, *The Emergence of the American University* (Chicago: University of Chicago Press, 1965), 21–56 for a discussion of the sterile religiosity and pious conservatism of the eastern colleges in the mid-decades of the nineteenth century.

31. Angell, *Reminiscences*, 227.

32. *The Chronicle* 4 (October 5, 1872): 10.

33. Women's acceptance as faculty in coeducational institutions was very limited until World War I. As Barbara Solomon has noted, "investing in female scholars seemed a great risk to the academic establishment," (Solomon, *Educated Women*, 137–38.) Michigan, despite its willingness to accord women equality as students, was no exception.

34. Angell's memorial address on the death of Alice Freeman Palmer. Palmer, *A Service*, 31ff.

35. Newcomer, *Higher Education*, 135.

36. Diary, 1872, 10.

37. Angell's memorial address, in Palmer, *A Service*, 33ff.

38. Diary, 1872, 10.

39. Ibid.

40. Alice Freeman to family, September 1872, in Palmer, *Life*, 58. Palmer reproduced heavily edited long passages from Freeman's letters, not all of which now can be found in her papers.

41. Diary, September 1872.

42. Palmer, *Life*, 58.

43. Peckham, *University of Michigan*, 69.

44. *Annual Calendar*, University of Michigan, 1872–76.

45. Ibid.

46. Diary, 1876, 14.

47. Palmer, *Life*, 47.

48. Alice Freeman to Elizabeth Freeman, November 7, 1875.

49. Alice Freeman to family, June 1873, as quoted in Palmer, *Life*, 59.

50. F. D. Haskell to Colman Hutson, February 17, 1876, Colman Hutson Papers, Bentley Historical Library.

51. Alice Freeman Palmer, *A Marriage Cycle* (Boston: Houghton Mifflin Co., 1915).

52. Anderson, *An American Girl*.

53. Alice Freeman to family, September 21, 1874.

54. Angell's address at the Alice Freeman Palmer Memorial Service in the program *A Memorial to Alice Freeman Palmer* (Chicago, 1903), 9.

55. Peckham, *University of Michigan*, 82.

56. *Pennsylvania School Journal*, 1881, in Woody, *Women's Education*, 236. Angell first refuted Clarke in the *Woman's Journal*, August 23, 1873, 267.

57. Alice Freeman to Lucy Andrews, December 29, 1874.

58. Helen Lefkowitz Horowitz, *Campus Life: Undergraduate Cultures from the End of the Eighteenth Century to the Present* (Chicago: University of Chicago Press, 1987). Others have agreed with Horowitz. Sally Schwager argues that women consistently received second-class status at coeducational colleges and universities in the nineteenth century, basing this conclusion on a number of studies of women's experience at Oberlin, Grinnell, Cornell, Wisconsin, Berkeley, Stanford and Michigan (Schwager, "Educating Women," 361–72); Glenn C. Altschuler, *Better than Second Best: Love and Work in the Life of Helen Magill* (Urbana: University of Illinois Press, 1990) reports male students "pointedly shunned" coeds and sees men and women mixing freely only after 1900, (5, 189); Helen Horowitz in *Campus Life* (201) seems to lump the 1870s and the 1890s together.

59. Horowitz, *Campus Life*, 41.

60. Ibid., 29–30.

61. Ibid., 42.

62. Alice Freeman to Lucy Andrews, February 27, 1875.

63. *The Palladium*, 1873–74, 57.

64. *Oracle*, vol. 8 (February 1874): 25–27.

65. See Amy Hague, "What If the Power Does Lie Within Me: Women Students at the University of Wisconsin, 1875– 1900," *History of Higher Education Annual* 1984, 78–100; Lynn Gordon believes that women at the University of California, many of whom commuted from across the Bay, "sparked no interest in the faculty or community" and "had no access to the main currents of student life" (Gordon, *Higher Education*, 55). California was much smaller and much newer than Michigan with only 100 undergraduates. Women were present on campus from its beginnings in 1870, but campus life for both men and women in the first decade seems to have been minimal (Gordon, *Higher Education*, chap. 2.); Nonetheless a woman was one of the three original editors of the *University Echo* when it was first published in 1877 William W. Ferrier, *Origin and Development of the University of California* (Berkeley: Sather Gate Book Shop, 1930) 336.

66. Marjorie Housepian Dobkin, ed., *The Making of a Feminist: Early Letters and Journals of M. Carey Thomas* (Kent, Ohio: Kent State University Press, 1979), 107; Charlotte Williams Conable, *Women at Cornell: The Myth of Equal Education* (Ithaca: Cornell University Press, 1967), 70–126, sees Cornell as very hostile to women from the beginning. See also Frankfort, *Collegiate Women*, 31; Morris L. Bishop, *History of Cornell* (Ithaca: Cornell University Press, 1962), 151.

67. Dobkin, *Making of a Feminist*, 121.

68. Alice Palmer in Anna C. Brackett, ed., *Women and the Higher Education* (New York: Harper Bros., 1893), 112–13.

69. See Susan Ware, *Partner and I: Molly Dewson, Feminism, and New Deal Politics* (New Haven: Yale University Press, 1987), 192.

70. *The Chronicle* 7, (June 30, 1876): 211–13.

71. Ibid.

72. Peckham, *University of Michigan,* 75–76.

73. *The Chronicle* 7 (November 27, 1875): 43–44.

74. *President's Report,* 1872–73, University of Michigan Archives, Bentley Historical Library, 6.

75. Peckham, *University of Michigan,* 66–67; Shaw, ed., *Encyclopedic Survey.*

76. Solomon, *Educated Women,* 120.

77. Diary, November, December 1874, 12.

78. Mary Alice Williams to her family, 30 May 1873. Williams Papers, Bentley Historical Library, University of Michigan.

79. Diary, June 1876, 15..

80. Alice Freeman to family, as quoted in Palmer, *Life,* 63.

81. Ibid.

82. Alice Freeman to Lucy Andrews, February 14, 1875.

83. Anderson, *An American Girl,* 59–60.

84. Alice Freeman to Lucy Andrews, February 20, 1875.

85. Alice Freeman to Elizabeth Freeman as quoted in Palmer, *Life,* 63.

86. Alice Freeman Palmer to Elizabeth Freeman, November 7, 1875.

87. Angell as quoted in Palmer, *A Service,* 31.

88. Alice Freeman to Lucy Andrews, February 27, 1875.

89. As quoted in Palmer, *Life,* 61.

90. Mary Caswell to David Mackenzie, undated [ca. 1903], Alice Freeman Palmer Papers, Wellesley College Archives.

91. Diary, 1875, 11, 13.

92. Alice Freeman to Family [ca. fall 1872] as quoted in Palmer, *Life,* 64.

93. Palmer, *Life,* 64; The best discussion of the Sunday School movement is found in Anne M. Boylan, *Sunday School: The Formation of an American Institution, 1790– 1880* (New Haven: Yale University Press, 1988).

94. See Alice Freeman to "Hattie," April 17, 1875.

95. Ibid.

96. Alice Freeman to "Dear Ones at Home," September 25–27, 1874.

97. *The Chronicle* 4 (November 30, 1872): 56.

98. That the organization changed its name and allowed women to be members as soon as the university began admitting women is the official story. See Shaw, ed., *Encyclopedic Survey,* 4, 1885–1890. However I found an unidentified clipping among miscellaneous Freeman memorabilia in the Bentley Historical Library that states that Alice Freeman was responsible for the admission of women to the Student Christian Association and the change in name from the YMCA. The official story seems to me to be more likely correct.

99. Alice Freeman to Lucy Andrews, February 27, 1875.

100. Alice Freeman to Lucy Andrews, July 18, 1875.
101. Palmer, *Life*, 66.
102. Peckham, *University of Michigan*, 67.
103. Account book of Levi Lockwood Wheeler, 1872–73. Levi Lockwood Papers, Bentley Historical Library, University of Michigan.
104. University of Michigan, *Announcements*, 1872–73.
105. Shaw, ed., *Encyclopedic Survey*, 4, 1850, 1860.
106. See Rothstein, *American Physicians*, 98–113, 295.
107. Palmer, *Life*, 56.
108. Diary, 1874, 12.
109. Ibid.
110. Ibid., 15.
111. As quoted in Palmer, *Life*, 60.
112. Palmer, *Life*, 65.
113. Ibid., 65.
114. Ibid., 61.
115. Alice Freeman to Elizabeth Freeman, July 7, 1875.
116. Diary, 1875, 13. Although Alice implies her salary was for the period she worked, I suspect it may be the yearly stipend.
117. See Calvin Thomas Diary, January–April 1873. Bentley Historical Library, University of Michigan.
118. See especially Alice Freeman to Lucy Andrews, February 20, 1875 and April 5, 1875. Mary Marston to Mama, January 31, 1875, Mary Olive Marston Papers, Bentley Historical Library, University of Michigan.
119. Diary, 1875, 13.
120. Alice Freeman to Lucy Andrews, December 29, 1874.
121. Alice Freeman to Lucy Andrews [ca. February 1, 1875] as quoted in Palmer, *Life*, 67.
122. Alice Freeman to Lucy Andrews, February 20, 1875. Geraldine Jonich Clifford argues the importance of teaching as a power base for women in American society as well as emphasizing the importance of the teaching experience in the social history of American women [John Mack Faragher and Florence Howe, eds., *Women and Higher Education in American History: Essays from the Mount Holyoke College Sesquicentennial Symposia* (New York: W. W. Norton and Co., 1988), 165–82].
123. Alice Freeman to Lucy Andrews, February 20, 1875.
124. Alice Freeman to Lucy Andrews, March 24, 1875.
125. Alice Freeman to Lucy Andrews, April 5, 1875.
126. Alice Freeman to Lucy Andrews, March 4, 1875.
127. Ibid.
128. Ibid.
129. Alice Freeman to Lucy Andrews, March 28, 1875.
130. Alice Freeman to Elizabeth Freeman, ca. May 1875, as quoted in Palmer, *Life*, 70–71.
131. Alice Freeman to Lucy Andrews, May 15, 1875.
132. Alice Freeman to Lucy Andrews, July 15, 1875.

133. Alice Freeman to Elizabeth Freeman, November 7, 1875.
134. Diary, March 1876.
135. *The Chronicle* 7 (April 8, 1876): 139.
136. Ibid., (June 30, 1876): 218.
137. Ibid., 216–17.
138. Ibid., 222; Edward Barry Scrapbook, Bentley Historical Library, University of Michigan.

CHAPTER 4

Crucible

When Alice Freeman graduated from the University of Michigan she was only twenty-one, barely beyond adolescence. But during the next three years, until she again left Michigan for a Wellesley professorship, she faced the most difficult time of her life. During that brief interlude she assumed awesome burdens for a young woman still in her early twenties. She earned her own living; she provided for her sister's education; and she reestablished her bankrupt, ill, and probably demoralized, father in a new community where he could eventually recoup himself professionally and resume active leadership of the family. She taught school, she continued her professional training, she rented houses, arranged for the moving of furniture, attended teachers' institutes, tenderly cared for a fatally ill sister. The catalog of her cares and responsibilities is endless.

Alice Freeman's life was never characterized by a well-defined political philosophy. She was no ideologue as educator, citizen, or woman. Her approach to any problem was always pragmatic, and it was through personality rather than creed that she exerted her influence and wielded her power to shape educational opportunities for American women. That personality was crystalized in her postcollege years. All her life Alice Freeman had been a responsible, resilient, caring person. But the personality traits, the commitment, persistence, creativity, and a capacity for hard work, that were to serve her so well as a pioneer in women's higher education were tested, accentuated, and strengthened during three hard years, 1876–79.

George Palmer, who preferred to see Alice's life in two distinct and contrasting modes, one before and one after her marriage to him, described the years, from 1876 to 1879, as a time of drudgery. "She had too little fresh air and amusement, she was burdened with family anxieties."[1] He was right, and he might well have added that she also was almost always ill, exhausted, coughing, and feverish. It was not a healthy or happy time for Alice Freeman. The jobs she held were largely dictated by family considerations rather than personal needs or professional advancement.

However George Palmer also saw the whole decade, from 1876 to 1887, from college graduation to her marriage, as "her time of service. In her second period, from her entering Windsor Academy to her leaving the University of Michigan, she was—though with many distractions—accumulating knowledge and properly serving her own ends. Now [1876–87] what others require becomes her chief care."[2] For the first three years following graduation, her young life was certainly burdened by the needs and demands of others. But he errs in attributing such cares to the whole period until her marriage. Her Wellesley presidency (1881–87) with its opportunity for creative and stimulating work hardly deserves such an unmixed assessment. George used his biography of Alice to provide his own idealized and distorted view of Alice's life. He did not necessarily see her life course as she herself had experienced it.

Alice Freeman experienced no postgraduate identity crisis, at least in the sense of having to return home to be at her family's beck and call after she finished college.[3] Her family's claim was financial and their needs were so acute there was no question but that Alice must have an independent income. Only the daughters of the relatively well-off, such as Marion Talbot, Jane Addams, and M. Carey Thomas, were likely to be forced to return home. Nonetheless the family claim was there, albeit financial.

1

Alice began the crucible years happily enough. She spent the summer of 1876 in Otego with her family. Her father's financial troubles were temporarily on hold. He did not file bankruptcy until the fall of 1877. She and her sister had a few relatively carefree weeks, visiting with friends, refurbishing their wardrobes, and also preparing Ella for seminary studies and Alice for her teaching. In August they vacationed for two weeks in Philadelphia, staying with Mary Marston, a University of Michigan friend, whose father was a centennial commissioner for Wisconsin. They explored the great exposition of 1876 and its wondrous modern machines and glimpses into old world cultures.

A dozen Ann Arbor friends from the classes of '75 and '76 were in Philadelphia at the same time (possibly by prearrangement), and Ella's fiance, Charles Talmadge, was on hand to serve as escort.[4] Although no letters from this summer survive, the Philadelphia excursion must have been a major adventure. This was Alice's first visit to a great eastern city. Her strong interest in history would have been stimulated not only by the fair, but also by the American historic places all around her. And the reunion with her University of Michigan friends was an added pleasure. But these were to be her last carefree days for a long while.

Alice had already accepted a teaching position for the next year at Lake Geneva Seminary, a young ladies' secondary school, in Wisconsin. William Fay Warner, another of Alice's Michigan classmates, was the son of its proprietor, and he had persuaded Alice and a male classmate, Albert Pearson, to join him on its faculty. They called themselves "the three," and obviously expected to bring a bit of the Michigan ambience to Wisconsin and preserve some of the camaraderie of their college years. Also Lake Geneva Seminary had promised a free education to Alice's sister, Ella, who was unlikely to obtain training elsewhere due to the family's financial troubles.[5] After the Philadelphia visit, the two young women traveled by train to Lake Geneva, near the Illinois border, in the lake-studded southeast corner of Wisconsin that is still a major summer resort and recreation area.

Alice, however, had made an inauspicious choice of jobs, a mistake she was not to repeat. Lake Geneva Seminary, founded in 1869 as a Christian school for young ladies, was a struggling institution.[6] Private academies, like railroads and toll roads, were overbuilt in the post–Civil War period. Although Lake Geneva's new teachers, despite their youth and inexperience, were probably better prepared with their University of Michigan degrees than those employed by many small, private finishing schools, money (and possibly enrollment) were decidedly in short supply at Lake Geneva. Alice expected a salary of $500 plus free tuition and fees for Ella as an academy student. Even that small stipend was not to be forthcoming for months. However, both young women did receive room and board.

Alice Freeman needed cash desperately. She was in debt. She had borrowed to supplement her savings from the Ottawa job to see her through her senior year. She was far too prudent to have splurged on the Philadelphia trip unless she felt her new salary would prove adequate to support her, help her family, and meet her obligations to her creditors. Instead she was without cash and soon found herself even further in debt. What is more, she did not find boarding school life very congenial. To add to her troubles, her health was far from flourishing. She also missed her Ann Arbor friends and the happy friendships of her university years. Despite the presence of two classmates, she was more lonesome for campus life than for her family. She described her experience at Lake Geneva in a letter to her friend Lucy Andrews.

The days have been very trying to me for the last month. The weather has been remarkably unpleasant almost all of the time I have been here, and about six weeks ago I took a cold which has threatened me more than any I have had in years. After several days it went to my lungs, and you can believe that it took all my strength to do my usual work, and get well without getting decidedly sick first. . . . It isn't entire rest to teach in a boarding school, even to one who is *entirely* well.[7]

She went on to describe her work:

. . . it isn't so very hard or wearing. I ought and hope I shall grow rested and strong in it. But Lucy I am not used to boarding school life. I think being "slave to a bell and vassal of an hour" would grow irksome to me sometimes under any circumstances.[8]

Lucy had asked Alice if she was happy, and she answered:

I am not. . . . but I am content and that is better. I am at work, and great tasks with high aims more than fill the years that stretch out before me until "I shall awake in His likeness and be *satisfied*."[9]

This was a very sad letter; she was lonely and worried about her family. She looked for comfort and recompense in her work, "great tasks and high aims" that would fill the years until death took her. But what a far cry from the eager, exuberant girl of a few months before. Few young women could contend with an onerous new job and poor health at the same time. But Alice had no choice. Further on, she added:

Nobody is perfectly happy. How can we be really happy always when there is so much suffering and *sin*. . . . I have given up trying to be happy. I have not time to spend that way.[10]

In many ways Alice Freeman's financial problems set the tone of that unhappy year. As she wrote her father, "How unfortunate that I happened to get among people who don't have any money."[11] There was no money for railroad fare home, so she and her sister stayed in Wisconsin for Christmas. As yet she had received none of her salary. Fortunately, an Ann Arbor creditor was willing to "wait a little."[12] She sent no gifts to her family and even found it difficult to put her hands on the few cents for a postage stamp or two.[13] In February, she had still received no salary but was promised that what she was owed would be paid in March. She now was also in debt to Lucy's brother, Sam Andrews, whom she had known in Ann Arbor, and she hoped she could repay him before long.[14] As she had done in Ann Arbor, she added private lessons to her other duties, tutoring young men preparing for college in Latin and Greek.[15] This brought her a little ready cash.

Meanwhile, her father's troubles were compounding. She wrote Lucy that she "had a long letter from Papa this week which made me feel very sad indeed. His health is poor, his lungs, and I fear he will have to give up practicing. I want him to. He is thinking about going back to Windsor."[16] Nor was Alice's health satisfactory. She petitioned her father for medicines and gargles for her throat, because "I am afraid my voice will entirely fail me unless I do something to counteract the constant strain on it in the schoolrooms."[17] But that was the least alarming of her symptoms. To Lucy, not to her family, she complained about the much more frightening congestion in her lungs.

But somehow, always resilient, always optimistic, Alice found the strength to enjoy the natural beauty around her. She wrote her younger sister, Stella:

The lake is spread out like a great sheet of silver in the sunshine today and looking up towards the heads on either side, the hills rise in a blue autumn mist. I never tire of looking at the water and listening to its voices. Today it is so still and glassy that it hardly breaks in ripples, even on the further bank. But sometimes when the winds are high, it groans and pounds and dashes all night long so I cannot sleep.[18]

For young Alice there was always something to enjoy.

Until that winter, party politics did not figure much in her correspondence, nor would they ever in the larger sense. She was not, however, so caught up in her own problems as not to be engaged, like Americans everywhere, by the electoral crisis that followed the Hayes-Tilden contest of 1876.

I suppose this has been an exciting week in Otego as everywhere else. Flags are flying from all the principal buildings here and the town has been full since Tuesday. A letter from Ann Arbor says the college boys are out *en masse* every night, and the whole town is wild with excitement at every dispatch. It seems to me that I never waited for political news with such anxiety, and that no election was ever so long in being decided.[19]

Alice favored Rutherford B. Hayes and was distressed at reports of southern Democrats intimidating black voters. In fact, she saw the whole mess as discrediting republican institutions in the eyes of Europe.

2

In June Alice Freeman was finally free of Lake Geneva Seminary. Although she was probably paid all or much of her salary eventually, the financial rewards had been precarious at best. In the summer of 1877 she returned to Ann Arbor to do graduate study in history. Undoubtedly another loan or some kind of financial help from Sam Andrews made Ann Arbor possible, because her savings from her salary would have gone to her family. In any case, she lived in the Andrews' household. Lucy and Alice were together again, and for a brief period she found some respite from what she called her "perplexities."

Alice Freeman's friendship with Lucy Andrews was the most intense and abiding of her emotional relationships with women other than family. It began, of course, when the two appeared on the University of Michigan campus in the fall of 1872, and they shared the same boarding house and later the same rooms. Although their friendship endured until Alice's marriage in 1887 and possibly longer, it began as a typical college girl pairing or "crush," much like those described by Helen Horowitz in *Alma Mater*.[20] By the time Alice and Lucy were separated for several weeks during the 1873 summer holiday, they shared caring, supportive, nurturant, and sometimes passionately fervent feelings for each other. They thought of their partnership as a Boston marriage and called each other "my little wife." The freedom with which they expressed their love for each other in the following passage is not atypical of the tone of their correspondence during these years: "I want to put my arms around you, dear, all around you, and fold you in, and hold you close to my heart that aches so for you, my little one."[21]

Alice's intimacy with Lucy Andrews was a mainspring of her emotional support during the years she spent at the University of Michigan and teaching in secondary schools. Lucy, with Alice's help, joined the Wellesley faculty in 1880 and continued to teach there until 1887, and their friendship remained intimate until Alice became president.[22] Alice concealed nothing from Lucy, and Lucy seems to have confided fully in Alice. Hopes, fears, frustrations, and triumphs are poured out in their correspondence.

Lucy was engaged to be married when she and Alice met, and she expected to be wed soon after graduation. Alice was soon fighting off a plethora of Michigan suitors. Lucy still expected to be married at commencement, but her betrothal was terminated by the summer of 1877, not without trauma, for reasons I have not been able to ascertain. But Lucy's and Alice's romantic relationships with men, in true nineteenth-century fashion, had nothing to do with their feelings for women friends. Women overtly and freely expressed their love for each other, as they could never safely do with male attachments. The whole turmoil of late adolescence, commitment to a peer, separation from family, sharing new intellectual horizons, was more easily done with a close woman friend. Only one side of the Freeman-Andrews correspondence survives. Alice was not a saver (or perhaps George Palmer destroyed her accumulation), but Lucy kept Alice's letters.[23] Since Alice frequently responded to what Lucy wrote, much of what both felt and believed is clear from the letters.

Lucy Caroline Andrews was born in the Sandwich Islands.[24] She sometimes cited her birthplace as Maui and other times as Molokai.

Her father, Claudius B. Andrews, had been a missionary to the islands, and later taught in a theological seminary training native
clergy, but soon also became a major landowner. Alice later said in
one of her published pieces, *Why Go to College,* that higher education
brought together the daughters of New England farmers and heir-
esses of Hawaiian sugar plantations, and she was probably talking of
Lucy and herself. Lucy's parents are rarely mentioned in their correspondence. Her mother had died before she and Alice met. Her
father was alive, but very ill the winter of 1876–77.

Lucy and her brother had come to the United States (Hawaii was,
of course, still an independent kingdom) in 1870. They matriculated
together in the preparatory department of Oberlin College. After
three months at Oberlin, Lucy transferred to the high school at Flint,
Michigan, where she lived with an uncle. She received a diploma from
the Flint high school before matriculating at the University of Michigan in 1872.

Lucy's brother came to Ann Arbor in 1871 and pursued literary
studies over the next five years, never taking a degree, and also establishing himself in the stationery business. Lucy no doubt entered the
University of Michigan at least in part because her brother, Sam, was
already there. After graduation in 1876 and Alice's departure from
Ann Arbor, Sam and Lucy shared rooms and kept house. It was this
menage that Alice joined in the summer of 1877 when she returned
to Ann Arbor for graduate work. The three young people cooked
and studied and no doubt played together during that summer, as
Alice also looked for a more financially rewarding job. It seems prob-
able that Sam paid most if not all of the household's expenses.

Perhaps because she no longer expected to be married, Lucy followed Alice's example and began teaching in secondary schools that
next year. She briefly taught algebra at Ann Arbor High School,
whose mission in the 1870s included acting as a preparatory department for the university. The following year, she taught mathematics
and Latin in Detroit Female Seminary, after which she spent a year
as instructor at the Normal School in Oshkosh, Wisconsin. She joined
Alice at Wellesley College in 1880, where for the next six years she
taught ethics and logic. She left Wellesley when Alice resigned to be
married, but continued in higher education until 1900 when she went
into business as an importer of Armenian needlework at a time when
the Turks' harsh treatment of the Armenian people was a cause

closely embraced by organized women. From Alice's letters to her, it is clear that Lucy once more came close to marriage in 1879, but again the union did not take place. Unlike her friend, Lucy lived to be over eighty, and died in 1939 in Connecticut where she made her home with a niece.

During that Ann Arbor summer of graduate study, Alice was offered an instructorship in mathematics at Wellesley.[25] Henry Fowle Durant, Wellesley's founder, was a friend of James B. Angell and leaned heavily on Angell for advice and help on academic matters. Angell later urged Durant to bring Freeman to Wellesley, but it seems more likely that Mary Marston, Alice's University of Michigan friend who went to Wellesley on Angell's advice to Durant in 1877, triggered this offer. Wellesley may have tempted Alice but instead she had a compelling need to find a position that would permit her to assist her family. The Wellesley post may have paid as little as $500 and also required living in college and separation from her family. Through Angell, she received a better offer. In September, she began work at East Saginaw High School as preceptress at a salary of $700.[26] A month later, her sister Ella joined her as a teacher in a local elementary school. Between them they made $1,200 and could provide for the Freeman family.

That fall James Freeman assigned his assets to his creditors, but was still heavily in debt. His health was poor and Estelle's tuberculosis was again active. Alice wrote Lucy that "it seemed best that there should be an immediate change for their sakes. So I am to have them out here with me, and I suppose Fred will come when his school has closed in March. I am very anxious that he should enter college—probably the Medical Department next fall."[27] The Freemans were to join Alice and Ella in the West.

In the 1870s Saginaw was a raw and boisterous lumber town of less than 10,000 people, home to sawmills and roistering lumberjacks. The pine forests that flourished on the shores of Lake Huron a generation earlier were now cutover in the neighborhood of urban centers like Saginaw, leaving the landscape bleak and unattractive in stark contrast to the richly wooded hills of the Susquehanna Valley. Much later, still disenchanted by Saginaw, Alice told her New England husband he would "like the pines of your native land better after a ride through the treeless stretches about this city built on sawdust and bayous."[28] In later years, Alice was to believe that Saginaw's climate, hot and humid in summer and cold and damp in winter, was unhealthful, but she seems not to have worried about the weather's effect on her and her family when she made the decision to establish the Freemans in Saginaw in 1877. She needed a job and the pay was high. What's more, Alice Freeman was joining the faculty of a public high school, which meant she would be paid and need not worry about the vagaries of private academy financing. Saginaw must have looked a dreary place, but it represented security.

The Saginaw High School was suffering from severe disciplinary problems when Freeman arrived; she suspended the leading offender, dissipated the friction, and raised scholarly standards.[29] During her two years at Saginaw as principal, fourteen students from this raw lumber town went on to college.[30] To accomplish that reformation was in itself an impressive task for so young and inexperienced an educator.

But Alice's tasks were not confined to her work. She was also encumbered by family responsibilities. Lucy had invited Alice to spend part of the Christmas holidays with her, but Alice explained:

> It all sounds so sunny and restful, and I am so tired, so tired today—and I can't come. Wait a moment and listen. My school is out Friday night for two weeks. That morning my father, mother, and Estelle will get here. . . .

> During the vacation I must get our people settled. I have already rented a house. They will bring most of the furniture, and you well know it will not be a light task especially in the winter . . . .

> You see, dear, that my hands are very full . . . I have been in constant communication with the [bankruptcy] assignee, and have had much to do for Ella. And the school work is very wearing. There is so much of it.[31]

When she wrote that letter, Alice Freeman was twenty-two, a year and a half out of college, the functioning head of her family, making all the decisions, assuming all the financial responsibilities, acting as breadwinner, debt payer, and family planner. She was dealing with crises imposed by the real world, and those crises were severe indeed. The exact nature of all of James Freeman's financial problems is

The Freeman family home in Saginaw, Michigan. (Photo credit: Ruth Bordin.)

never stated explicitly in surviving correspondence. The economic downturn and his lumber losses contributed. But he was also involved in a speculative enterprise, possibly the Osborn Hollow Lead mines, that proved a colossal failure. Many years later, she wrote rather fully of the 1878 family crisis to her fiancé, George Palmer, at a time when her family was again making heavy financial and emotional demands on her.

> It is only about nine years since Father lost absolutely everything he had, and we all gathered together here [Saginaw], where I was teaching, with just enough money to get the family into the house which I had rented.... Since then, Stella's long illness and death, Ella's marriage, Fred's college course, and the making of a home here—and a part of the old indebtedness paid off, though there was no legal claim on Father—indeed no moral claim; yet Fred and I have always said—and said to them who suffered in the failure—that if they were not paid in full, we would do so.[32]

Small Alice had adored her father, an adoration probably reinforced by his long absences from home when he was studying medicine. Her adoration and affection made his temporary physical and financial collapse in the 1870s even more difficult for her to handle. She empathized with her father, she wanted to and did protect and nurture him in every possible way, taking over his responsibilities as head of the family and assuming his debts. But she continued to need some parental care herself, at least a bottle of pills once in a while for her ailing body. It was her father who had helped her on her independent way. He had taken her to Michigan, even driven her to Binghamton to hear Anna Dickinson. He had been her example, if not her mainstay. It must have been very difficult to find parental roles reversed.

But as Alice Freeman predicted, matters did begin to come right after awhile. The family moved into a pleasant, spacious house on Saginaw's Jefferson Street. Mrs. Freeman helped augment the family income with paying boarders. Dr. Freeman set up consulting rooms and eventually created a large and prosperous practice. Stella's health improved temporarily, enough so that she hoped to attend school, and Fred joined the rest of the family in March and found work in a store. Alice's salary was raised to $800 in the fall of 1878, and the following August, Ella and Charlie Talmadge were married.[33]

Alice used the wedding both to rejoice for her sister and to think about marriage. She had no serious suitor at the time. Her relationship with Abram Hostetter, a fellow Michigan student who had loaned her money, seems not to have been a romantic one, but she did receive a Christmas present from him the year she was at Lake Geneva.

On opening, I discovered that it contained the set of books entitled "Devout Classics," four in number. I wish I could describe to you the beautiful cases and exquisite binding but I must wait until you can see them. They are books for which I have long wished and than which I would prefer nothing. Three are in prose—Jeremy Taylor's "Holy Living," and "Holy Dying," and the "Imitation of Christ" by Thomas à Kempis, and one volume of poems, "The Christian Year" by [John] Keble. The only thing that troubles me is that it is such an expensive present.[34]

Saginaw, Michigan, in the 1870s was surrounded by cutover lands.
(Courtesy of Bentley Historical Library.)

Nonetheless she took it. It was something she really wanted. Her diary, while she lived in Saginaw, has two entries consisting only of a name with a plus mark above it on the left hand side which I suspect was her way of recording proposals. The two for Saginaw were possibly Hostetter and a male colleague. And when reporting to Lucy about Ella's wedding, Alice used the occasion to advise Lucy on how to treat her new romantic attachment:

> You must tell him to sympathize in the broad sense with you and to let you be with him in little as well as great things. Then you will feel always that you are bound up together—that everything you do is *full* of the other. That, it seems to me, must be being married, and that you know is not the work of an hour or a year. Then no matter what comes, you can never really be separated, and two souls loving each other so, cannot drift apart.[35]

Did Alice also wish for such an attachment? Was she constrained only by her promise to her parents to educate Fred, who had helped her to the extent that he could two years earlier, and now deserved his turn at education? Eventually, Ella's marriage may well have reinforced any doubts Alice had about relinquishing control over her own life. The Talmadges were chronically short of money, and childbearing seems to have left Ella in poor health. Ella's marriage was far from carefree and only added to Alice's family concerns. Unfortunately Ella lost her two children in the diphtheria epidemic of 1882.

Although Alice Freeman made her emotional commitments to women during that part of her life when she was not financially free to marry, this did not mean she eschewed male companionship. Men hovered around her, eager to convince her to marry and to ignore her commitments to her family. She did not discourage them, and she enjoyed their company. But she was very careful to keep her relationships with men within clear limits. She did not permit herself to become emotionally entangled beyond a manageable, although real and sometimes affectionate, friendship with her male friends. Women were safe. She could let herself go. She could love and commit herself without reservation because marriage was not an issue. Emotional ties to women did not threaten her economic independence and the obligations she felt to her family.

Unfortunately, Stella's improved health was only temporary, and she died in June of 1879. Alice Freeman was very attached to her younger sister. She saw her as the brightest and most beautiful of the Freeman daughters. Alice had hoped Stella too would take a university degree and enter the new world of women's work. She wrote Lucy a few days after Stella's funeral:

My heart is full but my lips are silent all these days. You know how we "sit silent" in the presence of a great sorrow and the silence of death has fallen into my life. It is a very quiet time in my soul, but oh! Lucy! Lucy![36]

George Palmer believed Alice mourned Stella all her life and heard her murmur Stella's name as she herself lay dying.[37]

The "perplexities" of the past three years had all been resolved one way or another. It was time for a new beginning. Ella was married, the elder Freemans were increasingly prosperous and had bought a handsome house on Webster Street, although Dr. Freeman continued to practice on Jefferson. Fred was off to the University of Michigan Medical School, and Alice could take up her own concerns again. Alice Freeman's heaviest period of financial and emotional involvement with her immediate family ended with her departure from Saginaw in 1879. She never again lived with them for more than a few weeks at a time, and when she looked to family for rest and recreation, she preferred her maternal aunts and cousins in the Susquehanna Valley. Perhaps one reason she returned to the old Windsor neighborhood rather then her parents was that she found Saginaw's smelly lumber mills, large population of underpaid immigrant workers, and treeless, cutover surroundings far less likely than western New York's rolling, wooded, green hills to uplift her spirit.

But Alice's family remained a burden. Despite their increasing prosperity, the Freemans continued to make financial demands. She provided some assistance to Fred for a few more years, and she was always called to help during crises when the family was ill. In fact, George Palmer helped Ella Freeman Talmadge even after Alice's death. But Alice was never again so directly tied to her family's needs as she had been in the years before she went to Wellesley. In a sense, she was finally set free—a professional woman doing a professional job for herself, working hard, harder than she wanted to, but organizing her own life and calculating the costs and the rewards. She had achieved status as an independent New Woman.

Had her family not needed her help so desperately, she might well have completed an advanced degree. She could easily have been the first Michigan woman to earn a Ph.D. But after the summer of 1877, family cares absorbed all school holidays, and she could not afford to sacrifice her salary for even a semester to pursue further training.

Had she earned the degree it would not have much changed the course her life took. Those qualities most important to her career were the coping skills she developed during the crucible years. By 1879 she had met creatively and well a host of crises and problems, proved herself a successful teacher and school administrator, and demonstrated her ability to take care of herself and pursue an independent professional career. The skills she had acquired were to stand her in good stead.

NOTES

1. Palmer, *Life*, 73.
2. Ibid.
3. Joyce Antler, "After College, What? New Graduates and the Family Claim," *American Quarterly* 32, no. 4 (Fall 1980): 409–34.

4. Diary, Summer 1876.

5. Ibid., Promotional brochure of Lake Geneva Seminary, January 12, 1877. Pearson's sister received the same free education.

6. Ibid., Diary, summer 1876. Lake Geneva Brochure, January 12, 1877.

7. Alice Freeman to Lucy Andrews, November 19, 1876.

8. Ibid.

9. Ibid.

10. Ibid.

11. Alice Freeman to James Freeman, December 30, 1876.

12. Ibid.

13. Ibid.

14. Alice Freeman to Sam Andrews, February 10, 1877.

15. Ibid.

16. Alice Freeman to Lucy Andrews, undated [ca. December 1876].

17. Alice Freeman to Stella Freeman, November 12, 1876.

18. Ibid.

19. Ibid.

20. Horowitz, Alma Mater, 166–67. For discussion of nineteenth-century women's relationships with women, see Carroll Smith-Rosenberg, "The Female World of Love and Ritual: Relations Between Women in Nineteenth Century America," Signs 1 (Autumn 1975): 1–30; Blanche Weisen Cook, "Female Support Networks and Political Activism: Lillian Wald, Crystal Eastman, Emma Goldman," Chrysalis 3 (1977); Nancy Sahli, "Smashing: Women's Relationships Before the Fall," Chrysalis 8 (1979): 17–27; Lillian Faderman, Surpassing the Love of Men: Romantic Friendship and Love Between Women from the Renaissance to the Present (New York: William Morrow and Co., 1982).

21. Alice Freeman to Lucy Andrews, November 19, 1876.

22. The letters Freeman wrote to Andrews were given to the Wellesley College Archives after Andrews' death.

23. Much of what I know of Lucy Andrews' life and professional career has been obtained from the University of Michigan Alumni Records Office files.

24. Diary, June 1877, 16. For material on the Andrews family see Patricia Grimshaw, Paths of Duty: American Missionary Wives in Nineteenth Century Hawaii (Honolulu: University of Hawaii Press, 1989), 1883; R. Anderson, History of the Sandwich Islands Mission (Boston: Congregational Publishing Society, 1890), 375.

25. Diary, 1877.

26. Ibid.

27. Alice Freeman to Lucy Andrews, December 15, 1877.

28. Alice Freeman to George Herbert Palmer, August 16, 1886. Wellesley Typescripts.

29. Palmer, Life, 79. Her successful direction of the school is still a Saginaw legend.

30. Alice Freeman to George Herbert Palmer, May 1, 1888. Wellesley Typescripts.

31. Alice Freeman to Lucy Andrews, November 2, 1877.
32. Alice Freeman to George Herbert Palmer, March 27, 1887. Wellesley Typescripts.
33. Diary, 1878.
34. Alice Freeman to James Freeman, December 30, 1876.
35. Alice Freeman to Lucy Andrews, August 24, 1878.
36. Alice Freeman to Lucy Andrews, July 1, 1879.
37. Palmer, *Life,* 81.

CHAPTER 5

Vocation

In June of 1879, Alice Freeman accepted the professorship of history at Wellesley College.[1] The previous June Wellesley had offered her a position in mathematics and in December she had received an offer to teach Greek. Both were declined.[2] Family needs both economic and emotional still tied her to Saginaw. But after her sister died in June, 1879, and her father's practice was sufficiently established, she could leave Saginaw in good conscience.

1

We do not know precisely why Henry Durant first attempted to recruit Alice Freeman for the Wellesley faculty. President Angell of Michigan believed that it was on his recommendation. After he had watched Freeman's work in the Saginaw school system, he suggested her to Durant, who was always looking for faculty.[3] The second and third Wellesley offers do coincide with Alice's successful work in Saginaw which Angell was in a position to judge as he visited Michigan secondary schools to accredit their diploma programs for admission to the university. However, Angell's papers throw little light on the Durant-Angell connection. No letters between them exist before June, 1879, and that letter does not mention Alice Freeman.[4] Certainly there is no evidence as one historian suggests that Durant courted Freeman for his faculty at Angell's urging as a way of containing the faculty rebellion that had erupted at Wellesley in 1876 against Durant's autocratic ways .[5]

Alice's connection with and knowledge of Wellesley must go back to the late summer of 1877. Her college friend, Mary Marston, joined the Wellesley staff in the fall of 1877 and taught there for two academic years.[6] The Michigan-Wellesley network probably was underway before Durant met President Angell and was to include a number of Wellesley College faculty who were trained at Michigan during the last decades of the nineteenth century, when sound undergraduate and graduate education for women was not easily attained. In addition to Marston and Freeman, the Michigan coterie included Angie Chapin, Alice's college housemate and friend, who was professor of Greek until her retirement in 1918; Lucy Andrews, professor of ethics from 1881 to 1887; Eva Chandler, professor of mathematics until 1921; Mary Sophia Case, professor of philosophy until 1924; and Katherine Coman, professor of economics until 1913. Others were added during the years Alice Freeman Palmer was a Wellesley trustee.

Overall the University of Michigan network in the 1870s and 1880s was active and far-reaching. At first I viewed this community of scholars as primarily a women's network. Women who came to Michigan in the early days of coeducation felt a bond that tied them together well beyond undergraduate life and that continued to function in their professional careers much like the eastern old-boy network. When positions were to be filled, appointments made, Michigan graduates looked to college friends. Although the women's network was cohesive and functioned well, the bond was not only among women but transcended sex to include male classmates. Or perhaps it was the other way around; the male network was enlarged in the 1870s to include women. In any case, Michigan graduates knew who and where they were, kept in touch, shared vacations and holidays, got each other jobs, and even assisted at each other's religious conversions.

There can be no doubt that University of Michigan friends as well as its president were among the influences that brought Freeman to Wellesley. Two of Alice's old friends and classmates had already found their way to Wellesley. And being with her friends was very important to Alice. Mary Marston had spent the two previous years at Wellesley when Alice came in 1879, and Alice's roommate when she joined the faculty was her friend and former housemate, Angie Chapin, Michigan class of '75.

Other personal and family reasons also contributed to Freeman's decision to leave Saginaw for Wellesley. Alice Freeman may well have felt a need to escape her family's encompassing demands, and her sister's death freed her from her most pressing family obligations.

But she also had been very close to her sister, and felt obliged to distance herself from her loss. Plus she needed a good income. By the fall of 1879 Wellesley offered her $1,000 and living expenses, $200 more in cash than her Saginaw salary.[7]

At the same time, Saginaw had much to offer Freeman. She was a well-paid, successful teacher and administrator in the Saginaw public school system. Her sole previous experience at a female boarding facility with a live-in faculty had been far from satisfactory. Still other considerations may have given her pause. In Saginaw she was relatively close to Ann Arbor, where she hoped to continue her graduate study. Nor had Wellesley College yet acquired its later prestige, and many of its students were still in the preparatory department. She must have weighed all these factors.

In the end, Alice took the final initiative to obtain the Wellesley appointment. She wrote in May, when her sister was dying, to her friend Lucy Andrews, then teaching in Oshkosh, Wisconsin, that

I make no plans. I have recently written Mr. Durant about the state of things and have not heard from him. You see it is extremely doubtful whether I go to Wellesley. Nothing is clear before me now. I am very tired. The year has worn upon me in the school and at home, but I think I shall go to the end without getting sick. I wish, how I wish, I could spend a still summer with you, that I could tell my own Lucy how glad I am for her kind thoughts of me.... Tell me what your plans are for the summer, and let me live with you in spirit anyway.[8]

Alice's sister died, her spirits did not improve much, but she had written to Durant, and when his reply arrived, she accepted. She wrote again to Lucy:

I am not well this week, nothing very serious, only too tired to sleep, and sometimes I must confess, too heartsick to want to rest.... I will leave Saginaw as soon as I can get ready, next week, I think, but before going to Wellesley spend a few days at the old home in Windsor and Osborn Hollow. I have not been back there in three years.[9]

She always found the Susquehanna Valley restoring, and sought succor more than once with her extended family amongst the old familiar hills. The Windsor neighborhood provided a measure of rest and peace before the train took her east to New England where she had never been before.

2

The village of Wellesley, fifteen miles due west of Boston, was composed of "a tasteful church, one or two stores of the common country kind," a few scattered dwellings and the station.[10] The college itself, a short distance from the village, was not immediately visible unless one knew where to look. Wellesley was rural New England at its best, neat, unobtrusive human habitation surrounded by rolling countryside. In the nineteenth century's clean, clear air Milton's hills were visible in one direction and Mount Monadnock in another.

Alice Freeman unpacked her trunk at a college almost, but not quite, formed. Wellesley had accepted its first candidates for the baccalaureate in September of 1875, and graduated its first class in 1879, the spring before she arrived. Henry Fowle Durant, entrepreneur, evangelist, and former Boston attorney who was its founder, had applied for a charter to create a women's seminary in 1870 and amended his request to authorization for a college in 1873.[11] Wellesley's great first building, College Hall, situated on the high ground overlooking Lake Waban, was already complete when the first class matriculated. When Alice Freeman joined its faculty, Durant's ladies' college had already set many patterns for itself, a commitment to evangelical Christianity, insistence on a staff composed almost entirely of women, devotion to the creation of teachers, a charge that "calico girls," the daughters of the working middle class, rather than the wealthy, search for learning and professional training within its walls.

Henry Fowle Durant[12] was born in 1822 in Hanover, New Hampshire, but he grew up in the newly industrialized town of Lowell, Massachusetts.[13] He prepared for Harvard at the private school of Samuel Ripley, a Waltham Unitarian minister, where he learned the classics from Ripley's wife, Lois, a self-taught woman educator and scholar. This experience helped to convince him of the active role

Henry Fowle Durant, founder of Wellesley College.
(Courtesy of Wellesley College Archives.)

educated women could play in American society.[14] After graduating
from Harvard, Durant became a Boston attorney and a strikingly
successful trial lawyer.[15] He was an aggressive advocate with a style a
bit shocking to Boston conservatives, and a hint of disapproval surrounded his mode of practice. Among his clients was the Goodrich
company, then a pioneer rubber manufacturer. Durant was astute
enough to see that vulcanization had a promising economic future,
and he took his fee in company stock. This clever move provided the
base from which he expanded the considerable business interests that

made his fortune and provided the wherewithal to support the philanthropies of his later years.[16]

Durant married his first cousin, Pauline Fowle, when he was thirty-two. She was ten years his junior.[17] Her grandfather was a member of the French Huguenot nobility whose ancestors chose exile in Geneva after the revocation of the Edict of Nantes. Her father was a United States Army major whose family accompanied him to his posts at Sault Ste. Marie and Fort Dearborn when Pauline was a very young child. He died when she was six, but his family was well provided for, and his surviving child (a son had died earlier) received a superior education, not only the music lessons and European travel usual for upper middle-class young women, but several years of formal training in a French boarding school in New York City.[18] Pauline Durant belonged to a family of well-educated women. Her grandmother was a respected Latin scholar, and Durant's appreciation of women's academic abilities was further enhanced by her accomplishments and those of her family.

Pauline Durant influenced her husband in many ways. Like many Huguenots whose backgrounds included deep sacrifice for their faith, she took her religious beliefs seriously. Durant, the casual, somewhat skeptical Unitarian, tolerated his wife's more ardent Christian devotion, but did not share her zeal until they lost their only son to diphtheria in 1863.[19] Durant then left Unitarianism for his wife's evangelical Christianity, where both found a measure of succor for their loss.[20] Also, Pauline Durant had been deeply involved in philanthropy from the time of her marriage. Like many pious women of her class and time, she affirmed her Christian beliefs through charitable work among prisoners and other unfortunates. She aided the Dedham Asylum, the Bridgewater Workhouse, and the Boston jail. After his conversion, Durant precipitately left the law, believing its practice incompatible with the gospel, and he too turned some of his released energies and talents toward philanthropy.[21]

As the Durants combined religious and philanthropic interests expanded, Mount Holyoke Seminary for women caught their attention. Durant became a lay preacher and in this capacity participated in several revivals at Mount Holyoke as part of his new religious enthusiasm. He joined the seminary's board of trustees in 1867, and he and Pauline began to make substantial gifts to Mary Lyon's pioneering venture in women's education, including a $10,000 contribution toward a new library building completed in 1868.

Henry Durant, however, was not a man who was content to follow in others' footsteps. He may have abandoned the law, but he was still an active business entrepreneur. Business, however, did not fully engage his organizational talents, and he looked for a philanthropic venture that would be wholly his own. Before the death of their son, the Durants had acquired a summer home in Wellesley. This Wellesley estate, planned as their son's inheritance, could no longer be passed to a direct heir, and Durant thought of using it instead as the site for a school. At first the Durants planned two schools, one for boys and another for girls, plus an orphanage, but as early as 1867 Durant changed his will, leaving his country place for an academy.[22] In 1870 Wellesley Female Seminary was incorporated, and three years later the name in its charter was changed to Wellesley College.

Why did the Durants, bent on commemorating the brief life of their only son and motivated by deep religious commitment to aiding the unfortunate, turn to women's education as the primary vehicle of their philanthropies? No doubt their connection with Mount Holyoke played a part. They had seen firsthand a long-lasting experiment in women's education at work. In fact, Durant chose five members of the Mount Holyoke Board of Trustees for the first board of his own college. Also, as we have seen, the Civil War had propelled women into teaching, and created a shortage of trained women educators to staff the rapidly growing American secondary school systems. Training women to teach met a real need.[23]

Furthermore, women's higher education was receiving much attention. Vassar had enrolled its first students in 1865 in a wholly new type of institution, a women's college. Henry Durant could not help but be aware that Matthew Vassar, in founding that college, had created an innovative and permanent memorial to himself. Durant, no doubt, felt he could do as well or better than Vassar and enlist the whole-hearted support of his adored wife in the process. But his would be a less self-serving gift. He stipulated from the beginning that his college was not to be named after its benefactor nor was it to contain any monument to him.

Women's academies or seminaries had flourished in the pre–Civil War period. For example, Emma Willard opened Troy Seminary in

1821, Catharine Beecher the Hartford Seminary in 1827, and Mary Lyons founded Mount Holyoke in 1837. Overall the number of academies and secondary schools doubled in the two decades from 1840 to 1860. Young women attending these academies were frequently expected to (and usually did) teach, at least for a few years, before marriage.[24] The seminary movement peaked in the 1850s after which the new normal schools, specifically designed to train teachers and offer pedagogical instruction, emerged as alternatives. The curricula of the better women's seminaries rivaled in scope the course offerings of the last two years at men's colleges, and they provided a substitute for the undergraduate training offered by men's colleges and universities, but they did not award degrees.

Women's colleges appeared in several parts of the country during the 1850s but proved ephemeral.[25] However, Vassar (1865) and Wellesley and Smith (1875) successfully and permanently reestablished the pattern of degree-granting institutions for women, modeled in many ways on the best of the ladies' seminaries. But there was a difference. The colleges granted baccalaureate degrees. However, all but Smith (and Smith, when it opened, enrolled only fourteen students) of the new women's colleges had preparatory departments because so few of the young women admitted were adequately trained to do college work.[26] Vassar did not abandon its preparatory department until 1880. Nonetheless, from their beginnings, Vassar, Wellesley, and Smith were colleges, not academies or seminaries, and never saw preparatory training as anything but a temporary expedient.

The Wellesley campus in September of 1879, to which Alice Freeman was driven in one of the college's lorries, was still very much the Durant's country estate, despite the brand-new ornate, betowered, and pinnacled red brick castle that dominated the rise above Lake Waban. A generation earlier its several hundred acres had been an abandoned farm, since transformed by the Durants into a landscape reminiscent of the grounds of an English country house with not a few features traceable to the influence of the great landscape designer Capability Brown and the architect Andrew Jackson Downing.[27] The principal roads had been laid and major plantings installed long before its role as a college campus had been envisioned. The Durants loved the natural grasses, trees, and wildflowers and added to, rather than tampered with, the natural beauty of the land. In the early years, the campus grounds were always called "the Park," and a thousand rhododendrons and seven thousand crocus and snow drops were planted to enhance the landscape the fall Alice Freeman arrived on campus.[28]

However, remnants of the campus's original use as a farm remained. In the 1870s and 1880s the college dining room received its milk from Jersey cows kept on campus. Farmhands tended pigs, horses, and chickens and grew the vegetables that appeared on the college's tables. The college's ice was cut in winter from Lake Waban, and a blacksmith shoed the farm's horses.[29] During Alice Freeman's tenure the Wellesley campus was almost a self-contained rural community, a bucolic, semi-paradise inhabited by eager young women. Lake Waban provided both vista and recreation. Many rooms in College Hall had views of the perfect little lake nestled in the rolling New England countryside. And the lake also furnished Wellesley with its first organized collegiate sport. College sculls crewed by young undergraduates entertained the writer Lyman Abbott on its quiet waters in 1880.

It was a curious experience to sit quietly in the stern and be rowed by a crew of young ladies, while the lake was dotted with the tasteful uniforms of the 14 crews, each in its own colors, and the setting sun painted a picture rare in its beauty.[30]

Henry Wadsworth Longfellow was also treated to a lake excursion when he visited the college.

College Hall, dominating the south shore of the lake was even grander than Vassar's Old Main. Hammatt Billings, Boston architect who had designed the Mount Holyoke Library, supplied the plans, but Durant, with Mrs. Durant's help, was his own general contractor and supervised every detail of its construction. Both Vassar's Old Main and Wellesley's College Hall encompassed all indoor college activities under one roof. Students, slept, ate, attended classes, and worshipped in a single structure. But Wellesley's College Hall, although its plan was in one sense borrowed from Vassar, was more ambitious, more consciously elegant, than Matthew Vassar had chosen to provide.[31] Its pillared center court and five-storied atrium, frescoed chapel, and imposing public spaces provided an almost palatial setting for women's education. Even the students' rooms with

College Hall with Lake Waban in the foreground.
(Courtesy of Wellesley College Archives.)

views of the lake, the sun, and reflections on the water were quite in
contrast to Vassar's more Spartan quarters. Although the growing
enrollment and attendant crowding which took place during Freeman's tenure on campus played havoc with the original plan of par-
lor-bedroom suites where each girl could have some privacy for meditation, the rooms continued to have black walnut furniture and good
carpets. Originally the dining room was furnished with Wedgewood
china, an early victim, unfortunately, to undergraduate dishwashing
carelessness. Young Alice Freeman had never seen nor lived in anything so grand before.

Wellesley was a strange meld of sybaritic luxury and "calico girl"
austerity. The same girls who slept in black walnut beds and studied
in paneled refectories were required to perform much of the college's
routine domestic labor, wash the dishes, sweep the floors, and set the
tables. Mr. Durant had intended Wellesley college "for poor girls."
He kept the price of board and tuition relatively low, compared to
Harvard, and students' contributions through "domestic work" were

designed to make possible the low fees. But no one could buy their way out of their domestic assignments, for he saw these compulsory household tasks as an equalizing force, another form of character building, another lesson to be learned, an "opportunity of doing something for the common good."[32] As Durant saw it, the "elevating and refining influences of a happy Christian home shall surround the students."[33] And that included a contribution via menial tasks to the "family's" welfare.

Students were not necessarily enthusiastic about Durant's experiment with leveling. One entering freshman wrote to a friend the same September that Alice Freeman joined the faculty:

> I have been down to the lake twice. The grounds and buildings are simply lovely, but that don't do me any good. My work is to remove the bread from the table after each meal, brush off the plates, and also carry off and clean the fruit dishes after dinner. You may laugh at first, but just think of it when there are tables for three hundred, and two plates on a table, and to do it three times a day.[34]

When the system was finally abandoned, long after Durant's death and after Alice Freeman had left the presidency, but with her approval, the Wellesley student *Annals* jubilantly reported, "Hereafter dishwashing is no longer part of the domestic economy and takes its place with the lost arts."[35]

Interestingly, in the letters that have survived, Alice Freeman never mentions the magnificent physical setting in which she found herself in September of 1879. Other than passing reference to finding solace on the lake after ten o'clock when the students retired, or listening to a katydid on a spring evening, she says almost nothing about her physical surroundings at Wellesley.[36] She wrote vividly of the Susquehanna Valley, its contours and changing seasons, and she describes in detail a spring ramble with her high school students at Ottawa. When she taught at Lake Geneva the vistas opened up by the water thrilled her. But the Durants' carefully contrived and nourished country estate now turned college campus, her home for eight years, receives almost no notice as a physical environment at all.

Perhaps at the beginning she was too overwhelmed with responsibility and work to experience her surroundings more than passively. Later it was a familiar, if pleasant, time-worn scene that solicited no attention in her letters. She described other places she met with in her excursions around the neighborhood. After all, she had never seen New England before. But nary a word about the splendors of the college building, or the autumn color reflected in Lake Waban's waters. She was much more likely to reminisce about the University of Michigan where her brother was now a medical student or describe an excursion to nearby Lexington.

3

When Alice Freeman arrived on campus in the fall of 1879, Wellesley had 375 students, 46 of whom were still in the preparatory department soon to be phased out. Another 48 were already practicing teachers, referred to as the "teacher specials," on campus to acquire further training in academic disciplines and pedagogy but not necessarily candidates for degrees, and 6 were postgraduates.

The curriculum these students studied was heavily classical. Barbara Solomon has commented that the new women's colleges "approached curricular decisions cautiously."[37] However, as was true at the University of Michigan during Alice Freeman's undergraduate years, the 1870s was a decade of curricular redefinition. The sciences grew in importance, electives in modern languages, history, and English literature appeared. The long emphasis on the classics was crumbling around the edges, and although Vassar and Smith were reluctant to abandon the old ways, science, modern languages, and history received considerable attention at Wellesley. By 1879 the freshmen among the 208 candidates for the baccalaureate studied Greek, Latin, mathematics, history, and English literature and were permitted to elect French or German. Science entered the curriculum in the second year when chemistry was required, as was physics for juniors. However chemistry, botany, and astronomy were available as electives for upperclasswomen.[38] Greek, Latin, mathematics, and history were required of all freshmen and sophomores and could be elected by juniors and seniors, and the range of science and modern language electives was broad for the time. And from its beginnings Wellesley had required a one-hour course in history in each of the four years.[39]

The number of courses seems excessive by modern standards, but classes were only forty-five minutes long and several classes, especially electives like modern literature and history, met only once or twice a week. Sixteen recitation rooms in College Hall, twenty feet square, serviced all these classes, supplemented by a chemistry lecture room with adjoining laboratory, a natural history exhibit, an art gallery, and lecture and laboratory rooms for physics and natural history.[40] The chemistry lab was fitted for ninety-six students, four sections of twenty-four each, and each student had her own drawer and cupboard and worked out her own experiments.[41]

In fashioning the curriculum, Henry Fowle Durant had taken great care to provide ample resources for training in the sciences. Wellesley was the second college in the country to provide a laboratory for undergraduate work in physics.[42] Only two years after Alice Freeman's arrival, in September of 1881, the general course was split into classical and science courses with quite different requirements.[43]

Durant's concern with science and technology was also reflected in Wellesley's physical plant which was state of the art with every modern gadget available. College Hall was heated with steam, every study parlor had its own flue and the degree of moisture in the rooms was carefully regulated.[44] The building was lighted by gas, manufactured on the premises, but also every study was equipped with German student lamps "that give the softest and purest light known."[45] A steam passenger elevator was available for those who needed it. Hot and cold water was piped throughout the building, and the number of bathrooms was generous, the water supply a pure artesian well. College Hall itself attested to the rising importance of science in the late nineteenth century. As Durant was quick to point out, Wellesley's location was healthy with no malaria, plenty of sunshine, and good drainage.[46]

Durant himself was interested in science and technology, but his natural proclivities were nourished by his friendship with Eben Norton Horsford, his closest friend and the college's second-most important early benefactor. Horsford, an eminent chemist and Harvard professor who trained in Germany, had invented Rumsford's baking powder, the source of his fortune. Like Durant, his wealth was the result of mid-nineteenth-century commercial use of chemical processes in the rapidly industrializing American economy. Durant had consulted Horsford as early as 1871 about his plans and relied heavily on his advice with the science curriculum and equipment. Horsford's attachment to the college became almost as deep as Durant's, and his gifts to Wellesley included the electric lighting that replaced the original gas lights, a substantial library endowment, and the furnishing of a faculty parlor.[47]

Durant's and Horsford's concern for a healthy environment for Wellesley's students did not necessarily ensure a healthy faculty. Unfortunately Durant did not see overwork as a health hazard. Teachers carried grueling teaching loads as well as dormitory responsibilities. The result was that among the faculty, tuberculosis was rampant, hemorrhages frequent, unexpected leaves for poor health a constant. Alice herself was not to escape and was forced by acute tuberculosis to retire briefly from classroom responsibilities during her second spring on campus.

In the 1870s and 1880s faculty and students participated together in Wellesley College life. They shared the same two-room suites in College Hall and the same simple suppers of bread, butter, cookies, molasses, and milk in the college dining room.[48] Students were explicitly forbidden food from home and eating between meals. Henry Durant believed in health through a diet of wholesome, simple food, and he was intent on keeping "his girls" healthy.[49] Whether teachers were expected to be equally rigorous in eschewing favorite treats is not clear, but everyone, students and teachers, was free to pick the flowers, berries, and other fruits that grew abundantly on the spacious college acres. During the growing season they were not bereft.

Already in the 1870s a number of Wellesley traditions, shared by faculty and students, were in place. "Flower Sunday," the first Sunday of the college year when the chapel was decked with flowers and the text was "God is Love," dated from 1876. "Tree Day" was first celebrated in 1877 when two Japanese golden evergreens were planted, and the festival later grew increasingly elaborate with costumes, marches, orations, and odes. "Float Day" celebrated the lake and the rowing crews, simply at first, and then enhanced by fancy uniforms, banners, and original ditties. With the elaboration, hundreds of spectators made their appearance.[50]

Alice Freeman mentions some of these occasions in her letters and seems to have enjoyed them, but Henry Fowle Durant was of two minds about festivities. He expedited "Tree Day," providing the first trees to be planted. Such commemoration of "the Park" he had so carefully nurtured fit his own design. "Flower Sunday" pleased Pauline Durant, and she contributed the riches of her garden and

A College Hall suite, in which faculty and students lived.
(Courtesy of Wellesley College Archives.)

greenhouse to its celebration. But when commencement turned into another festival, Durant had second thoughts. In June of 1881 he informed the board of trustees that he felt the "excitement" attending post commencement ceremonies was "out of harmony with all the plans and purposes of the College in placing God first in all things." Diplomas should be given "as a token of the sealing to the service of God on earth of each graduate who went forth prepared for the work God would give her to do." Durant asked that diplomas henceforth be given at the close of baccalaureate services and commencement exercises dispensed with.[51] But Durant was no longer the governing force in the college when the 1882 commencement came round, and Alice Freeman liked ceremony.

4

When Alice Freeman arrived on the Wellesley campus in the fall of 1879, the college was still in many ways Henry Durant's private fiefdom. He had given the land, financed and planned the physical plant, developed the curriculum and hired the teachers. A board of trustees had existed since 1871, but met infrequently, was poorly attended, and exercised what authority it had almost solely on business and legal matters. Even business was controlled by the Durants, as he served as treasurer and she as secretary of the board. The only decisions regarding faculty and curriculum appearing in the trustees' minutes during Henry Durant's lifetime is mention of the appointment of two committees at the third annual meeting in 1873. The two Durants and Rev. Dr. Nathaniel C. Clark were appointed a committee to select teachers and Henry Durant and Edward N. Kirk a committee to prepare a curriculum.[52]

At least some of the students seem to have regarded Durant not only as founding father, benefactor, or even autocratic busybody, but as something of a tyrant. One Wellesley historian quotes a student journal of 1875, "Mr. Durant rules the college, from the amount of Latin we shall read to the kind of meat we shall have for dinner."[53] Another early student observed that he played favorites and that he had precious little experience in dealing with young people.[54] But his paternal benevolence also came through in another journal. The portrait is more benign:

> First, comes the father of the College, Mr. Durant, the leading spirit and the motive power; active and vivacious, he seems always flitting along the corridors, bound on some errand, for he is in touch with everything in the life of the place, from the dinner menu and the dish-washing, through examinations, sports, and the decoration of rooms to the students' spiritual welfare; with his keen questioning eyes, sweet smile, and pleasant greeting, he seems the parent of us all.[55]

Despite his despotic benevolence, Durant's educational ideas represented the very best the 1870s had to offer. He opposed the then current methodology of rote memorization from textbooks with the inevitable cribs and feeble understanding. He believed academics should be studied by close systematic observation, that mathematics was a tool for developing reasoning and original thinking in which merely memorizing propositions and equations was inappropriate, and he believed languages should be taught to be used and understood.[56] What is more, he was committed to a faculty of women, not an easy proposition to implement at a time when few academically trained women were available. But he did not compromise. As Lucy Stone commented on a visit to Wellesley in 1879, at this college "the cooks are men, the professors are women."[57] Possibly Durant's strong commitment to an all-woman faculty was only another evidence of patriarchy, that he wished the role of the dominant male at his college exclusively for himself. But his early death ensured that he did create a nineteenth-century college for women, taught by women, and administered by women. Durant found his faculty in high schools, seminaries or academies, and at home. Some had been trained at midwestern colleges and the University of Michigan. Others were essentially self-educated or sent out to acquire training after their selection. Ada Howard, whom he chose as president of the faculty, was a graduate of Mount Holyoke Seminary and had been on the staff of Western College for Women and Knox College, both in the Midwest, and was proprietor of a private school in New Jersey when she was offered her Wellesley post.[58] Only Frances Lord, with seven years at Vassar behind her, had real experience with college teaching. Jenny Nelson, a friend of the Durants, had been a tutor, Mary Horton was self-trained and lived across the street from the campus. Few of the faculty had baccalaureate degrees when Wellesley opened its doors in 1875.[59] But this changed as the Michigan contingent joined the college, Mary Sheldon in 1876, Mary Marston in 1877, and a bit later the famous "Michigan Six."

Durant expected a high degree of subservience from the teachers he so carefully selected. Ada Howard's authority was little more than that of a house mother. Florence Kingsley, an early student, describes her as "Miss Howard, of the stately black silk gown and crown of silver puffs" with frail health who sometimes for days "would be invisible to students."[60] Durant's word was law. Three of the faculty were arbitrarily fired by Durant at the end of the first year for supporting student opposition to performing as model scholars in a staged exhibition before official visitors.[61] As one college historian puts it, "It is clearly inconceivable that anyone could have been president in the true sense of the word in Mr. Durant's lifetime."[62]

However, Durant's will could be restrained if met with equal strength. Alice Freeman was his loyal admirer, but was also intent on maintaining her own integrity. George Palmer described an incident when Durant asked Freeman to talk with a senior "who was not a Christian" about her soul.[63] She refused. Although Freeman earlier was eager to personally intervene with her friends for religious ends, she now saw such faculty interference as an assault upon personality that she could neither countenance nor join and quite contrary to her method of interacting with students. Durant resisted her refusal but eventually accepted it. Durant admired strong people and could tolerate disagreement from Freeman as did his wife later. No doubt this mutual respect played a role in his desire to see her someday elevated to the presidency.

Alice Freeman could oppose Durant, but she also was admiring of his great gifts. She wrote to her mother:

> Mr. Durant preached to-day! If you only could have heard it, all of you! But it seems as if some great strange thing had happened, and we must speak and walk softly, as when someone has died. There was an atmosphere of sacredness about it all. . . . I never heard and never shall hear again anything quite like it for clear logic and tender appealing. This is the second time I have heard him preach.[64]

Later, as president, she commemorated Durant's life on the occasion of his death with an annual chapel service designed to help new students know and understand him. In the fall of 1883 she spoke for three-quarters of an hour on his relationship to the cause of higher education for women, reviewing his life story and showing how its course had inexorably moved toward the founding of Wellesley. However, there may well have been more Freeman than Durant in her assertion that Durant believed that women's influence was essential to solve pressing social questions if they were to be well solved.[65]

5

Alice and Angie Chapin shared quarters in College Hall, probably a two-room suite much like those inhabited by the students who lived around them. Despite having the companionship of her old Michigan friend and housemate, her letters to her family and friends during her teaching years at Wellesley displayed less than boundless enthusiasm for her new position. She repeatedly complained how hard it was to find time to write letters, of the constant interruptions by students, of the time taken by supervision of "domestic work."

She was grossly overextended in the classroom. She taught fifteen hours of history classes per week plus a daily Bible class, gave a weekly public lecture, served as advisor to the senior class, and, of course, oversaw her share of household tasks. And a residential facility like Wellesley's ensured that the faculty was always at the mercy of perfectly legitimate student needs for advice, counsel, and just plain companionship. In a notebook she kept at the time, which no longer exists but was quoted by her husband, she described a hectic day spent in a faculty meeting, examining new books, grading examinations, and taking a short walk to the village, "It is so hard to do neglected work!"[66] And a letter to her family said: "I don't feel at all satisfied with what I am doing or with the distribution of my time. What with domestic work, corridor care, section meetings, and all the unexpected breaks that will come, I seem to accomplish very little, and there is so much of everything to be done here before things are as they ought to be."[67] In another quote from the missing notebooks she complained: "Everything has gone wrong today. My Roman history did not do well this morning. Worked at the library on references. Could not get exercise, but had a little sleep this afternoon. Must improve at once in health and work."[68] She was harried and overextended.

Sharing meals and living quarters with almost the whole faculty and student body compounded the demands on faculty time. On one occasion Freeman wrote: "I have just sent the girls out of my room, telling them they must give me a chance to write a birthday letter to my father. The truth is, an individual girl is a lively and bewitching creature, but five hundred come to be a trifle, just a trifle, tiresome once in a long time."[69] And less than a week later she tells of "a beautiful day but full of disappointments and downright badness. When shall I conquer my besetting sins. Wasted the evening with Emily, Marion, Helen, and Jane."[70] Durant's close knit community of scholars engaged in a single common task sometimes proved a prison to the participants who could not escape the demands of collegial life for even an hour.

The frantic pace never let up. Alice wrote her mother in the spring of 1880 as her first year at Wellesley drew to a close:

Tomorrow I go into Boston to the library, and to do the spring shopping which cannot be neglected until I get home. Tuesday is "Tree Day" with out of door exercises. Thursday, Mary Marston and her mother come for a week's visit, and a week from next Thursday I expect Electa [her cousin] and her friend Miss Allen for several days. May 27th is our great day, when Mrs. Hayes of the White House is to be here with over seven hundred other distinguished people.[71]

Along with the festivities were field trips, a party of fifty-six students escorted to Waltham, "where the famous watches are made," then on to Lexington, where they lunched on the old battleground. Visiting professors spoke at chapel and required personal attention. A colleague's father died and her classes must be taught. "I don't know how I ever shall get through this week and next!"[72] And a month later, as her first year at Wellesley drew to a close, she had examinations to give, papers to correct, courses of reading to arrange, and

tomorrow I take my section on a little excursion over the lake to the point for a strawberry supper (the strawberries furnished by the college). Wednesday night three meetings to attend. Thursday Mr. McDivitt [a University of Michigan friend] expects to be in Boston in the morning and comes out in the afternoon. The next day is Class Day and I hope he can stay for at least part of the exercises. I have to give a lecture to the whole History Department Saturday morning on "Historical Books: How to select and read them." It isn't begun yet, and I am getting a little anxious about it.[73]

Life was not less hectic when college opened the next fall:

The American Scientific Association has been in session [in Boston] for the past week, and we have seen distinguished people here "too numerous to mention." I have really enjoyed entertaining those who came in twos or threes, especially the Princeton professors. But tonight there is a most welcome silence over the whole building.[74]

Two vivid descriptions of Alice Freeman as a Wellesley teacher supplement the harried, burdened woman she described in her letters to family and friends. She does not comment on teaching per se in her letters, only the frantic search for preparation time. Her students, however, vividly describe her teaching. One girl who was among the first to be enrolled in 1879 in her history classes describes "her wonderful sympathy with each student, amounting almost to power of divination, and her rare tact in dealing with each mind before her." She said that Freeman always treated her students with "warm personal interest," expecting each to think for herself and do original and vigorous work, appealed to the best and also took the best for granted. "All history lived and glowed, as we sat entranced for the briefest hour in all the day, as with her we traced the finger of God through all the records of men and nations."[75]

Alice Freeman's history lectures to the freshman class were so popular that upperclassmen attended as well. Martha Conant, one of her students, wrote to her family that "in hearing her speak you seem to have the whole scene before you and be one of those Grecian soldiers eighteen or twenty centuries ago, ready to charge the Persians in defense of home and country."[76]

Another student described an all-day excursion on which Freeman escorted her history students to Concord and Lexington in three carriages with forty-nine students in all. They visited the Mason house, Lexington common with its monument, the Harrington house, and relived Paul Revere's ride. They passed by the houses of Emerson and Louisa May Alcott and toured the battlefield at Concord.[77] This excursion to investigate the artifacts firsthand must have impressed the whole campus, because Carrie Park, another freshman, wrote her father about the trip. She was not Freeman's student and not part of the group, but complained, "I wish I had a membership in the class!"[78] Freeman's fellow teachers were impressed with her success as a teacher. Mary Caswell who taught with Freeman reported that "she won all because she understood and sympathized with all."[79] She was closest to those students who were "least blessed in regard to the goods of this world."[80] She remembered, no doubt, her own struggles as a student.

One of the seniors remembered Freeman when she arrived on campus as the new professor of history. She was "youthful as the youngest of us, bright, alert, charming, her fine, soft, brown hair

combed back from her brow to a dainty coil behind,... escaping in
waves, making merry here and there, her round, full face shining
with delight to be counted one of us."[81] Mary Caswell described her as

> not in the strict sense of the word beautiful in appearance. Her
> charm was rather in her whole expression. Her hair was brown and
> very pretty. It was hair of the kind that always looked fresh and
> well cared for without much attention. Her eyes were brown and
> fine. Her features were not especially well moulded or strong, but
> when she spoke, the light that played upon her face was something
> rare. Her whole being, figure, and voice and gesture, pose, joined
> in the magical effect.[82]

She may have been harried, overworked, and uncertain, but her
students and colleagues at Wellesley saw her as a radiant, vibrant,
assured woman.

In February of 1881 Alice Freeman suffered a severe hemorrhage
in the upper lobe of her right lung.[83] She was hospitalized, her doctors predicted she would not live six months and advised her to seek
a cure in southern France. Instead she retired once more to the
ancestral farm in the Susquehanna Valley where she stayed with her
Aunt Sarah until the first week in April after the Easter recess, when
she resumed her full load of Wellesley tasks. Although later in her
Wellesley career her health was again threatened by extreme fatigue
and overwork, the lesion of 1881 had completely disappeared when
Alice Freeman was examined nine years later and it never reap-
peared.[84]

Alice Freeman's health was mended, but the crisis placed a severe,
if temporary, strain not only on her health, but on her relationship
with both her family and Lucy Andrews. Soon after she had retreated
to Aunt Sarah's she wrote to reassure Lucy that she was sleeping late,
breakfasting at ten, and remaining indoors during inclement
weather, but she chided Lucy for alarming Alice's parents who threatened to come East in response to the panicky letter Lucy sent them.
Alice was more than annoyed:

> I have kept them constantly posted as to the exact condition I was
> in, sent my father a report of Dr. Parker's examination. Dr. Jones
> wrote them his opinion.... [but] the fact that you had recently seen

me, made it possible for your alarming letters to throw the whole family into an agony of suspense and fear, in which they suffer for me in anticipation the sorrow we have endured over our Stella. Ah, Lucy, Lucy! I know your love for me prompted this action, but if you had known me as well as I thought, and if you had known my father and brother at all, you would never have taken this step.... Be assured, hereafter, dear Lucy, that I fully comprehend my case, that I shall always be under the best practical medical advice, and that my father and I are in the most perfect understanding, and as long as he and my brother live, I shall never want anything which my health requires.[85]

Lucy was concerned, but Alice insisted on handling her problems without assistance.

Although she returned to Wellesley after the Easter break, her health continued to be precarious. Her illness also created financial problems. She wrote her mother:

I never was in quite such a fix before. Last year when a teacher was sick either in the hospital or away from college—if even for a limited time—salary went on. Last summer the trustees passed a law that when a teacher was away, her salary was stopped. There are four of us who have been overworked and had to leave, and none of us think it is a very generous policy, considering the way teachers are worked here, but there is nothing to be done now. And I am out of a month's salary, beside all the expenses of medicine, doctors, and travelling.[86]

Her loss of salary meant she could not meet all her obligations to Fred, who was then in medical school, and that she needed repayment of loans she had made to her sister's husband. Her illness had taken a fifth of her year's salary and family needs would have to give a little.

In many ways Alice's family was a burden she could not escape. She loved them deeply. Along with her Michigan friends they provided her with emotional support during these years. But they asked much of her in return for their affection and support. And during this period of her life, money and gifts seem to have flowed only one way, from her to them. Alice probably regarded all funds received from her family during her college years as a loan she was to repay either directly or by supporting her brother Fred during his medical school training. She also seemed to consider her father's debts as her obligation. By 1879 she had already provided her sister Ella's seminary education and assumed major financial responsibility for the whole family when they moved to Saginaw. Despite Dr. Freeman's growing practice and prosperity, Alice continued to assist the family financially during her years at Wellesley, not just Fred but her parents and sister Ella and her husband.[87] The burden was sufficiently onerous that she felt the need on occasion to distance herself from her family. The summer of 1881 was such a time. She did not go to Saginaw that summer as planned but in August returned again to Osborn Hollow, exhausted and much in need of further rest before taking up her academic duties in September.[88]

The spring and summer of 1881 were stressful in another way. Henry Durant's health was failing rapidly. The college physician's diagnosis the previous fall was Bright's disease, and although Durant continued to be active, he found it increasingly difficult to keep his usual close control on his business interests and the college. A winter vacation in Mexico had not helped much.[89] Alice Freeman's worry over Durant's health and what this would mean to the future of Wellesley was complicated by the fact that her old friend Lucy Andrews was eager to join the Wellesley faculty. Alice wanted to help her. But just where control lay and who made decisions was somewhat ambiguous and very troubling. Alice wrote Lucy:

> Gertrude Woodcock [a student] is here wandering around the table like an uneasy ghost, and getting her arms around me frequently. So don't expect a letter. And yet I must send her to bed, close my ears to that whip-poor-will, singing in the moonlight across the lake, and tell you two things at least before I go to sleep. And first, Mr. Durant is very ill today.... As soon as he is better, I shall see him again [about Lucy's position].[90]

Meanwhile Alice had arranged for one of the trustees to interview Lucy in New York. All went well with Lucy's appointment, and she took her place as instructor in classics in September of 1881.

Mr. Durant continued to fail. Alice had written her mother in June of 1881, "There are to be radical changes, some overtwinings, and it is a question of how some things will end. But I do not propose to worry."[91] Of course she did worry and one wonders if she had any notion of how things would come out. About the time of President Garfield's death in late September, when Durant was no longer able to leave his home, he presumably left final instructions about the college.[92] But whether those instructions specifically named Alice Freeman as Wellesley's next president, we do not know. As she wrote to her parents, her "own prospects have never looked so bright," but she saw only dark days ahead for the college.[93]

Alice Freeman's two years as a Wellesley teacher resulted in her being well-informed about the college and fully cognizant of its strengths and weaknesses. She knew the faculty and student body and, probably most important of all, had earned Pauline Durant's respect and affection. She was still a very young woman, only twenty-six, but she had acquired administrative skills as a Saginaw principal and had demonstrated her gifts as a teacher at Wellesley. Unlike Ada Howard, who was not particularly well liked by either faculty or students, the whole Wellesley community loved Alice Freeman. What is more they had had enough of Durant's benevolent patriarchy and were ready for a different kind of governance.

NOTES

1. Diary, July 1879, 22.
2. Diary, June 1878, December 1878, 18, 22.
3. Angell's memorial address in Palmer, *A Service*, 39.
4. H. F. Durant to J. B. Angell, June 12, 1879. James B. Angell Papers, Bentley Historical Library, University of Michigan. Much has been made on very slim evidence of the Angell-Durant connection. For example, see Palmieri, "Adamless Eden," chap. 1. I am convinced that the Michigan-Wellesley connection was less an Angell-Durant liaison and much more the result of the Michigan women's network.
5. Palmieri, "Adamless Eden," chap. 1.
6. No correspondence between Freeman and Mary Marston survives, but undoubtedly letters between the two University of Michigan friends were exchanged.
7. Trustees Ledgers, 1879–80. Wellesley College Archives.
8. Alice Freeman to Lucy Andrews, May 24, 1879.
9. Alice Freemen to Lucy Andrews, July 1, 1879.
10. Edward Abbott, "Wellesley College," *Harper's New Monthly Magazine* 53 (August 1876): 322–23.

11. Several biographical accounts of Durant exist. The most complete is Florence Morse Kingsley, *The Life of Henry Fowle Durant: Founder of Wellesley College* (New York: Century Co., 1924). Although eulogistic and sentimental, it is useful for its detail. The best brief account of Durant is in Horowitz, *Alma Mater*, 42–55; see also Elizabeth Donnan's article in the *Dictionary of American Biography*, 3: 541–42; Glasscock, *Wellesley*, 3–10; and Palmieri, "Adamless Eden," chap. 1.

12. Durant was born Henry Welles Smith. He changed his name in 1847 to avoid confusion with other Boston lawyers named Smith. Both Durant and Fowle were family names. See Kingsley, *Durant*, 77–78.

13. Ibid., 23–28.

14. Ibid., 37–45.

15. Ibid., 67–71.

16. Ibid., 138.

17. Ibid., 94–98.

18. Ibid., 56–65, 71–75.

19. Ibid., 125–26.

20. The Durants were members of the Wellesley Congregational Church, but also had close ties to Methodism through evangelist Dwight Moody.

21. Thomas Wentworth Higginson, one of Durant's Harvard classmates, recounted an incident that occurred before Durant ceased practicing law in which he expressed utter contempt for the legal profession, "'Law', said Durant, 'is the most degrading of all professions. All human law is a system of fossilized injustice, and the habitual study of it only demoralizes'" (*Woman's Journal*, October 15, 1881, 1).

22. Kingsley, *Durant*, 157–70; Glasscock, *Wellesley*, 9–10; Palmieri, "Adamless Eden," chap. 1.

23. The academies saw themselves first and foremost as preparing women to be better wives and mothers and therefore enhancing their ability to perform well in their allotted sphere, but in fact they trained many teachers.

24. See Kathryn Kish Sklar, *Catharine Beecher: A Study in Domesticity* (New Haven: Yale University Press, 1973), chap. 12; Solomon, *Educated Women*, chap. 2; and Anne Firor Scott, "The Ever-Widening Circle: The Diffusion of Feminist Values from the Troy Seminary 1822-1872," *History of Education Quarterly* 19 (Spring 1979): 3–25, for a discussion of women's secondary education in the nineteenth century.

25. Solomon, *Educated Women*, 47.

26. Ibid., 20–21.

27. Glasscock, *Wellesley*, 265ff; Horowitz, *Alma Mater*, 50ff; and Abbott, "Wellesley College," contain vivid descriptions of the early Wellesley campus, as does Montgomery Schuyler, "Architecture of American Colleges: Three Women's Colleges, Vassar, Wellesley, and Smith," *Architectural Record* 31 (1912): 512–37.

28. Lyman Abbott in the *Christian Union*, June 9, 1880, as quoted in Glasscock, *Wellesley*, 285.

29. Glasscock, *Wellesley*, 467–68.

30. Lyman Abbott in the *Christian Union,* June 9, 1880, as quoted in Glasscock, *Wellesley,* 241.

31. See Horowitz, *Alma Mater,* chap. 3, for a thoughtful description of College Hall and its effect on educational practice. College Hall, which burned March 17, 1914, is also described in Kingsley, *Durant,* 197–204; and Glasscock, *Wellesley,* 14–16.

32. Kingsley, *Durant,* 216.

33. *Wellesley College Catalog,* 1879–80, 78.

34. Carrie Rose Park Huntington to Ella and Angie [ca. September 30, 1879]. Carrie Huntington Papers, Wellesley College Archives.

35. *Wellesley Annals,* 1888–89. Wellesley College Archives. Hereafter cited as *Wellesley Annals.*

36. Alice Freeman to "Dear Ones at Home," September 3, 1880. Carla Wenckebach, the young German educator hired by Alice Freeman as head teacher of German, responded quite differently to Wellesley's opulent quarters. She "could hardly recognize its being merely a school." She thought the Royal Palace in Berlin small in comparison to College Hall "which in length and stateliness of appearance surpasses even the great Winter Palace in St. Petersburg." [Margarethe Mueller, *Carla Wenckebach: Pioneer* (Boston: Merrymount Press, 1908), 218.]

37. Solomon, *Educated Women,* 80. See also Rosalind Rosenberg, *Beyond Separate Spheres,* 52, who contends that the women's colleges tried to emulate the classical curricula of the men's colleges just as those colleges were discarding the classical emphasis for the sciences.

38. *Wellesley College Catalog,* 1879–80, 12–18.

39. This represents innovation. In the 1870s Vassar had no courses in history or economics (Campbell, *Liberated Woman,* 38).

40. Abbott, "Wellesley College," 328.

41. Ibid., 330.

42. Glasscock, *Wellesley,* 126.

43. Ibid., 124.

44. Kingsley, *Durant,* 226.

45. *Wellesley College Catalog,* 1878–80, 79.

46. Ibid., 1879–80, 78–79.

47. Glasscock, *Wellesley,* 18–19; Kingsley, *Durant,* 117–19.

48. Alice Payne Hackett, *Wellesley: Part of the American Story* (New York: E. P. Dutton, 1949), 55.

49. Ibid., 56. For an analysis of Durant's beliefs about health see Martha H. Verbrugge, *Able-Bodied Womanhood: Personal Health and Social Change in Nineteenth Century Boston* (New York: Oxford University Press, 1988), chap. 6. Breakfast was baked beans and brown bread, oatmeal, milk, fruit, and coffee only twice a week. Lunch was again heavy on the carbohydrates, bread, cake and cookies, cold meat, fruit, milk, and sometimes soup (Martha Pike Conant, *A Girl of the Eighties* [Boston: Houghton Mifflin Co., 1931], 99).

50. Glasscock, *Wellesley,* 236–40.

51. Minutes of the Board of Trustees, June 21, 1881, Wellesley College Archives.

52. Minutes of the Board of Trustees, June 17, 1873, Wellesley College Archives.

53. Glasscock, *Wellesley*, 16.

54. Kingsley, *Durant*, 229.

55. Elizabeth Stillwell student letter, 1875, as quoted in Florence Converse, *Wellesley College: A Chronicle of the Years 1875–1938* (Wellesley, Mass.: Hathaway House Bookshop, 1939), 27.

56. Kingsley, *Durant*, 191–92.

57. As quoted in Glasscock, *Wellesley*, 164.

58. Glasscock, 11–12, 87.

59. Ibid., 87–88. The most comprehensive analysis of the early Wellesley faculty is to be found in Palmieri, "Adamless Eden." chap. 4.

60. Kingsley, *Durant*, 227.

61. Palmieri, "Adamless Eden," 63–69. Palmieri suggests that Durant brought Freeman to Wellesley in 1879 to help contain student rebellion. The rebellion was earlier, and there is no evidence of any such motive by Durant.

62. Glasscock, *Wellesley*, 22.

63. Palmer, *Life*, 98.

64. Alice Freeman to Elizabeth Freeman, November 14, 1880.

65. Unidentified clipping in Catherine McCamant scrapbook, Class of 1887 Papers, Wellesley College Archives.

66. Palmer, *Life*, 96.

67. As quoted in Palmer, *Life*, 112–13. The letter is no longer in her papers.

68. Palmer, *Life*, 96. Very few of the letters that George Palmer reproduced in his memoir are now in her papers. I suspect that the letters as published by him were heavily edited, because their tone and style are different from the original letters that still exist. Both samples of letters, however, show a harried, overworked, fatigued woman whose zest for life is limited by too many demands on her time and energies.

69. Ibid., 104.

70. Ibid., 96.

71. Alice Freeman to Elizabeth Freeman, May 16, 1880.

72. Ibid.

73. Alice Freeman to Elizabeth Freeman, June, 14, 1880.

74. Alice Freeman to "Dear Ones at Home," September 3, 1880.

75. Lila S. McKee to Miss Perkins, February 5, 1903. Alice Freeman Palmer Papers, Wellesley College Archives. McKee was president of the Western College for Women at the time she wrote this letter soon after Alice Freeman Palmer's death.

76. Conant, *Girl of the Eighties*, 110–11.

77. Notebook of Helen B. Hart, 1880, Records of the Class of 1883. Wellesley College Archives.

78. C. P. Huntington to Papa, May 10, 1880. Carrie Huntington Papers, Wellesley College Archives.

79. Mary Caswell to David MacKenzie, undated [ca. 1903]. Alice Freeman Palmer Papers, Wellesley College Archives.

80. Ibid.

81. Adeline Emerson Thompson's remarks at the Alice Freeman Palmer Memorial Service, University of Chicago, 1903.

82. Mary Caswell to David MacKenzie, undated [ca. 1903]. Alice Freeman Palmer Papers, Wellesley College Archives.

83. In the retrospective joint diary, Alice Freeman mistakenly dates this event 1880 as does George Palmer in his *Life*.

84. Diary, February 1880; Palmer, *Life*, 99–100.

85. Alice Freeman to Lucy Andrews, March 19, 1881.

86. Alice Freeman to Elizabeth Freeman, May 6, 1881.

87. See especially Alice Freeman to family, May 16, 1880, Alice Freeman to Ella Freeman, November 14, 1880, and Alice Freeman to parents, June 5, July 5, 1881.

88. Alice Freeman to family, August 15, 1881.

89. Kingsley, *Durant*, chap. 27.

90. Alice Freeman to Lucy Andrews, May 10, 1881.

91. Palmer, *Life*, 112.

92. Ibid., 114; Kingsley, *Durant*, 347.

93. Alice Freeman to Elizabeth and Fred Freeman, July 5, 1881.

CHAPTER 6

Fulfillment

The year 1881 marked a dramatic change in Alice Freeman's life course. Until then, she had pursued a promising if undistinguished career as an intelligent, creative, hardworking woman educator. She had pioneered as an early participant in university coeducation, done yeoman service as a seminary and high school teacher and principal, and contributed meaningfully as an early member of the Wellesley faculty. But in no way was she a national figure.

If Henry Fowle Durant had lived another ten years, it seems unlikely Freeman would have achieved the position in education she held for the rest of the century. Either she would have married or continued as a Wellesley professor, popular and beloved, but lacking the academic distinction brought to Wellesley by a Mary Calkins, founder of one of the first psychological laboratories in the country, or a Sarah Whiting who presided over the second physics laboratory in the United States. She provided part of the succor that made possible the accomplishments of both these women, but, even in her chosen field, she did not begin to rival her University of Michigan colleague Lucy Salmon, whose analytical studies of American constitutional history represented major scholarly advances.

1

Henry Fowle Durant's early death at fifty-nine (his wife Pauline lived another thirty-six years) provided the opportunity for Alice Freeman to become, during the last two decades of the nineteenth century, the most distinguished woman educator in the United States. Freeman set the pattern of what a woman president should be for a women's college. With her election to the Wellesley presidency, she became the only woman to head an independent, nationally known college.[1] Vas-

Alice Freeman when she became president of Wellesley
College. (Courtesy of Wellesley College Archives.)

sar and Smith had men as presidents. Mount Holyoke had not yet
moved beyond academy or seminary status. Radcliffe's ambiguous
role as a Harvard annex was still tenuous and included no power to
grant degrees. Bryn Mawr and Barnard did not exist.

What is more, Alice Freeman's visibility coincided with the golden
age of the American university presidency. As Hamilton Mabie, *Gilded
Age* editor and critic, commented in 1893: "There is no class in the
community more influential today. None commands greater respect
on public questions no less than on academic and educational questions; they [college presidents] are credited with large intelligence,
with disinterestedness, and with high aims."[2] The high prestige of
college presidents was abetted by the fact that the hundred-year-old
republic was beginning to have major intellectual pretensions. In the

1880s the United States routinely sent its best scholars abroad to the sources of European culture and science for training. At the same time Americans rightly believed that their mobile social system provided the most open avenue to higher education in the world. Simultaneously, Old World learning was respected, and the United States was proud of its unique democratic opportunities. At no other time in its history had the United States so revered and listened to its educators, put them in positions of trust, and seen them as incubators of public policy. James Burrill Angell alternated educational leadership at the University of Michigan with sensitive diplomatic missions to China and Turkey and important negotiations on Pacific fisheries. Cornell's Andrew Dickson White served as American minister to Russia, minister and ambassador to Germany, and was a major force in the early Hague peace conferences. Charles W. Eliot of Harvard made his chief contribution to public policy in the area of civil service reform.

Alice Freeman was the only woman in a galaxy of academic giants, all of whom were making pronouncements on the proper course of the republic. Alice Freeman did not rival Angell, White, or Eliot as an arbiter of major public questions. She largely confined her public role to matters of educational policy, but in the 1880s and early 1890s higher education had no other woman's voice that could match Freeman's in prestige and breadth of audience. And certainly no other voice that could rival hers for eloquence and charm. Now the college girl who had basked in her fellow students' affections, the teacher who had seduced her pupils into loving loyalty and strong commitment, had a larger role to play. She was neither radical nor aggressively assertive, except that she believed with zeal that women should be educated. Had she been a "shaker" rather than a "mover" she would have been neither chosen for her role nor listened to when she achieved it. And she was certainly not among the first of her sex to champion higher education. Instead she belonged to the consolidating generation that made higher education for women a part of the mainstream.

Freeman was women's strongest voice in a number of academic battles. And academic battles of importance were fought during the years she functioned as women's representative in college- and university-governing councils. The American university was being shaped in a mold that lasted for at least seventy-five years, and Alice

Freeman was of great importance in shaping admission standards, implemented eventually by college boards; curricular reform, substituting science and the infant social sciences for the heavy dependence on classics (and an earlier departure, literature); and professional standards, including research degrees, tenure, and sabbaticals for faculty. She fought all those fights, gracefully, for Wellesley and in so doing assisted the acceptance of new standards in academe as a whole.

2

On October 3, 1881, after a long illness, Henry Fowle Durant died of Bright's disease at his home on the Wellesley campus. In what Pauline Durant later called "a sacred hour," he indicated on his death bed that he wished to see Alice Freeman as his successor, or as Mrs. Durant chose to view it, "God had given you [Alice Freeman] to us in our great need."[3] Whether he specifically designated that she should become president is not known. Ada Howard, president of the faculty, was ill that fall and had frequently suffered periods of invalidism in the past.[4] In any case Howard was incapable of providing real educational leadership. Pauline Durant had shared her husband's concern with every facet of the college's development, and she undoubtedly hoped to play as active a leadership role as Henry. However, her real concern was with the individual student and her needs, not the larger purpose of the college.[5] Had educational leadership fallen into Pauline Durant's hands and Wellesley followed her chosen path it would have become a parochial, self-consciously religious institution, probably focused on training missionaries and clergymen's wives, not the leader in the professionalization of education for women that Alice Freeman shaped.

Over a month elapsed between Durant's death and Alice Freeman's appointment as acting president and vice-president. Not until the Executive Committee of the Board of Trustees met on November 14, 1881, was formal action taken.[6] Freeman replied to a letter she had received from Eben Horsford that suggests he had been talking with her about accepting the presidency, but the trustees' minutes are sketchy for this period and Alice wrote no letters that survive to family or friends.[7] Lucy Andrews had joined the Wellesley faculty that fall. Alice had no need to correspond with her; they could consult and confide in person. Had she actively hoped for the appointment, she may not have chosen to confide in her family. In any case, we do not know if Alice Freeman expected or hoped for the responsibilities she was about to assume. She certainly was aware of Henry Durant's confidence and trust. She must have known that Mrs. Durant felt comfortable working with her. Alice never shirked the responsibility necessary to give her control over outcome. By now she had a substantial investment in the success of Wellesley as an experiment in higher education for women.

This was an uncertain, fearful time for the college. Undoubtedly Durant's prolonged ill health contributed to the deterioration of his financial affairs. Just before he died the New York Belting Company in which he was a heavy investor was in danger of bankruptcy and also tainted by corrupt practices not of his doing.[8] The college had consistently lost money (approximately $50,000 per annum) since it opened its doors, deficits that Durant personally absorbed. Enrollment was growing and faculty increasing in size, but no realistic long-term financing had been provided. Without Durant's business acumen and open purse, could Wellesley carry on?

If Wellesley was to flourish, leadership was needed. Alice Freeman rose to the challenge and provided that leadership, but whether she sought leadership or had it thrust upon her, we can only speculate. Her friends thought the proffered appointment came as a surprise, that she hesitated a bit before accepting, conferring first with Ada Howard, the Executive Committee of the Board of Trustees, and Pauline Durant.[9] But her acceptance seemed enthusiastic. And as we saw earlier, she had written her mother in July that her own prospects had never seemed so bright. Ada Howard, in feeble health, was to go away for a rest, and Howard's absence from campus would assure that Alice was in undisputed control. Although Freeman's teaching load was reduced, she continued as head of the history department.

When the announcement was made in chapel the evening of November 15, the enthusiastic good wishes and congratulations of faculty and students did not conceal that she faced a back-breaking job. Alice Freeman was only twenty-six, but if a trained woman, a product of the university system dominating higher education in the last quarter of the nineteenth century, was to head Wellesley, she would have to be young. There were no others. As one of her contemporaries put it, "It was not only that *we* [the students] were young, the college was young, too, and so was our president."[10]

3

There were two aspects to the Wellesley presidency as assumed by Alice Freeman in 1881. First, Wellesley had never before had a president in a real sense. Ada Howard had been little more than a house mother. Henry Fowle Durant had presided over the college as chairman of the board and treasurer. The presidency itself had to be defined and delineated, and Freeman did it with dispatch. Secondly, Wellesley's academic mission had to be redefined and broadened to include clearly the new professional and scholarly training of women.

First came the delineation of the office of the presidency. What were the duties and responsibilities that went with that office? How much of the governance of the college did the president assume? And this in the face of Henry Fowle Durant's adoring and strong-minded widow inheriting his mantle as treasurer of the college, the person with absolute and intimate control of the purse strings. It was this aspect of her job, delineating the powers of the office itself, that fully engaged Alice Freeman at the beginning of her tenure and that was never clearly and cleanly resolved, especially in terms of the power and influence of Pauline Durant. This problem recurred later when Freeman relinquished her presidential duties.

Nonetheless Alice Freeman was able to shape the contours of the Wellesley presidency in very significant ways. Her contributions fall into two categories, substance and style. Wellesley lore abounds in stories about the young professor summoning her senior students and asking them to help her, because only with their help could she assume the presidency.[11] And, undoubtedly, she did just that, because it would be true to her style, making others believe her projects were their own treasured goals meriting their sacrifice and dedication. Henry Durant imposed his standards on the college; Alice Freeman made her goals something everyone else soon knew to be what they had always wanted and worked for.

Both Durant and Freeman had what the nineteenth century called magnetic personalities, and both got their own way, but Alice Freeman had the lighter, easier touch. Durant had governed Wellesley

Alice Freeman, second from left, with a group of students on the steps of College Hall. (Courtesy of Wellesley College Archives.)

College with a heavy evangelical hand. For example, he remained to the end of his life part of a mid-century tradition of a crusading Protestantism that militantly demanded total commitment to a personal savior and an overt conversion experience. And he actively proselytized students to that end. Alice was a believing devoted Christian, but the late-nineteenth-century winds of tolerance had softened her approach. When it came to religion, she did not believe it right to impose; she could only convince, and that she did gently.

Both Henry Durant and Alice Freeman interacted closely with students, but Henry Durant's style was patriarchal and authoritarian, albeit kindly and caring. Alice Freeman treated students as cohorts marching under the same banner toward the same goals. If Henry Durant's style was far more authoritarian than Freeman's, Ada Howard's had been much more remote. Poor health, her age (she was in her fifties), and her lack of teaching responsibilities tended to distance her from students even though she lived closely among them in College Hall. Ada Howard had no nickname, at least none that found its way into the written record, but to the Wellesley community of the 1880s, Alice Freeman was "the Princess," one of this community of women and yet also apart.

As historians of education have long pointed out, American institutions of higher education stem from two roots, the Germanic tradition which emphasizes the responsibility of the professor to his academic discipline, and the English system where the emphasis is on developing the person, nurturing the responsible citizen, and of course, incidentally training the clergy and later the British civil service. In the English system the don's primary responsibility was the "formation" of his students.[12] Under Henry Durant, the English tradition had supplied the Wellesley pattern, albeit training the clergy was interpreted as training Christian teachers, missionaries, and clergymen's wives. Alice Freeman perpetuated this tradition in the style, but not the substance, of her presidency. Her close, almost maternal, relationship to students, the familial residential patterns she found congenial, the intimate interaction between campus life and academic learning all belong to the English pattern. But her determination to professionalize the faculty and her emphasis on science in the curriculum fit the Germanic tradition.[13]

The cottage system beloved by both Alice Freeman and Pauline Durant also smacked of the English nurturant ideal. Cottages already had a foothold on campus when Freeman took the helm. However, the first cottage, Waban, had been more a convenient solution to the crowding in College Hall than a reversal of Henry Durant's centralized patriarchy. And Stone Hall already housed "teacher specials" in the fall of 1881.[14] But it was Alice Freeman who exalted the cottages (three more were opened during her tenure) to embody the best in college life. Students were promised at least a year of cottage living, expected, of course, to be the best year of all, and Freeman herself moved her residence from College Hall to Norumbega Cottage when it opened in 1886.[15] Norumbega opened with a sentimental housewarming that symbolized the cozy familial quality of cottage life. The president received guests in "her new and beautiful rooms." Eben Horsford talked about the possible early Norse settlement nearby after which the cottage was named. John Greenleaf Whittier sent a poem, a ceremonial fire was lit on each of the house's several hearths, and hot maple syrup on ice, apples, and doughnuts were the eminently suitable refreshments.[16] Alice Freeman participated faithfully in the Norumbega "family's" life, entertaining her friends in its dining room, attending its many theatricals, and joining student discussions. She truly accepted Norumbega as her home.

But Alice Freeman not only lived with her students, she also followed the English system in taking responsibility for their moral and spiritual welfare. She conducted daily chapel services, assisted on Sundays by clergymen from elsewhere. She encouraged the organized religious life of the campus. Following the University of Michigan pattern, as she often did, she and several of her colleagues who also were Michigan graduates organized the nondenominational Student Christian Association in 1884.[17] She supported Wellesley's devotion to missions. By 1883 twenty-four Wellesley students had entered the mission field, and she took pride in the high percentage of students who professed Christianity and were church members.[18]

But it was her personal intervention in religious questions that set the tone for her influence on the religious lives of Wellesley students. Religion rather than politics was the focus for student ferment in the 1880s. Vida Scudder, who attended Smith from 1880 to 1884 and later joined the Wellesley faculty, told how in the 1880s religion provided the prime subject for late-night undergraduate discussions. The curfew was defied "to confide to one another those awful Doubts.... Separate at 10 o'clock? Why, the result might be a lost

Norumbega Cottage, erected during Alice Freeman's Wellesley presidency.
(Courtesy of Wellesley College Archives.)

soul."[19] Alice Freeman played a central role in this process of religious questioning. Much of her one-on-one counseling of students involved religion; for example, she wrote George Palmer when he was courting her:

> One of the Freshmen has just left me after an hour of eager talk about God's will. She is a wonderfully bright, attractive mind, sensitive but timid, afraid lest her "sins are too stultifying to leave enough soul-life to be worth saving." How I like to talk of these things with such girls, so honest and simple, so unwilling to run any risk of shirking duty or failing of the truth."[20]

As president, Alice Freeman was Wellesley's chief disciplinary officer. Nothing resembling student government existed before 1887, but her discipline was administered with such grace and tact that no one could resent it. One freshman wrote her family that the good-natured college physician was overfree with giving excused absences to delinquent students for all sorts of trumped-up illnesses. Class attendance was compulsory, but the rule was rapidly becoming a farce. Something had to be done. President Freeman announced at chapel that the regular Monday evening programs of entertainment would cease because class absences were so great that "there must be too much strain on the girls." And the freshman insightfully added, "This is just like Miss Freeman, such a delicate and yet forcible way of giving us a lesson."[21] Go to class or lose other privileges, but not as punishment. No one is accused of wrongdoing. The curtailment of their fun was only to protect their health which they themselves had demonstrated was in jeopardy.

In general student reactions to Freeman give evidence of the new spirit of cooperation and affectionate camaraderie, but also attest to the strong leadership that she brought to the campus. In 1884, students complained that the interval between breakfast and "silent time" was too short to complete their chores. Like normal high-spirited undergraduates they undoubtedly hoped to get "silent time" abolished or shortened, but their wily president announced that instead extra time would be provided "in future by having the morning bell before breakfast ring fifteen minutes earlier," and the student reporter adds: "A less vivid imagination than Miss Freeman's would hardly have construed the general exclamation which followed her announcement as one of joy: but we could not help smiling when she added, 'There, I knew you would be glad.' And so we were in time."[22]

On another occasion, Freeman's easy grace facilitated the painless adoption of a political position. In 1887 the Wellesley Microscopical Society had a mass meeting in the interest of the birds being killed for "fashion." After the cause, which ran counter to the tastes of the well-dressed audience, had been pled, Alice Freeman closed the exercises and brought them to a practical conclusion.

She made a kind of confession and promise for the Wellesley women which, in brief, was this. They had gotten the pretty ornaments they had seen in the shops without thinking of what millions of women were doing to our beautiful birds. They would do this thoughtless thing no more, but would do all they could to demand of fashion something which more befitted the enlightened women of the nineteenth century. . . . Several birds that came into the chapel on hats went out rolled up out of sight in handkerchiefs.[23]

Freeman's skillful handling of students inspired warm affection as well as admiration and respect. Freeman addressed the international meeting of the Young Women's Christian Association (YWCA) when its final session was held on the Wellesley campus in 1884. Students observed her polished performance on the platform and commented, "How proud we were of our president that afternoon when she addressed the ladies and students in chapel!" And later: "The serenade that 'came upon the midnight clear,' after the excitements of the day were over, was only a faint expression of the loyal tribute each heart paid to our beloved 'Princess Ida.'"[24] Students obviously saw her as more than young and attractive, but as beautiful. They courted her like lovers, serenading her frequently to show their affection. One student wrote her family about such an occasion, that after a song or two the blinds were opened and "Miss Freeman was disclosed to view, standing on a chair, smiling and looking so pleased and gratified and every way lovely that we cheered and cheered and cheered."[25] Then Freeman opened the window, said it was too cold to make a speech, invited them into her rooms, and probably fed them hot chocolate.

Students watched what she wore and worried about her health. On Tree Day when she donned the Oxford cap and gown the seniors had chosen for the ceremony, they noticed "how distractingly becoming the costume was to Miss Freeman."[26] And when she was ill in 1885, "we all carried a heavy burden on our hearts while the face of our dear president was missed from its accustomed places in chapel and office. . . . And when at last Our Lady was released from North Hospital, it seemed as if spring had suddenly come with birds and sunshine," but all in snowy December.[27]

Living together as they did, Wellesley faculty took full parental responsibility for the students during their years in college, but the responsibility did not end with graduation. Alice Freeman also led the Wellesley staff in taking active charge of finding suitable employment for graduates. Wherever she was, placing her "girls" was uppermost in her mind. She wrote Louise Hodgkins, professor of literature, from a train crossing Illinois in a spring blizzard:

Lena Heath would be a good governess for Mrs. Stuke's little relative. Lena H. is so very fond of children that she thinks of an "orphan asylum." If someone is wanted at once, please look over the present candidates for positions on the Registry and see if any names strike you as desirable for this particular place? Verna Sheldon may need a place very much—in the east. There are others to whom such a home would be a heaven![28]

And on another occasion she wrote a recent graduate who asked for advice on what position to take:

> I am inclined to advise the Pittsfield High School for your parents sake. You have been away from them for so long, and so far away lately, that, if you do not return to Menominee which I would be very glad to have you do, and if the way should open, I should be in favor of Pittsfield. They need college influence there, also, and you can do very valuable work in introducing enthusiasm and desire of better things.[29]

It was Alice Freeman's daily presence on campus, her interaction with the total Wellesley community, that defined the Wellesley ambience. As one of the faculty described it: "Of all this ardent work and play our young president was the center. The grace of thought, the glowing imagination, the bubbling wit which made her classrooms places of joy to throngs of eager girls and charmed her public audiences were poured forth like sparking wine in the glad hours of personal friendship."[30]

4

Although she lived in college and participated as a mother and mentor in the life of the students, Alice Freeman also saw the president as governing the college, supplying its direction, presiding actively over its staff. However, at the same time that she exerted her own leadership, she fostered faculty collegiality and responsibility. The faculty began to take shape as an intellectual force. Simultaneously the role of the board of trustees changed overnight. No longer was Wellesley a private fiefdom run according to the views and wishes of its "proprietor."

In delineating the leadership functions of the president, Alice Freeman made skillful use of the board of trustees. Had she encouraged (or permitted) Pauline Durant to inherit her husband's patriarchal mantle, the president's power would have been much circumscribed. But instead Freeman turned to the trustees as the logical successors of Durant's decision-making authority and thereby provided a legitimate avenue through which she could exert her own influence.

The role of the board of trustees changed dramatically. Under the Durant regime the trustees met infrequently and sessions were poorly attended. Since the founder made the decisions, there was little for them to do. And Ada Howard, as president of the faculty, played no part at all in their deliberations. Under Alice Freeman's leadership, the frequency of meetings increased, attendance improved, and the president was present at all meetings of both the board and its executive committee and influenced the decision-making process directly. From her first year, Freeman made a comprehensive report to the trustees on the state of the college.[31] Faculty appointments and salaries became part of the regular business of the trustees. Overall the board assumed the role Durant had played in decisions that involved money. But the board was firmly guided in the decision-making process by the young president who from the beginning attended trustees and executive committee meetings and who formally became an ex officio member of the board and its executive committee in by-laws adopted in February, 1884.[32] At the same time the functions of the executive committee were regularized as "general management of the institution," and defined as determining, along with the president, the course of study, the preparation of calendars and other publications, the appointment of emergency faculty, and the nomination to the trustees of faculty for permanent positions.[33] The functions of the board of visitors, a body of competent professionals who visited classes and reported on the adequacy of the academic program, had been regularized the previous November. At the same time, Alice Freeman's old mentor, James Burrill Angell, joined its roster.[34]

The trustees were the means. However, it was the Germanic influence, with its emphasis on scholarship and research so rapidly gaining ascendency at the best American universities in the late nineteenth century, that shaped Alice Freeman's curricular and institutional contributions to Wellesley. It was Freeman who brought Wellesley into the mainstream of higher education in the 1880s, fostered secularization, professionalism, high admission standards, and rigorous training and graduate degrees for faculty.

A curricular revolution took place in the American colleges and universities in the last decades of the nineteenth century. One historian has described those years as "an arena of continual dispute, of spirited conflicts over deeply held ideas, of partisan alignments and sharp individual thrusts, which gentlemanly [womanly?] loyalties might soften but could never wholly subdue."[35] Freeman did not shy away from these fights. And she was clear about which side should triumph in the end. She slowly shifted the emphasis at Wellesley from training Christian womanhood to preparing young women to work professionally in the natural and physical sciences, the new social sciences, education, and the humanities. She presided over Wellesley's transition to the new academia. And the Wellesley College she eventually transferred to Carolyn Hazard's stewardship, not long before her death, was forged out of her own struggles with and accommodations to the new world of twentieth-century higher education.

The Wellesley faculty Freeman inherited in the fall of 1881 was entirely Henry Fowle Durant's creation. The board of trustees had not even ratified his appointments. He was sole recruiter, hirer, and firer. When Alice Freeman became acting president, ten faculty members carried professorial rank. Much of the teaching was done by twenty-two teachers and assistant teachers (the school of music had its own faculty of ten).[36] During Freeman's last academic year as president the number of faculty holding professorial rank had doubled to twenty. Twenty-six instructors played the role formerly played by teachers and were aided by thirteen tutors and assistants. Academic titles had been upgraded, but most of the teaching was still being done by underlings. However, sixteen of the faculty had M.A. degrees, one had earned a Ph.D., and thirty-five possessed B.A.s.[37] Faculty size increased markedly during those six years, as did its quality as measured by formal academic training.

When Alice Freeman became president, the principle of tenure was not recognized and appointments were made annually. For example, in June of 1882 the trustees invited all professors and teachers to stay on at their present salaries for the following year.[38] But the next year at Freeman's initiative the trustees instructed the executive committee "to consider whether it was desirable to make more permanent appointment of the Faculty and Instructors of the College, than the plan heretofore followed of reengagement from year to year."[39] The following winter a new manual for faculty governance specified that after three years of acceptable service professors, associate professors, instructors, and the physician could all consider their positions permanent.[40] By this time, all faculty appointments, salaries, resignations, and dismissals were ratified by the full board although the president and the executive committee were empowered to secure candidates and make recommendations. And in 1884 the president suggested that the listing of the faculty in the *Calendar* be by rank in order of appointment, a clear recognition of the principle of seniority.[41] That same fall, the rank of teacher was changed to instructor.[42] The previous June, Alice Freeman's title had been changed to reflect the role she actually played—from president of the faculty to president of Wellesley College.[43]

In the 1870s faculty leaves had been granted almost entirely for reasons of health and, except for brief periods, were unpaid. By 1884, however, advanced study had replaced illness as the most frequent reason for absence from campus. Sabbatical policy was regularized in 1886 when another gift from the Eben Horsford endowment made it possible for two half salaries to be allowed each year for professors who wished to travel and study abroad.[44]

Significant changes in the curriculum also took place during the six years of Alice Freeman's presidency. Science played an increasing role. By June, 1886, twenty seniors had elected to receive the new bachelor of science degree.[45] But so much instruction in science required increased laboratory facilities, and by the mid-1880s these were already in short supply. As early as her 1883 report on the state of the college, President Freeman was begging for larger quarters for botany, chemistry, and mineralogy as well as pointing to the need for an observatory and botanical gardens.[46] That same year, Freeman's old Michigan friend, Eliza Mosher, was engaged to give a course in practical physiology. Freeman was unsuccessful in enlarging exercise facilities because they would require major capital outlay.[47]

Although teachers had been trained at Wellesley from the beginning, it was President Freeman who initiated a course in pedagogy and drew on the new head of the German department, Carla Wenckebach, because of her experience with German educational ideas and systems, to teach it.[48] By June of 1887, 122 students were availing themselves of this opportunity.[49] Wenckebach was an ardent disciple of the new pedagogy. Soon after her arrival in the United States she wrote to a teacher friend in Hamburg that she was thoroughly disappointed in American schools and colleges. Despite splendid buildings, generous equipment, and good salaries, the teaching methods were antediluvian, memorization "just as if Pestalozzi and Froebel and Herbart had never lived."[50] Her tutelage ensured the professionalization of teacher training at Wellesley. Anglo-Saxon, Italian, and Spanish were added to the language curriculum, and Wellesley added that new discipline, political economy, to its offerings in 1883–84.[51] The candidates for the B.S. degree were required to have a year of German, the language of science, and the classics had to give a little in the competition. Latin and Greek were made elective in the sophomore year.[52]

Another new discipline, psychology, introduced into the Department of Mental and Moral Philosophy in the 1880s, caused overt concern on the board of trustees and open conflict in the department itself. Eventually the department was divided, a compromise Freeman favored from the beginning, and the president was authorized "to secure independent instruction for Logic and Psychology."[53] No one was peremptorily fired, as looked likely for awhile, although Lucy Andrews and another instructor left at the end of the academic year. Lucy and Alice were never again to be close. Lucy did not fit with the new research-trained younger faculty, but exactly why she left is unclear. Alice admitted that after one stormy faculty meeting, "I did feel strongly inclined to say that 'this place was too narrow for me.'"[54] The unspoken problem was at least partly religious. Were secular attitudes toward human behavior replacing religious faith? Mrs. Durant was firmly on the side of religion; faculty and trustees were divided, and Alice Freeman by this time was firmly convinced that Wellesley must be part of the new academia pursuing intellectual and secular ideas wherever they might lead.

Although President Freeman was meticulous in bringing matters of curriculum and faculty appointments and status changes to the attention of the executive committee, they generally followed her recommendations. Occasionally their governance was intrusive. They refused Frances Lord's request for appointment of a recent graduate as an assistant in her department, demanding someone with more experience.[55] They suggested the classical curriculum include more lectures on art and literature.[56] Eben Horsford exercised strong paternal care over the sciences. As chairman of the board of visitors he reported to the executive committee in the spring of 1886 that he felt Maria Eaton, the professor of chemistry, was not providing the quality of instruction necessary. Eaton resigned, and her resignation was accepted after she was interviewed by the committee and given a chance to present her case.[57]

Although no direct evidence exists, I suspect the seemingly intrusive behavior of the executive committee was really Freeman's way to exert control over the faculty, that it was Freeman who was disturbed over Professor Lord's choice of an assistant or felt the need for more attention to art and literature in the classical curriculum. It is clear that it was Freeman who wanted changes in chemistry and asked Horsford, whose qualifications were impeccable, to investigate. As he reported to the executive committee, he found Eaton's course in qualitative analysis far below standard. And as Eaton explained in her own defense, each year brought large increases in number of students and new branches of instruction.[58] She had been brought to Wellesley in 1876 by Henry Durant and the field of chemistry was obviously moving too rapidly for her comfort. One member of the executive committee voted against accepting her resignation. The vote was cast by Pauline Durant, a clear chastisement of those who wanted to change her dear husband's college.

Another skirmish between the old and new orders involved Vida Scudder. Scudder, one of the first generation trained at the women's colleges (Smith class of '84), joined the Wellesley faculty after graduate work at Oxford. Her superior was Louise Hodgkins, who had been brought to Wellesley by Henry Durant when the department of English literature was organized. Scudder was brilliant, radical, and creative, and her Wellesley career was more than once singed by fiery controversy, but the question in 1887 was about Scudder's tenure. Clearly Freeman was on Scudder's side. She saw Hodgkins as "commonplace" and Wellesley as needing Vida Scudder's spark.[59] And Freeman, as usual, won. Friction between older faculty and the new professionals recruited by Freeman continued for many years. Ellen Hayes, appointed to the chair of mathematics by Henry Durant in 1878, was eventually seen as such a problem that a separate department of applied mathematics was created for her in 1897.[60]

Although the change was made with tact and kindness, Alice Freeman converted the Wellesley faculty from a group of relatively untrained, bright, well-meaning educators into a professional faculty that prized research and scholarship. She herself was not part of that new order. Her graduate work in history at the University of Michigan was scarcely begun, much less completed. However, Michigan awarded her a Ph.D. at its first June commencement after her election as president.[61] Actually, as late as 1900, one-third of all American Ph.D.'s were awarded for unsupervised work done off-campus or for no work at all. In 1884 only 10 percent of Harvard's professors had received a Ph.D.[62] Freeman's degree was not considered honorary at the time, and she proudly used the letters after her name for the rest of her life.

Other changes, somewhat less abrasive, involved curricular organization and faculty status. At Alice Freeman's request, the bachelor of science degree was awarded at her first commencement as president, formal recognition of Wellesley's strong science curriculum especially in physics.[63] The library was catalogued on the brand new Dewey decimal system. Freeman was familiar with library cataloging from Michigan, and had Wellesley's done in the best new process.[64] The music school, whose teachers had been paid on a fee-for-service basis, was forced to accept salaries for its faculty, and its organization was tied more closely to the college as a whole.[65] The departmental system was strengthened. Standing committees of the faculty were developed to deal with entrance examinations, preparatory schools, curriculum, academic schedules, and the library.[66] The academic council grew out of the regular meetings of department heads called by Freeman.

The faculty met on Tuesdays in the evenings, and its meetings frequently were lively affairs.

9 P.M. Faculty meeting, two hours long, well attended. Our proposed classification of the undergraduates unanimously voted, and a good discussion on the students' work, taken up heartily.[67]

Although Alice Freeman well understood the killing work load under which the Wellesley faculty labored, she was unable to do much about it. Faculty size almost doubled during her tenure but so did the size of the student body. The constant toll of serious illness, at a time when tuberculosis was the scourge of young people everywhere, meant faculty were always having to assume someone else's responsibilities as well as their own.

Faculty salaries also seem to have remained about the same during Freeman's administration. Henry Durant had been generous to se-

nior faculty from the beginning, and in the early 1880s they continued to receive salaries ranging from $1,200 to $1,500 per annum
and, of course, a "home."[68] In 1885 regular raises were provided
until professional salaries reached $1,500.[69] Instructors were paid
$500 to $800, with an occasional recent Wellesley graduate receiving
a mere $400 plus "home."[70] Women's professorial salaries were cer-
tainly adequate, but far below those received by the only full-time
male professor on campus. When Junius W. Hill came to head the
music school in 1884 his salary was $3,000, but of course he received
no "home."[71] Single women could have done no better anywhere, and
the average family income in Massachusetts in 1880 was only $1,000.

Alice Freeman's own salary was generous. In June of 1885, a mo-
tion was made to the trustees, perhaps at her instigation, that it be
increased to $4,000 per annum.[72] The motion was referred to the
executive committee who scaled down the request to take fuller account of the college's distressed financial position. In 1885–86 she
was raised from $1,700 to $3,000, and received an increase of $500
for each of the next two years, bringing her stipend to the $4,000
first requested.[73]

Changes inevitably meant tensions. Few personal documents have
survived from the early years of Alice Freeman's presidency. For the
later years we have her correspondence with George Palmer. When
she was away from campus she wrote freely of college problems to
her secretary, Anna McCoy, but she could afford few other
confidants. For example, she now exercised a leadership role over
her old Michigan network and could hardly confide in them about
college policy.

Eben Horsford was her closest advisor. She consulted him constantly about college business, everything from custodial crises like
an outbreak of scarlet fever or a suspicious water supply to substantive questions like Melvil Dewey's recommendations for the arrangement and cataloging of the library.[74] Their personal relationship was
extraordinarily warm and intimate. He gave her the kind of gifts she
might have received from a family member, gloves for Christmas, a
furry rug to warm her feet, and a soft lamp to make "a cozy, happy
place of this working room."[75] Eben Horsford was, after Henry
Durant, Wellesley's most generous early benefactor. His generosity
to the college, its staff, and its students was endless. He provided
funds for faculty sabbaticals, library acquisitions, and the construc-

Eben Horsford, Harvard chemist, and President
Freeman's closest advisor. (Courtesy of Wellesley
College Archives.)

tion of Norumbega Cottage.[76] President Freeman was not averse to exploiting his concern for the college. When the need arose to replace the original gas illumination in College Hall with electric light, Horsford was consulted about the problem.[77] What Freeman wrote him on his birthday in 1886 was true: "Wellesley is full of you and the signs of your loving life are everywhere."[78]

5

One of the most subtle and difficult changes during Freeman's tenure took place in the college's relation to its roots in evangelical Protestantism. As Ernest Boyer has pointed out, "issues of values and religion have been central to the tradition of higher education in America."[79] Alice Freeman was part of that tradition as was Wellesley. However, Christian service as a major aim of higher education was losing status as the nineteenth century drew to a close. Pauline Durant continued to uphold that goal. Alice Freeman in the spirit of the times moved away from it.

Alice Freeman's Wellesley presidency cannot be discussed without facing that nineteenth-century bugaboo, how does one arrive at and test religious faith. Alice did everything as good church people thought it ought to be done, presiding over weekly chapel (the iconoclast Carla Wenckebach confessed she came to a service so alien to her German soul only because "it was such fun to hear Alice Freeman chat with the Lord!"[80]), to religious counseling of disturbed students. But she drew the line at severe proscriptions.

Henry Durant had founded his college "for the glory of God and the service of Jesus Christ."[81] Daily chapel services, Bible study classes taught by the whole faculty, two periods of silent meditation, and a religious test (membership in an evangelical church) for all faculty and officers, imbued Wellesley with a religious orientation that was rigid and all-embracing. One could argue that Alice Freeman did not change this very much. However, Vida Scudder, socialist and ritualistic Anglican, but with impeccable scholarly qualifications, was not lost to the Wellesley faculty because of her non-evangelical views. Daily chapel services and silent periods continued, Bible study was retained, and every meeting of every committee including the board of trustees opened with prayer. President Freeman's annual reports to the trustees always included a paragraph like this: "As a body the students have been thoughtful and responsive, the religious feeling deep. Out of 444 students at the time of the inquiry, 219 were church members and 400 believed themselves to be Christians."[82]

But there was a subtle difference from the Durant regime. Even Lyman Abbott, a prominent Boston clergyman who preached occasionally at Sunday chapel, was aware of a new liberalism. He wrote that religious doubts "were no longer discouraged.... The eager quest for truth had taken the place of an acceptance of authority more apparent than real."[83] Alice Freeman defined "Christian" somewhat differently from Henry Durant. She listed the churches to which the students were attached and they included Episcopalians, Lutherans, Friends, and Roman Catholics, all Christians in her eyes, but not necessarily Durant's evangelicals. In fact, as time went on, she found more and more professing Christians among the students. In recommending the 1886 senior class for degrees, she stated that "all but two were professing Christians, and not a weak or doubtful member."[84] To achieve such unanimity, a broader interpretation was inevitable, but one still wonders about the two non-believers. Perhaps it was a student who was confirmed the next year, and "who never had a Bible until two years ago when she came to College. How many times she had been to me to talk of her astonishment in finding the 'truth of the other side' as she says. She had been brought up on [Thomas] Paine and his class, and feels now that she is in a new world. There are so many compensations for the long toil of these years."[85]

Before Alice Freeman's presidency not only was Bible study mandated throughout the four years of the college course, but all teachers were required to give instruction in it. Eliza Kendrick reported that on her first Sunday as a freshman, in the fall of 1881, she got her Bible lesson from "Miss Hollowell of the Department of Botany and her talk was on the opening chapter of Genesis."[86] One cannot imagine this obligation was high on Hollowell's list of priorities. The faculty resented the Bible study classes and found them burdensome, and the students by 1881 found them less than serious and sometimes amusing. Kendrick speculated that at the end of her senior year they would reach Revelation. But Pauline Durant could hardly be expected to accept tampering with the founder's clear intentions. Nor did Alice Freeman ask her to.

It took time, but by 1886 Henry Durant's evangelical Bible study was on its way toward conversion into an academically respectable department of biblical studies. A two-hour course in Greek New Testament, taught by Angie Chapin, professor of Greek or a course in Hebrew (as a language) was substituted for Bible study for juniors and seniors. Bible study had become a department, and its courses were taught by professionals.[87] Chapel was left untouched as it acted as a unifying force for the college and a way for Alice to chat not only "with the Lord" but with the students. No revolution had occurred, but one might categorize the result as a modest secularization of Wellesley's religious roots.

Pauline Durant, although appeased, was not always happy with this new academic semi-secularism, nor did she understand Alice Freeman's intention to make Wellesley part of the larger, rapidly changing academic world. But Alice Freeman found ways to include Pauline Durant in the process. She took her to an important Canadian educational conference where they were entertained by the Canadian minister of education at a state dinner. Canadian leaders eager to modernize Canadian higher education consulted Freeman about coeducation, colleges for women, admission standards, and adequate preparatory schools. Durant was present as trusted advisor and friend and shared Alice's glory.[88] Alice Freeman always kept Pauline Durant as her friend. Durant would vote against Freeman in trustees meetings, but would continue to depend on Alice as a loving daughter. Alice gave Durant both time and affection, and was considerate of her always.

Increasing acceptance of varied religious viewpoints was not the only kind of tolerance Freeman encouraged at Wellesley. Sophonisba Breckenridge, daughter of the Kentucky aristocracy, entered Wellesley in 1884. Her parents escorted her to the college and "as we approached the entrance a handsome, handsomely dressed couple of the Negro race with an attractive daughter [Ella Smith who later taught at Howard University] approached the door." The friend who was with the Breckenridges asked if they would allow Nisba to go to school with a Negro. Her father replied that she'd got on all right with the boys and would get on all right with the colored. Nonetheless Nisba could not swallow her food when the Fiske singers entertained at the college and some were placed at the table. Freeman tried to help her overcome her prejudice and Sophonisba Breckenridge was able with Freeman's help to squash the opposition to Smith's being given equal privileges at the Junior Promenade.[89]

One of the problems facing American colleges and universities in the late nineteenth century was the raising and standardization of entrance requirements. Wellesley, like other academic institutions, first solved the problem by itself. Again Freeman had watched the University of Michigan experiment with accrediting Michigan public high schools that met its standards and admitting their graduates by diploma. Wellesley had acquired easy access to a preparatory school, Dana Hall, in 1880 when it phased out its own preparatory department, but Freeman greatly expanded the system of what she called "fitting schools." Wellesley inspired preparatory schools that opened in Philadelphia and Auburndale, Massachusetts, in 1883. By November of 1884 seventeen "fitting schools" had been organized.[90] Although Wellesley took no financial responsibility for any of these schools, Freeman actively supervised their curricula and staffing, and most of their faculty were recent Wellesley graduates. The physical toll taken by setting up this network of feeder schools was enormous, especially because of the traveling required. For example, she visited Philadelphia to supervise the opening of its fitting school, writing the circular herself, arranging newspaper publicity, and helping to choose the faculty.[91]

A less cumbersome system of dealing with entrance requirements supplemented the fitting schools by 1885. A Conference of College Officers had been organized and had met with principals of various preparatory schools on admission standards. Standardized requirements were agreed on, a paid secretary hired and a fee for service assessed to the participating colleges. At Freeman's urging, Wellesley was a part of this group from the beginning.[92]

Alice Freeman had aspirations for a graduate school at Wellesley. In this, she was unsuccessful. The Ph.D. degree was still a rarity among male scholars when women seriously began seeking a college education. Only 25 women had received Ph.D.s by 1890 although the next decade saw over 200 more join their ranks.[93] Durant made provision for graduate study as early as 1876 when the *Calendar* announced that "graduates of this and other colleges" would be received for further study, and two M.A.s in Greek were awarded in 1882, the first commencement at which Alice Freeman presided.[94] Some students pursued graduate study but were never candidates for an advanced degree and others continued their study while not in residence. By 1887 there were 24 master's candidates.[95] However, Alice

Freeman lost her enthusiasm for investing the very limited resources of the faculty in graduate training.[96] Freeman was right. As Margaret Rossiter has pointed out, the women's colleges did not have the financial resources to expand into graduate work. Certainly Wellesley did not. And there was also substantial sentiment among women scholars that graduate studies was not the place for a sex-segregated educational experience.[97] Wellesley remained a college for undergraduate women.

Unfortunately one of Wellesley's primary needs in the 1880s was financial planning and fund-raising. These were needs Alice Freeman was unable to fill. She could successfully inspire ice cream socials to support a lecture series or ladies' bazaars for student aid funds. But Wellesley needed a substantial endowment, and that was not forthcoming. Although she was later to develop such skills, at this period of her life Freeman was not an effective money raiser. Perhaps her many duties did not allow her the time. Perhaps she did not know how.

Durant money was less and less available. Over the years the Durant fortune had been eroded by business losses and expendable capital gifts to Wellesley. Tuition and fees had never covered costs. Enrollment could not be increased except by converting dormitory space in College Hall to classrooms and laboratories, but then where would the students live? Wellesley village was not large enough to absorb many students into private homes. The new cottages helped, but not enough. The trustees were forced to borrow consistently against designated funds to meet expenses so that the small capital endowment for scholarships and special purposes most of the time existed only on paper.[98] Pauline Durant as treasurer was no better able than Alice Freeman to provide sound financial management.[99] She resisted tuition increases fearing her husband's plan for a college for "calico girls" was being violated. However, one contribution the president made now was to assist Wellesley financially decades later. Freeman, while president, founded Wellesley Alumnae Clubs around the country, and while the alumnae were not yet rich enough to be an immediate help, someday they would be. Meanwhile, the problem got worse. And no solutions presented themselves. Lack of financial leadership was Alice Freeman's greatest failure as president of Wellesley.

Alice Freeman in June, 1884. One of the annual portraits she had made as gifts for each graduating class. (Courtesy of Wellesley College Archives.)

6

At the same time that Alice Freeman was moving Wellesley into the Germanic-influenced avant-garde of American academia, she was gradually taking her place as the most visible woman educator in the United States, possibly the world. She was active in various types of educational associations. She was one of the founders of the Association of Collegiate Alumnae (ACA; later the American Association of University Women) organized in Boston in 1882. Collegiate Alumnae played a major role in defining a community of educated women. Not only did it provide college graduates with association with their peers, but it also created an organ for establishing scholarships for women, especially to finance graduate studies. Alice Freeman was active in ACA all her life.[100] She also was active in the Commission of New England Colleges. She was one of the directors of the Classical School at Athens, and we have already noted her participation in the Conference on Admissions Requirements. She spoke frequently before various educational bodies. Her appearance in the fall of 1886 before the Canadian educators in Montreal was designed to coincide with a heated controversy over admitting women to McGill University.[101] In June of that same year, she spoke before the Milford Teacher's Association and gave the commencement address at Tilden Seminary where two former Wellesley students were teachers.[102]

She was a friend to the famous, which also helped to create for her a public audience and nationwide attention. John Greenleaf Whittier, then the United States' unofficial poet laureate, had a visit from her on his deathbed. "I had a rare hour with Mr. Whittier this week. This morning he talked of death, holding my hand, and saying, 'I have written always thinking only of the friends I love.'" When she left him, he took her hands and kissed her repeatedly. She feared she would not see him again.[103]

Her activities on campus often attracted media attention to both her and Wellesley. The Queen of Hawaii, on a state visit to the United States, came to call, partly because she had known Lucy Andrews since childhood. As the students saw it, "the Queen of Wellesley spoke beautiful words of welcome to the Queen of the Sandwich Islands," as Liliuokani planted a tree on campus.[104] However, their weary president was less enthusiastic in private.

I am informed today that the Queen of the Hawaiian Islands wishes to visit the College. So, Wednesday or Thursday, the Royal Party must be received, but I am too sleepy at this moment to care that I know only half a dozen sentences of her language, and she little more of mine, and that I never was presented at her court.[105]

Pundita Ramabai, the charismatic Indian educator and reformer, also paid Wellesley a visit and, since her visit tapped some of Alice Freeman's larger purposes, she inspired more enthusiasm on Alice's part. Ramabai raised $200 from the students for her work. "They are full of enthusiasm and respond in the hearty way I like to cultivate in women who have money. If these girls only learn to think of others, instead of spending so much upon themselves."[106]

More important for the future of women's higher education was the visit of M. Carey Thomas, then dean and professor of English (and later president) at about-to-be-opened Bryn Mawr College. Thomas was one of the new breed of academicians with a European Ph.D. and the high scholarly standards that Freeman herself could not match but attempted to recruit for her faculty. Nonetheless Thomas was impressed as she sat in Wellesley's chapel listening to a woman president reading prayers to an audience of 600 women and seventy professors, all women, "not a man's influence seen or felt." She felt Wellesley "ushers in a new day."[107] However, Thomas's reservations about any vocational emphasis at Bryn Mawr were confirmed by Wellesley's teacher's department, which she quite rightly attributed to Durant although Freeman had not hesitated to strengthen the pedagogical training.[108] Nonetheless Bryn Mawr and Thomas were to build on Wellesley's experience.

The public side of Alice Freeman's life during her term as Wellesley's president was full of rich rewards and public applause that helped to counteract the grueling hard work and dearth of free time or privacy that marked her days. After she moved to Norumbega Cottage, she was able to breakfast in her rooms rather than with her housemates, but 8:30 chapel was a service she routinely conducted, including the homily. Her mail plus the usual appointments with students and others kept her busy through the morning, and she lunched in College Hall with faculty and students. Meetings, more letters, callers, interviews, and many trips to Boston, where the college's boards often met and where influential trustees could be wooed and consulted, occupied hours and days. She continued to teach and offer public lectures on campus as well as in the larger community. She dined with her Norumbega housemates and frequently joined their pre-study hall fun. In 1887 she wrote a revealing letter while proctoring an examination in one of her courses. She had conducted three services on Sunday (two of them because the men who were supposed to have presided did not show up). She spent much of Monday arranging for a meeting of the faculty council, no doubt carefully plotting how its discussions would go; Tuesday was faculty meeting, another exercise in diplomacy and tact. Wednesday she met with the executive committee of the trustees, no doubt to advance an agenda to which she was committed, and Thursday she was to preside over a "Day of Prayer."[109] Wellesley's evangelical origins were irrepressible.

She lightened her load a little by obtaining clerical assistance. She acquired a stenographer sometime in 1881. By 1884 she was requesting an additional secretary and an assistant secretary was appointed in 1885. Before she left the presidency she was seriously considering the addition of a dean who would be in charge of the college's correspondence and possibly be in training as a future president.[110] The mail followed her wherever she went. The receptions at which she presided as Wellesley College president were endless. On June 10, 1886, "from three to five P.M. Professor Horsford and President Freeman received in the library," the *Wellesley Courant* reported. On the 19th she presided at a reception for the graduating seniors. Baccalaureate followed on the 20th with another reception, and the next Monday still another receiving line for the sculptor Anne Whitney.[111] She made biennial trips to Saginaw to visit her family but these represented duty rather than vacation. Her one substantial holiday was her first journey to Europe in the summer of 1884 and that was justified by ill health and professional duties.

7

On July 12, 1884, Alice Freeman sailed on the *City of Rome* with her father and her cousin Electa Dye for Keswick, England. Electa Dye was the closest personal companion of Alice's presidential years when her administrative responsibilities required that the old Michigan network be used less freely. She and Electa, daughter of Alice's mother's sister Sarah, met several times a year at Electa's mother's home in Osborn Hollow, where Alice always retreated for real rest when her health was threatened or her responsibilities overwhelmed her energy, or they met in New York City where Electa worked in an educational program for young working women. Theirs was a happy companionship. Both had strong professional interests and commitments. Both enjoyed the out-of-doors and gardening during their brief respite from other cares. When they arrived at Sarah Dye's home, roses were pruned, flower beds weeded, and the neighboring hills climbed to admire pleasant vistas. Alice loved the Susquehanna Valley and its small mountains with an intensity she never could muster for the elegantly contrived Wellesley campus, perhaps because care was her constant companion at Wellesley. At Osborn Hollow, she was free.

For one reason or another Alice needed her father on this journey or perhaps he needed her. Her health had been poor that spring and she did not want to undertake so strenuous a venture without medical supervision. Or perhaps his periodic restlessness demanded a new outlet. In any case her father's companionship posed problems. Her mother, frequently in ill health, thought he belonged at home with her. James Freeman was torn between two strong-minded women. Alice may have exaggerated her physical problems to carry him with her. After all, she had Electa to rely on, and the possibility that her mother also travel with them seems not to have been seriously considered. Undoubtedly Alice paid her father's passage, but also he would be earning nothing, and Elizabeth Freeman would be left to fend for herself.[112]

Three academic years in the presidency had left Alice Freeman scarred and worn. Tuberculosis again threatened, and she herself was convinced that she needed a true holiday "if I am to save a bad breakdown and go on with my work."[113] Her fatigue was real. A student who knew her when she came to Wellesley as a teacher in 1879 and who had not seen her until after her first year as president reported that she did not recognize Freeman at first glance. Although a greater Wellesley had evolved, "our lady showed marks of the effort. . . . The evolution of the new Wellesley had drawn lines over the round, mobile face, lines of character, of strength, great, great lines to be welcomed, for they stood for development and growth."[114] But these lines also stood for weariness, overwork, and ill health. So much communicating one-on-one with students, struggling with administrative and curricular problems, appeasing an increasingly diverse faculty, worrying about fiscal dilemmas she could not solve, to say nothing of the endless receiving lines at receptions, had all taken their toll. She needed, as the Victorians would say, a change of air, and she got it. On June 5, 1884, the executive committee gave its approval for President Freeman to go abroad for several weeks of rest.[115]

Never before had she been quite so self-indulgent. She wrote her secretary Anna McCoy and her Wellesley colleagues as the voyage drew to a close:

> The truth is I have the experience of having done absolutely nothing since we left New York a week ago this morning, and now the Irish cliffs are looming off at the left, and in a few hours we shall touch Queenstown. I have not had an uncomfortable hour, have slept ten hours a night, and eaten four meals a day and worn water lilies around my neck, and walked from three to five miles on deck everyday, and played ball, etc., and am quite another woman than the one who left Wellesley ten days ago.[116]

The travelers stopped at Oxford and Cambridge to examine the great British universities where several of Freeman's faculty were soon to study. They walked in the Lake District, journeyed on to Scotland where James Freeman explored his mother's origins, and returned to London September 1st after stops at Durham and York. James Freeman then returned home. Alice had been appointed as a delegate by the United States commissioner of education to represent American colleges at the International Conference on Education held in London that September at which "I was called on to speak three times."[117] This was her first appearance outside the United States on the international educational scene. After the conference she spent a week at Newnham College with Anne Jemima Clough, pioneer in British higher education for women, after which she and Electa walked for a few days in the Shakespeare country. Alice had completed her first substantial holiday as well as had her first exposure to travel abroad.

8

On April 13, 1887, Alice Freeman was awarded an honorary doctor of humane literature degree by Columbia University, the first honorary degree given by a great eastern university to a woman. This recognition exemplified the preeminence Alice Freeman had reached in American educational circles. She was by far the best-known, the most respected, and the most influential woman educator in the United States. She had presided over and helped to implement the movement of women's higher education from experiment to mainstream.

Typically, she worried about what she would wear for the occasion. Should the street costume, mantel, and bonnet that she would need for the public exercises in the Metropolitan Opera House in the morning be black or a color?[118] She decided on a simple black silk, but she had her dresses for the ceremony and the evening reception made in New York. Alice Freeman was never dowdy.

The ceremonies were colorful and impressive. The *New York Times* reported that the orchestra chairs were filled "with well-known men [but there was a woman, unmentioned by the *Times* among them], most of whom had assembled to receive honorary degrees at the hands of the college."[119] Among the other recipients were Andrew Dickson White, whom she had heard lecture as a Michigan student, and Moses Coit Tyler, who had then been on Michigan's faculty. Her brother, Fred, watched pridefully, the only family member able to be present.

Alice Freeman was pleased but not overwhelmed by accolades that came her way. She wrote:

I am having some very pleasant letters about the degree. That is the pleasant thing—if others like it. I wonder if I ought to care more about it. I am afraid I am too indifferent. I am going to try to be more interested,—to feel that it is an honor, but somehow I can't remember it. I hate to see people who are not sensitive to the courtesy and kindnesses of others, public or private. I must not be one of them.[120]

Alice Freeman's success and recognition as an educator were assured, but already she knew that quite possibly her days at Wellesley were numbered.

NOTES

1. Frances Willard had claimed the title earlier but the pattern in which she operated was different. Hers was a coordinate college, not an independent institution. Much of its work was clearly preparatory and in that sense, she was only following the well-worn path of the earlier prefectresses of women's seminaries (Ruth Bordin, *Frances Willard: A Biography* [Chapel Hill: University of North Carolina Press, 1986], 54–56).

2. As quoted in Bledstein, *Culture of Professionalism*, 131–32.

3. Pauline Durant to Alice Freeman, May 23, 1887. Wellesley Typescripts. Alice Freeman to Eben Horsford, October 20, 1881. Photocopies in the Wellesley College Archives of original Eben Horsford Papers in the possession of Andrew Fiske. Hereafter cited as photocopies, Eben Horsford Papers.

4. Glasscock, *Wellesley College*, 22.

5. Horowitz points this out. *Alma Mater*, 85.

6. See the Minutes of the Board of Trustees, Report of the Executive Committee, June 1, 1882, 94. Wellesley College Archives; Hackett, *Wellesley*, 69.

7. Alice Freeman to Eben Horsford, October 20, 1881. Photocopies, Eben Horsford Papers.

8. Kingsley, *Durant*, 337.

9. An Ann Arbor friend, probably Lucy Andrews or Angie Chapin, to Elizabeth Freeman, November 15, 1881, as quoted in Palmer, *Life*, 115–16.

10. Mueller, *Wenckebach*, 221.

11. The original version of this story is probably the one in Palmer, *Life*, 101–2.

12. A recent statement of this is to be found in Ernest L. Boyer, *College: The Undergraduate Experience in America* (New York: Harper and Row, 1987), 125.

13. I do not find Roberta Frankfort's analysis of Alice Freeman Palmer in (*Collegiate Women*, chaps. 1, 3, 4) very helpful nor do I agree with many of its conclusions. It is true that Alice Freeman often articulated the Wellesley community as a family but the academic ideal of training the whole person was not peculiar to women's colleges. Men's schools still cherished the English pattern in the 1880s, and Freeman's choice of language was largely a matter of semantics. She was as devoted to professorial professionalism, the increased emphasis on science, the new social sciences, and the American translation of the Germanic ideal as any of her male colleagues.

14. Glasscock, *Wellesley*, 22.

15. See Horowitz, *Alma Mater*, 88–90, for a discussion of the influence of the "cottage system" on college life.

16. Clipping, April 22, 1886, in C. McCamant Scrapbook, Class of 1887 Papers, Wellesley College Archives.

17. Converse, *Wellesley College*, 134; Palmer, *Life*, 146. Liberal Protestants found the Y's uncongenial, in part because they would not accept Unitarians.

18. President's Report, 1883, 5, 11, Wellesley College Archives; Minutes of the Board of Trustees, June 19, 1883, 117; June 22, 1886, 200, Wellesley College Archives; *Wellesley Annals*, 1886–87, 6.

19. Scudder, *On Journey*, 71.

20. Alice Freeman to George Palmer, January 9, 1887. Wellesley Typescripts.

21. Clara D. Carron to family, October 28, 1883, Class of 1887 Papers, Wellesley College Archives.

22. *Wellesley Annals*, 1884–85, 3.

23. *Wellesley Courant*, April 26, 1886 as clipped in C. McCamant's Scrapbook, Class of 1887 Papers, Wellesley College Archives.

24. *Wellesley Annals*, 1883–84, 4. Sometimes the students used Tennyson's princess as a reference, sometimes Princess Ida.

25. Clare D. Carron to her family, October 28, 1883. Class of 1887 Papers, Wellesley College Archives.

26. *Wellesley Annals*, 1883–84, 5–6.

27. *Wellesley Annals*, 1885–86, 2.

28. Alice Freeman to Louise Hodgkins, April 6, 1887.

29. Alice Freeman to Anna Fuller, July 21, 1885.

30. Louise McCoy North as quoted in Hackett, *Wellesley*, 89.

31. Minutes of the Board of Trustees, June 27, 1882, 102. Wellesley College Archives.

32. Minutes of the Board of Trustees, February 29, 1884, 125. Wellesley College Archives.

33. Ibid., 125.

34. Minutes of the Board of Trustees, November 12, 1883, 123. Wellesley College Archives.

35. Vesey, *Emergence*. Although he almost completely ignores women, probably the best account of the changes in higher education in the late nineteenth century is still to be found in Vesey's book, especially pt. 1, "Rival Conceptions of Higher Learning," 21–251.

36. Wellesley College Catalog, 1881–82. Wellesley College Archives.

37. President's Report, 1887–88, 3. Wellesley College Archives. At this time Vassar had many teachers but only eight full professors, [Louise Fargo Brown, *Apostle of Democracy: The Life of Lucy Maynard Salmon* (New York: Harper Bros., 1943), 106].

38. Minutes of the Executive Committee of the Board of Trustees, June 1, 1882. Wellesley College Archives. Cited hereafter as Minutes of the Executive Committee.

39. Minutes of the Board of Trustees, February 12, 1883, 125. Wellesley College Archives.

40. Minutes of the Board of Trustees, February 29, 1884, 127. Wellesley College Archives.

41. Minutes of the Executive Committee, October 31, 1884. Wellesley College Archives.

42. Minutes of the Board of Trustees, November 21, 1884, 151. Wellesley College Archives.

43. Minutes of the Board of Trustees, June 5, 1884. Wellesley College Archives.

44. Minutes of the Board of Trustees, February 4, 1886, 188, 192. Wellesley College Archives.

45. Minutes of the Board of Trustees, June 26, 1886. Alice Freeman to Eben Horsford, October 27, 1884, February 11, 1886. Photocopies, Eben Horsford Papers.

46. President's Report, 1883, 8. Wellesley College Archives. The other women's colleges were less receptive than Wellesley to the increased emphasis on science and the addition of psychology and the social sciences to the curriculum, and continued to stress the old classical course. (See Rosenberg, "Academic Prism," 324–25). Freeman had experienced James Burrill Angell's promotion of science at Michigan, and of course Durant had opened the path.

47. President's Report, 1883, 7, 8. Wellesley College Archives.

48. Hackett, *Wellesley*, 113.

49. Minutes of the Board of Trustees, June 28, 1887, 145. Wellesley College Archives.

50. Mueller, *Wenckebach*, 204–5.

51. *Calendar of Wellesley College*, 1883–84.

52. Minutes of the Board of Trustees, June 3, 1886, 196. Wellesley College Archives.

53. Minutes of the Executive Committee, December 30, 1886. Wellesley College Archives.

54. Minutes of the Executive Committee, December 30, 1886, January 26, 1887, February 23, 1887, April 27, 1887, May 14, 1887, June 1, 1887; Alice Freeman to George Palmer, April 24, 1887, May 1, 1887, May 8, 1887, May 15, 1887. Wellesley Typescripts.

55. Minutes of the Executive Committee, February 15, 1884. Wellesley College Archives.

56. Ibid.

57. Minutes of the Executive Committee, March 10, 1886, Wellesley College Archives; Alice Freeman to Eben Horsford, March 12, 1886. Photocopyies, Eben Horsford Papers.

58. Minutes of the Executive Committee, March 10, 1886, Wellesley College Archives.

59. George Palmer to Alice Freeman, March 13, 1887. Wellesley Typescripts.

60. Margaret Rossiter, *Women Scientists in America* (Baltimore: Johns Hopkins University Press, 1982), 22.

61. *Annual Calendar*, 1881–82, of the University of Michigan.

62. Patricia M. Hummer, *The Decade of Elusive Promise: Proper Women in the United States, 1920–1930* (Ann Arbor, Mich.: UMI Research Press, 1979), 33–39; Bledstein, *Culture of Professionalism*, 277. Helen Magill, who received

the first American Ph.D. earned by a woman (Boston University 1877), studied at Boston University for only two years, taking classes with upperclassmen because there were no graduate courses and spending her second year writing her thesis on Greek drama (Glenn C. Altschuler, *Better Than Second Best,* 38–40). This was a cursory regimen at best and her training was probably no better than Alice had received under Charles Kendall Adams in his seminar.

63. Minutes of the Board of Trustees, June 1, 1882, 95– 96; Rossiter, *Women Scientists,* 18.

64. President's Report, 1883, 8. Wellesley College Archives.

65. Minutes of the Board of Trustees, June 5, 1884, 132. Wellesley College Archives.

66. Palmer, *Life,* 129–30; Glasscock, *Wellesley,* 25– 26.

67. Alice Freemen to George Palmer, October 4, 1887. Wellesley Typescripts.

68. Minutes of the Board of Trustees, June 21, 1881, 80–81. Wellesley College Archives.

69. Minutes of the Board of Trustees, November 5, 1885, 177. Wellesley College Archives.

70. Minutes of the Board of Trustees, June 5, 1884, 130–31; November 5, 1885, 177; February 4, 1886, 184; June 28, 1887, 145–46.

71. Minutes of the Board of Trustees, June 5, 1884, 132. Moses Coit Tyler also received $3,000 at Cornell (Michael Kammen, *Selvedges and Biases: The Fabric of History in American Culture* [Ithaca, N.Y.: Cornell University Press, 1987], 232).

72. Minutes of the Board of Trustees, June 25, 1885. Wellesley College Archives.

73. Minutes of the Board of Trustees, November 5, 1885. Wellesley College Archives.

74. Alice Freeman to Eben Horsford, October 28, November 19, 1884. Photocopies, Eben Horsford Papers.

75. Alice Freeman to Eben Horsford, February 23, October 28, 1884. Photocopies, Eben Horsford Papers.

76. Alice Freeman to Eben Horsford, April 8, July 15, 1886; Pauline Durant to Eben Horsford, March 29, 1886; Marion Pelton to Eben Horsford, February 8, 1886; James B. Angell to Eben Horsford, February 9, 1886. Photocopies, Eben Horsford Papers.

77. Alice Freeman to Eben Horsford, April 17, 21, June 12, 1885. Photocopies, Eben Horsford Papers.

78. Alice Freeman to Eben Horsford, July 26, 1886. Photocopies, Eben Horsford Papers.

79. Boyer, *College* (New York: Harper and Row, 1987), xiii.

80. Mueller, *Wenckebach,* 243.

81. As quoted in Hackett, *Wellesley,* 31.

82. Minutes of the Board of Trustees, June 19, 1883, 117. Wellesley College Archives.

83. Abbott, *Silhouettes,* 70.

84. Minutes of the Board of Trustees, June 22, 1886, 200. Wellesley College Archives.

85. Alice Freeman to George Palmer, January 16, 1887. Wellesley Typescripts.

86. As quoted in Glasscock, *Wellesley,* 131.

87. Palmer, *Life,* 145–46; Glasscock, *Wellesley,* 32.

88. Alice Freeman to George Palmer, October 8, 1886. Wellesley Typescripts.

89. Sophonisba Breckenridge, Manuscript Autobiography, University of Chicago Archives [ca. 1930s].

90. Palmer, *Life,* 125–26; President's Report 1883, 9, Wellesley College Archives; Minutes of the Board of Trustees, November 21, 1884, 150, Wellesley College Archives. Alice Freeman to George H. Palmer, October 19, 1886. Wellesley Typescripts. Alice Freeman to Anna McCoy, July 12, 1882.

91. See, for example, President's Report, 1883. Wellesley College Archives.

92. Minutes of the Executive Committee, December 2, 1885, December 30, 1886; Minutes of the Board of Trustees, June 3, 1886, 194. Wellesley College Archives.

93. Rossiter, *Women Scientists,* 35; Solomon, *Educated Women,* 134–36.

94. *Calendar of Wellesley College,* 1876; Glasscock, *Wellesley,* 136–37.

95. President's Report, 1887–88, 12. Wellesley College Archives.

96. Ibid.

97. Rossiter, *Women Scientists,* 30. M. Carey Thomas was not to agree. She believed all women's colleges should have graduate schools (Barbara M. Cross, ed., *The Educated Woman in America: Selected Writings of Catharine Beecher, Margaret Fuller, and M. Carey Thomas* [New York: Teacher's College Press, 1965], 167).

98. Minutes of the Board of Trustees, June 1, 1882, June 22, 1886, 214, Wellesley College Archives, provides an example.

99. See Palmer, *Life,* 127; George Palmer to Alice Freeman, June 12, 1887, 101; Alice Freeman to George Palmer, May 8, 1887, Wellesley Typescripts.

100. Marion Talbot and Lois Kimball Mathews Rosenberry, *The History of the American Association of University Women* (New York: Houghton Mifflin Co., 1931), is still the most complete study of the organization.

101. Alice Freemen to George Palmer, October 6, 1886, October 8, 1886. Wellesley Typescripts.

102. *Wellesley Courant,* June 3, 1886, as clipped in C. McCamant's Scrapbook, Class of 1887 Papers, Wellesley College Archives.

103. Alice Freeman to George Palmer, December 3, 1886. Wellesley Typescripts.

104. *Wellesley Annals,* 1886–87, 8–9.

105. Alice Freeman to George Palmer, May 5, 1887. Wellesley Typescripts.

106. Alice Freeman to George Palmer, February 12, 1887. Wellesley Type-scripts.

107. M. Carey Thomas to Mary Garrett, May 3, 1884. M. Carey Thomas Papers, Bryn Mawr Archives.

108. M. Carey Thomas's notes on Wellesley College. Reel no. 166. M. Carey Thomas Papers, Bryn Mawr Archives.

109. Palmer, *Life*, 152; Alice Freeman to George Palmer, January 25, 1887. Wellesley Typescripts.

110. Minutes of the Executive Committee, October 15, 1884; Minutes of the Board of Trustees, June 14, 1885; George Palmer to Alice Freeman as quoted in Palmer, *Life*, 170.

111. *Wellesley Courant*, June 10, 1886, June 24, 1886, as clipped in C. McCamant's Scrapbook, Class of 1887 Papers. Wellesley College Archives.

112. Alice Freeman to Elizabeth Freeman, July 8, 1884; James W. Freeman to Elizabeth Freeman, July 9, 1884.

113. Alice Freeman to Elizabeth Freeman, July 8, 1884.

114. Adaline Emerson Thompson's remarks at the Alice Freeman Palmer Memorial Service, University of Chicago, 1903. These appear in slightly different form in Palmer, *Life*, 165.

115. Minutes of the Executive Committee, June 5, 1884. Wellesley College Archives.

116. Alice Freeman to Anna McCoy, July 19, 1882.

117. Diary, 1884.

118. Alice Freeman to George Palmer, March 28, 1887. Wellesley Type-scripts.

119. *New York Times*, April 14, 1887.

120. Alice Freeman to George Palmer, April 24, 1887. Wellesley Type-scripts.

CHAPTER 7

Dilemma

Sometime in the spring of 1886, probably early May, George Herbert Palmer, a relatively young but rapidly advancing and highly ambitious Harvard professor of philosophy, and Alice Freeman, president of Wellesley College, were invited to dinner. Their hosts were the former Governor of Massachusetts, William Claflin, and his wife, Mary Bucklin Claflin, one of five women who were members of the board of trustees of Wellesley College.[1] The Claflins lived in Boston where their social milieu was the intellectual, academic, political power clique that governed part of the Boston social scene.

Mary Claflin and Alice Freeman had enjoyed for several years a relationship that on Claflin's side combined easy communication with respect and admiration. Freeman, who needed all the help she could get for remaking Wellesley, linked a genuine liking for a well-connected, helpful, semi-powerful woman with a touch of self-serving but necessary cultivation of the prominent. The Claflins knew both Freeman and Palmer, liked them both, and also knew that both were comers in the academic world. Boston society enjoyed mixing old blood and new talent, and the Claflins dropped Freeman and Palmer like a couple of plums into one of their proper, carefully orchestrated dinners. Neither Alice Freeman nor George Palmer was averse to being used that way. Calculated friendship and measured intimacy were integral parts of their lives.

But no one expected what happened. They fell in love. Within ten days the debate that lasted for a year and a half was underway. Together, with pain, understanding, and immediate sacrifice on the part of Alice, Palmer and Freeman worked out the bargain that defined the dilemma. Where did the New Woman belong?

Since the couple seldom met, the bargain was largely negotiated through a voluminous correspondence, sometimes several letters a

153

day.[2] And wonderful letters they are. So articulate were both of them that they used words as rapiers, shining in the sun. As George sharpened his arguments and perfected his metaphors, Alice rose to the challenge and replied in kind. Caroline Hazard, a later Wellesley president, compared the Palmers to the Brownings, participants in the nineteenth century's great literary romance.[3] The analogy is apt. Quite possibly both Alice and George cast themselves in such a role. Alice's rather hapless attempt at poetry, *A Marriage Cycle,* although lacking literary merit, may quite well have been inspired by Elizabeth Barrett Browning's *Sonnets From the Portuguese.*

Through their letters one can follow the intricacies of the relationship. Two successful, independent people both reached for and confronted each other. For a year and a half they cannily bargained, guiltily reassured, shamelessly adored, and very occasionally withdrew from their overwhelming need for each other. They loved, they doubted, and they fought with infinite politeness and great skill. And underneath pulsed the ever-present major theme: Alice must preserve her independence within her surrender, and George was determined his life plan should not be changed.

Their courtship had many aspects.[4] One was a power struggle. Would Alice become George's wife, bright but subordinate, and perform her marital duties in a conventional way? Or, would George recognize his wife's great achievements and make allowances that would permit her to continue her career? Another dimension was sex. The sexual tension that emanates from their hundred-year-old correspondence is palpable. One can feel the hormones of this less-than-youthful couple racing back and forth between Wellesley and Cambridge. As good Victorians they could hardly admit to being governed by the flesh, but the flesh was calling loud and clear within each of them. Still another aspect was duty. What were Alice's obligations to fifteen-year-old Wellesley which was just beginning to establish itself as a viable and prestigious institution. George's duties seem less compelling to a twentieth-century feminist, but he strongly cherished obligations to his discipline and to his academic institutional connections. He was a devotee of the new German-inspired university system and felt he exerted important and necessary influences in Cambridge. To George, a new women's college could hardly make comparable demands.

For eighteen months they hammered out the answers to these

questions, never quite phrasing them as they have been framed here, but bit by bit resolving their differences, Alice eventually found a resolution that was probably inevitable for the nineteenth-century New Woman. Although she fought hard, it was clear from the beginning that, for the first time, she was ready to surrender and abrogate obligations both to her family and to her own independence. She was tired. She had had almost enough of making her own way. And George was a persistent and an able strategist. He saw what he wanted and he went after it with zeal.

1

A few days after their first encounter Alice received a letter from George, "Do you ever have such a thing as leisure? If within the next weeks you should discover an unoccupied half hour, might I ask the privilege of depriving you of it?"[5] His excuse for seeing her was a bit unconvincing but easily accepted by Alice. He wanted to discuss the possible further education of the daughter of the farmer who tilled his Boxford farm. Ten days later Alice answered that either the next Friday or Monday she would be at liberty.[6] And she encouraged him further. She invited him to a Wellesley fete on June 4th in honor of Eben Horsford, who was, of course, not only a benefactor of Wellesley, but one of George Palmer's Harvard colleagues.

George went, and in his thank-you note written after his train brought him back to Cambridge that evening, he took up a theme, Alice's health, on which he would improvise variations for the next year and a half. "I was distressed to see you look so worn, and to find you were having little appetite and sleep," and he proposed that she "become a girl again and come like a child to our [Harvard's] Class Day?" But she must not "let this invitation be one more burden." She should simply not answer unless she truly wanted to come.[7]

She accepted with alacrity: "What a delight to sit in the midst of a class day for whose arrangements I made no plans, and could have no responsibility."[8] And the serious wooing began. She was willing. He was both ardent and determined. George escorted her back to Wellesley that evening laden with water lilies, roses, and laurel and pressed upon her invitations to join him for a holiday at his Boxford farm. She had not had a serious suitor (or at least one she had permitted to be serious) for some time.[9] For the last five years, she had carried crushing responsibilities. She had been working, probably beyond her physical strength, since she was nineteen. The temptation to lighten her life with a touch of romance was more than attractive. He offered a change of pace, and she responded eagerly.

In July, she spent a week at Boxford, north of Boston, where George owned a farmhouse that had been in his mother's family for two centuries.[10] Mrs. Claflin, the unsuspecting matchmaker, accompanied her as chaperone. Alice and George walked alone in the woods when Mrs. Claflin was resting, played with his dog Barnes, and got well past polite banter to intimate friendship. It was clear that their emotions were now involved. She wrote to George on her return to Wellesley, "Whatever you may think when you think this day over, you certainly will know this, that from the beginning you have seen my heart, and I have concealed nothing from you."[11] When the "week of peace," as they called it was over, he wrote to her about his work (he was then translating Homer), sent her Jonas Very sonnets to read, and as he strolled the farm, "came out on the hard green turf which encircled the old cellar, where we and the moon looked at one another a few nights ago."[12] Friendship it may still have been, but their relationship now included moonlight and roses.

By the end of July, George was declaring his love and probably pressing her to marry him. He wrote: "It was horrible not to kiss you in the wood today, to claim you as my own and to protect you against the wounds that I made. But then it is you that I want, you with all your splendid powers and high aims, you entire, your charm, your beauty, your clinging love. We could say anything for a minute, but what shall we say for a lifetime? That we belong together—I think—."[13] He had declared his love, and that distressed her. She was not ready for love and commitment, and he promised that "I will not speak again of what I spoke today. I will only be near you and we will share the many interests which fill our busy lives."[14]

By August the love George had declared in July was mutual. He followed her to Saginaw on her annual summer visit to her family, dismissing her objections because "before our terms begin we must have a definite and clearly considered policy about our intercourse during the year. It is a complicated matter which we must arrange together. For meeting its perplexities, letters are quite insufficient."[15] She was not yet prepared to tell her family of their relationship but, of course, her family guessed when her mother surprised Alice in the upstairs sitting room on George's lap.[16]

To marry or not to marry, that was the question. Here came the hard thought and the bargaining. As George wrote Alice: "There is no simple solution. . . . Time is necessary and the most unselfish care." He saw two elements in their problem: "(1) Wellesley must not suffer. (2) We must come together. We cannot neglect one of these and expect to preserve the other."[17] She was not so sure they could achieve both those aims. And, of course, George left out the third condition, that George's professional life must remain autonomous and intact.

Alice Freeman had been attracted to intellectual men since she was fourteen and her Windsor Academy tutor had persuaded her to betroth herself to him. He was followed by a score of Michigan suitors, some of whom continued to pursue her after she went to Wellesley. Many of the male administrators who had hired or worked with her had been avid for marriage. She had withdrawn. Now when she had everything—power, position, a comfortable income—marriage became an almost irresistible prospect.

2

Was George Palmer so attractive, so powerful, that he could break the pattern that had governed Alice Freeman's romantic attachments thus far—attraction and withdrawal? He was probably the most prestigious man who had yet courted her. He certainly outshone high school superintendents and Michigan undergraduates. Palmer, in turn, had always been attracted to intellectual women, but this time he had a monkey on his back. Alice Freeman was not only something of an intellectual, but the incumbent in one of the most important posts occupied by an American woman of her time.

In 1886, George Palmer was forty-four. Three years before he had received his full professorship at Harvard where he had been teaching classics and philosophy since 1870. Although Palmer was never ordained or licensed to preach, he chose theological training after graduating from Harvard as the one way then available to study philosophy. Palmer also studied, as did many of the new university professional academics, in Germany at the University of Tübingen.

George Palmer at about the time of his marriage.
(Courtesy of Wellesley College Archives.)

His education had been interrupted by a stint in his family's wholesale dry goods business and a year of high school teaching, but he had chosen college teaching as his life work before his marriage in 1871 to Ellen Margaret Wellman of Brookline.[18] Theirs had been a difficult courtship. She was an intimate of his sister as well as the sister of a college friend. Ellen was several years older than he and in poor health. They long carried on an intellectual correspondence (with infrequent meetings) about books and ideas. Ellen was an intellectual, a self-taught student of philosophy and literature, and probably had a truer concern with ideas than Alice. George and Ellen shared rich and varied interests. Aside from the impact of two years at the University of Tübingen, Ellen probably contributed as much as anyone to George Palmer's intellectual development before he came to Harvard to teach.

But when they decided to marry, both their families were strongly opposed. The Palmers disliked intensely Ellen's Swedenborgian religious ideas, that she was older than their son, and that she was already stricken with active tuberculosis which had plagued her much of her adult life. Eventually, however, everyone was reconciled. The marriage seemed happy and fulfilling for both, marred only by Ellen's ill health. Always frail, Ellen died in 1879 of tuberculosis. Thereafter George Palmer lived the bachelor life of an academic don near Harvard Yard.[19]

George and Alice were an incongruous pair. Physically George Palmer was unimpressive. While he had been frail and chronically ill as a child, careful habits including regular exercise and a healthful diet had helped him achieve a vigorous adulthood. Nonetheless, he was a small man, not much over five foot two inches, and rarely weighed over 130 pounds. And Alice had not shrunk over the years. Although George always called her his "little girl," she was certainly considerably taller than he, and while still slender when they met and married, she, more than he, put on weight over the years. Nonetheless as his biographer states, George Palmer had "a personal force which made its impression."[20] Alice responded to that force, rather than his height, and there is no evidence that she ever worried about any physical incongruities, nor that her Wellesley students, who were not always reverent, made fun of an "odd couple" when their engagement was announced and wedding celebrated. Longish, dark hair, handlebar mustaches, and a pair of bushy eyebrows over deep-set, startling pale blue eyes, helped to create a face that no Harvard undergraduate would ever forget.[21]

It was his voice that was Palmer's most remarkable feature. Vida Scudder, who knew him at the time that Alice first met him, called it "one of the most beautiful voices ever granted a man" as he read Shakespeare's sonnets or the *Odyssey* to her mother on summer evenings.[22] Lucy Sprague, the Palmer's surrogate daughter who lived with the Palmers during her Radcliffe days and later traveled with them in Europe, described George's "wonderful, cultured voice that could make Milton sound like an organ."[23] Wellesley girls were also entranced by his voice and his readings. Harvard men flocked to chapel when it was announced he would speak. George Palmer was no physical Adonis, but he combined his wonderful musical voice with a penetrating way with words that left few immune to his personality. Both Alice and George responded to each other's voices. In an era when reading aloud was the middle-class family's chief form of evening entertainment, the musical, resonant speaking voice, plus a few histrionics, was a treasure to be carefully cultivated. Both Alice and George were great readers, for each other, as well as others.

George Palmer's interest in the education of women long antedated his relationship with Alice Freeman. His first wife, Ellen, had helped arouse that interest; his mentor, the Scottish philosopher Edward Caird, further encouraged it. Palmer was an early lecturer at the unofficial Harvard Annex (later Radcliffe College), not an unusual means for a junior, underpaid Harvard teacher to pick up a bit of extra money. In fact, President Charles Eliot often held out such employment as bait when hiring promising young men at ridiculously low salaries. But Palmer, unlike the other grubbers after a few hundred dollars, always gave his best to the Annex and credited its students as being among the most stimulating he would teach in Cambridge. He continued to appear on its roster long after he had established himself at the Yard and had no need for extra income. In fact, when George Palmer was scheduled to give a series of Greek readings at Harvard in the spring of 1887, he pressed the authorities to permit the Annex women to attend. Harvard bigwigs protested that the occasion would seem less serious "if bonnets were present." Palmer's rejoinder was to promise that if they were not allowed he would read all six books over again for the Annex.[24]

Vida Scudder, who as a young girl knew George Palmer intimately when she and her mother were summer tenants at the Boxford farm and who continued as a close colleague and friend throughout both their lives, saw him as possessing a culture as wide and sensitive as anyone she had ever known. But she also saw in him a certain humility, and she quoted a heartfelt remark he had once made to her, "I am defeated, and I know it, if I meet any human being from whom I am unable to learn anything."[25] George Palmer had his faults. In his old age (and he lived for over thirty years after Alice died), he became quaint and eccentric and perhaps pompous and rigid. But the man Alice Freeman met in 1886 was none of these. He was spontaneous, venturesome, and very ambitious. He knew he was confronting the New Woman. At least most of the time, he relished taking her on.

At the time that Alice Freeman and George Palmer met, she was a much more prominent public figure than he. As the only woman who was president of a well-known educational institution, she had attracted considerable attention. The Harvard faculty viewed the exotic, charismatic young educator from the Midwest with curious interest and made occasional tentative overtures to welcome her into their academic fraternity. Popular magazines sent journalists to write celebrity sketches based on interviews about her life and work. Although publicity made her uncomfortable, it attested to her national prominence. As we have seen, she was in demand as a public speaker, both in the United States and in Canada. George Palmer was hardly known outside Cambridge and Boston and certainly not a man to attract the notice of the public press. He had received no honorary degrees when Columbia conferred one on Freeman. What is more, she earned more than he did. In 1887 her salary was $4,000 to his $3,500.[26]

George Palmer was not a jealous man, and he took great pleasure in Alice Freeman's fame and accomplishments. When her Columbia degree was announced, he wrote: "I rejoice that you are so broadly known. The universal honor in which you are held will make both our lives wealthier and more productive."[27] In fact, George would have preferred to announce their engagement at the time she was receiving all the public attention, an idea that horrified Alice. In the same letter he remarked: "I shall be delighted too to have the degree announced at just about the time of our engagement. . . . I welcome a racket. We can't get engaged everyday, sweetheart, and I don't object to getting all the fun out of it that is possible."[28]

George Palmer belonged to the liberal intellectual community that welcomed new ideas, including a change in the role of women. He was also an exponent of the religious liberalism that was sweeping American universities in the last quarter of the nineteenth century. As early as 1882 he opposed Harvard College's stuffing compulsory religious practices down undergraduate throats.[29] He bridled at religious tests for academic appointments and encouraged Alice Freeman in her attempt to modify Durant's rigidly sectarian qualifications for the Wellesley faculty and trustees. In a weak moment, when the Wellesley presidency was being urged on him, he considered possibly accepting "if the College could be placed on an independent basis and become genuinely unsectarian."[30] Alice had encountered a worthy partner, capable of recognizing her ambitions and talents and fully meriting her respect. But he had reservations.

As the academic year 1886–87 got underway, the little excursion into purely personal pleasure and satisfaction on which Alice Freeman had embarked the previous spring left her with an additional large problem, one that dwarfed those old problems she inherited from previous years, such as building a competent faculty, constructing physical facilities to house a rapidly expanding enrollment, securing prestigious and informed trustees, and acquiring a firm financial base for Wellesley. Now a new question was added. Would she, should she, could she marry? For Alice Freeman was ambitious, not only for herself but for the enterprise with which she was most closely associated. Perhaps Wellesley would have become Wellesley no matter what Alice Freeman did, given the place, the time, and the circumstances. But she certainly facilitated its transformation from Mr. Durant's missionary enterprise into a viable force in the new academia. And as she repeatedly said to George, her work remained unfinished.

As she looked at the college and herself, the old problems and the new one became intertwined. There was no way she could escape her duty to Wellesley, as she saw it. She could not retreat into marriage and leave the college to fend for itself. Nor could she simply add marriage to the roles she already played because, when it came to final choices, George Palmer could not and would not permit it. Only by solving the college's problems could she solve her own dilemma.

Consciously or unconsciously George Palmer adopted a pair of strategies that advanced his suit and tied Alice Freeman more closely to him. Very early in their relationship George began to play an active, if publicly unacknowledged part in policy-making at Wellesley. His first clear intervention occurred in August of 1886 when he urged an overworked Freeman to create a deanship to relieve her of administrative duties beyond the secretarial level, someone, as he said, who would have sufficient academic status to answer policy correspondence and be "in training for a future president." In doing so he asked, "now have I been very meddlesome?"[31] But his advice was to flow freely thereafter. For example, in September he suggested a candidate for Wellesley's professorship of ethics.[32] By October Alice

Freeman was clearly dependent on him for advice and succor in managing the burdens of the presidency that she had handled alone for nearly five years before they met. Her need was so great that she risked gossip to have him come to her rooms because it "has been a destructive week.... For the second time in my life I have had to dismiss a student publicly," and another student showed signs of mania and must be constantly guarded until she could be got home.[33] Even her relationship with students became part of his ken, and his advice on the composition and handling of the board of trustees, selection of new faculty, and the management of Pauline Durant was specific and constant.

But Alice had not yet agreed to marry George. That commitment was not made until January (possibly early February) of 1887. Meanwhile her ambivalence kept them both in a turmoil. On the first of September in 1886 she wrote him: "We must stop here.... Upon the closest thought that I can give the subject from all sides, no other course seems open to me." And she added that: "I will never run the risk of spoiling your dear life and my work at the same time until both He [Christ] and you and my own heart make it clear that taking that risk is greater service than anything else He has in store for you and me."[34]

Only solving Wellesley's problems would lead to her surrender, and he willingly acquiesced in that necessity, especially as time went on and he realized that it was his only hope of success. In November he wrote: "All your obligations are mine.... And until they are wisely treated I could not welcome you."[35] Throughout the fall she vacillated between involving him more deeply in college affairs and attempting to free herself from him. Part of the time she vowed she would try "not to press the burdens and joys of College life upon you so."[36] At the same time she had arranged for him to give a series of Greek readings to Wellesley students, and rejoiced "to have you *in* Wellesley, and instructing our students, do you know how much it means to me? You come into my daily life then; you stand beside me in my beautiful work here and have a part in it. It seems as if you belong to me in a new way."[37]

George tried to be patient and not push her toward commitment too rapidly. On one occasion he wrote: "I have been thinking much about our possible intercourse lately, in this long week. I do not want our approaches to have anything feverish, anything disturbing, about

them. We are man and woman, not children. We mean to be strong."
He suggested they write only once or twice a week but try to see each
other in public places like the art museum in Boston or the college
(but not Norumbega, the cottage where she resided) more frequently.[38]

As the new year began Alice Freeman was unable to free herself
of her dependence on George Palmer's advice. She wanted to discuss
with him the plans for the new art building, the problems in the
philosophy department, the Furness Shakespeare fund, and a half-
dozen other matters, and again she risked gossip by asking him to
come on a Saturday evening to her college office by the seldom-used
east door.[39]

There were times when neither thought they could resolve the
dilemma. How could she possibly leave the work she had really just
begun? He suggested that "administration may be now your genuine
life. If it is so, do find it out and tell me, and do not let me spoil a
life—two lives—that I want to enlarge. Would you not be happier,
and in your judgement more useful, darling, as president of Wellesley than as my wife?"[40] And in the same letter he revealed clearly
that if they married he would expect her to subordinate her needs to
his, "Have you any such desire to be always by my side that studying
how to help me [italics mine] could ever seem to you the greatest of
duties, for which all others might wait?"[41] His acceptance of the goals
of the New Woman with her need to control her own life was wearing
thin in those sentences. But actually he was as ambivalent as she for
he wrote next day, saying: "I would far rather you never came to me
than that you should come and find your great powers in any respect
lessened. For I do not seek to get you, not for myself. Only that by
joining, we two together make up one more righteous person than
either could be alone."[42] Part of the time they were ordinary Victorians unable to see beyond the conventional marriages they saw all
around them; part of the time they believed they could meet as equals
and forge a new kind of relationship that permitted both of them to
fully incorporate professional lives.

There also was truth in George's statement, "I am a shadowy being
who has lent a romance to your life." Alice did find escape into romance much more attractive than the realities of marriage. As
George said: "In my presence you like to forget all realities and live

in the rapturous moment. But the feeling gone, hard facts are waiting and these do not include me."[43]

During the first year of the Freeman-Palmer courtship, until their impending marriage was publicly announced, where and when to meet was a constant problem. Had they met frequently speculation about a romance would have been rife on both campuses, and since they had made no firm plans and saw Wellesley's need for steady, stable leadership as essential, they felt they must keep their relationship a secret. As George wrote his sister-in-law that first summer: "We are not allowed to know each other's daily lives. We cannot share or even hear minutely each other's work. . . . Our meetings are infrequent."[44] Except for formal public occasions they met secretly. Just before school began in the fall of 1886 they rendezvoused in the woods near Wellesley. George brought a picnic lunch. Alice was to make sure her horse would make no trouble by seeing that he was fed and watered beforehand. Afterwards George walked back alone to the Wellesley station and she went off on a round of errands.[45] That October they met at Boxford with Mrs. Claflin serving once more as unsuspecting chaperone.[46] Later that month Alice attended the Collegiate Alumnae Association meetings at Bryn Mawr, and he joined her on the overnight steamer from Fall River, Massachusetts, to New York City. He brought "rolls to feed us both again before we go to bed," and reserved two staterooms side by side. They had three hours alone together that evening and he promised to "purr and coo, to lay my head on your breast, and talk quietly and be talked to."[47] At least once that fall (during Thanksgiving weekend) they met in her hotel room at the Vendome where she stayed when in Boston on business, "where once your door is locked nobody knows whether you are at home or not."[48] They considered spending a few days together at a mountain resort during the Christmas holidays, but she eventually vetoed that excursion as too risky.[49] In January he complained, "What is to be done about these enforced separations?" and he suggested they arrange to meet in his brother Julius's law offices in Boston. Julius would have to be told about their relationship, but he would be completely trustworthy. They contrived to invite Fred Palmer as a guest preacher to Wellesley which served as an excuse for two easily explained meetings.[50] It was not easy. Sometimes they did not see each other, publicly or privately, for two or three weeks. After he had taken a solitary, starry stroll on a November night, he lamented that "we have never walked together outside Boxford."[51]

Their correspondence made explicit their physical intimacy. He wrote more openly than she, as in "only a day or two and you will be sitting in my lap," or "were you only here I would kiss you and lay you in bed and you should rest beside me."[52] Or, on another occasion: "How close we have been, sweet love, and what peace that closeness contained! Did I tell you as you lay sleeping in my arms, you murmured, 'You will not go away, dear,—not to Germany again?'"[53] But despite these intimacies they seem not to have fully consummated their union. In March he wrote: "I will keep your dear flesh to myself, if you please. Already I have claimed it all as mine. And I am glad to think that when at parting we knew how truly our spirits were one, we dared rejoicingly to own that our bodies were so too."[54] However, in May, he wrote: "Since I left you yesterday I have been full of self reproaches and resolves. I shall not come so near you any more, for I am sure that instead of calming you with assurance of our immense present wealth, I am only stirring longings for the greater blessings which we neither of us believe to be honorably ours at present."[55] His meaning seems clear. There were limits (despite its intensity) to their physical relationship before their marriage.

Although the terms were unresolved, Alice Freeman, early in the new year, made a firm decision to marry George Palmer. She let him give her a ruby and diamond engagement ring on her birthday, February 21, and she wore it at once, although she explained it to curious students as a birthday present from her family. She refused to make a public announcement and had not yet told her parents. And despite George's impatient urging she would not commit herself to a date. Her decision had not been made easily. For months she toyed with the idea of a European trip with her friend, Lillian Horsford, to put some distance between herself, Wellesley, and George to better assess her dilemma. But she postponed that possible separation repeatedly until her family's problems made it impossible, and she made her decision without this hiatus.

Alice Freeman decided to marry at a time when her problems with the college were compounding. Relations with Pauline Durant "were never more uncomfortable, and with all the work the friction becomes more difficult to bear. If the subjects of dispute were only great interests [which in many ways they were soon to be] there would be a dignity and value in variety of opinion, or even in strenuous opposition."[56] But Freeman saw the strain resulting from petty matters—how the farm's produce should be used, campus rules, chapel attendance, faculty custodial duties.

The trustees were a major problem. Most of the active trustees were original Durant appointees and joined Pauline Durant in emphasizing the strict "evangelical" point of view. But when Sarah Houghton and Caroline A. Wood, two of the five women trustees, died in January of 1887, the opportunity arose for Alice Freeman to create a board more to her liking.[57] Two vacancies existed. Since some of the trustees, such as the evangelist Dwight Moody, were almost completely inactive, additional strong, involved trustees that shared Freeman's view of the college could probably control policy. Her first choice was Lillian Horsford, her close personal friend and Eben Horsford's unmarried daughter.[58] She would bring both the Horsford money and a liberal point of view to the board.

Pauline Durant, however, did not want any new trustees. She thought the board was already too large and interfered too much with running her dear husband's college, and Alice complained to George, "These are discouraging days whenever I get a glimpse of her feeling concerning the management." Mrs. Durant rejected most of the names proposed by Freeman as not "evangelically sound." Alice felt that Durant was so sensitive to change that any rash word would endanger the college.[59] It was George who was assigned the job of checking the opinions of Judge Bradley, the only potential trustee to whom Mrs. Durant reacted favorably.[60] A week later George provided Alice with an annotated list of possible trustees all of whom would back Freeman in a crisis.[61] George suggested she let Durant pick three from this list. She replied: "You help me so much in my trustee work as in every item of all my affairs. Thank you for this letter so full of your heart and head."[62] By this time managing Wellesley College was clearly a joint enterprise. Freeman could no longer, or at least thought she could no longer, handle her administrative responsibilities without Palmer's help.

Meanwhile, slowly but surely, through the combined efforts of Alice and George, progress was made in long-range plans for Wellesley's future. The trustee issue came to a head at the February meeting, an all-day session where the president put forth her nominees: Lillian Horsford, John William White, and Daniel Sharp Ford. An-

Pauline Durant, cofounder of Wellesley College.
(Courtesy of Wellesley College Archives.)

other trustee nominated a conservative Baptist whose daughter had attended Wellesley. Pauline Durant protested that there were too many nominations, and anyway she would vote against some. George Palmer's advice on strategy flowed freely at this time. He thought Horsford, the Claflins, Hovey, and McKenzie would provide enough support so that Freeman could get what she wanted from the board.[63] And he was right. New trustees were not elected until the June meeting when Lillian Horsford won a place over Pauline Durant's strong objections, and Eustace Fitts, another person on whom Freeman could count, joined the board.[64] Henceforth Pauline Durant's power definitely was shaken.

The next major question dealt with the administrative leadership of the college. Palmer still favored a dean who would assume many immediate burdens and be in training for the presidency itself. And by late winter Freeman had found a candidate for the job, another midwesterner, Margaret Evans, preceptress and professor of English at Carleton College in Northfield, Minnesota. The two met in Chicago for an interview in early spring. Evans was attracted by the offer but decided prior obligations compelled her refusal.[65] In the end the question of administrative leadership was postponed until fall. Whether he was aware of it or not, George Palmer's strategy to make himself indispensable to Alice Freeman in her role as president of Wellesley had worked. She needed and used him every step of the way.

During their courtship George Palmer discussed his work fully with Alice Freeman; his trials and triumphs with publishers, his survey (with an eye to keeping Harvard College a viable option for the poor) of the financial status of Harvard students, his slowly growing acceptance by the Harvard establishment both as scholar and as friend. He talked of what his contributions to Harvard were and might be in the future, and where his scholarly interests would take him, his discourse with students, even the examination papers he read. He did not, however, ask Alice Freeman's advice about his career. That counsel which she frequently asked for herself and which he gave so freely was not expected to be reciprocal.

Another strategy that George Palmer used to lead Alice Freeman both toward marriage and away from the Wellesley presidency was to emphasize the risks of stress and overwork to Alice's health. Her physical condition, which had been relatively stable for several years, began to deteriorate during the fall of 1886. In November she caught a feverish cold that persisted for months. Adding her personal dilemma to her professional problems undoubtedly contributed to the physical stress under which she lived. But long before her illness, George Palmer argued that by marrying him she could ensure her future good health. "In my home you will be stronger for Wellesley, for yourself, for every good purpose for which the Lord made you, than you can possibly be by continuing longer as a public functionary."[66] In that same letter George proposed for the first time that

Alice marry him, live in Cambridge, and guide Wellesley from the board of trustees rather than as president. His argument was based on the need to preserve her fragile health. It was an argument that he continued to put forth with persistent vigor until she resigned the presidency.

George Palmer was undoubtedly sincere in his concern that if Alice stayed on campus as Wellesley's full-time administrator, tuberculosis would claim her. He had lost one young wife to that disease. Alice's family had a history of fatal consumption. Alice was overworked and overextended, and it was impossible for her to rest in her residential situation. By spring of 1887, when they had already decided to marry, the doctors reported that her disease was accelerating, reinforcing George's conviction that it was "imprudent for your health to manage the college any longer . . . I shall fight stoutly. And I shall not be put off by makeshifts, those pretty plans that demonstrate that while you are still to continue as president, you will have nothing at all to do."[67] Her health failed to improve. In summer she was so ill that she had to interrupt her Saginaw-to-Wellesley trip by stopping at a friend's home in New York state. The doctors then advised her that only after a long and complete rest could she continue her work.[68] In September she was in bed again and spent many days confined to her room during the fall of 1887.

Since her junior year at Michigan Alice Freeman had frequently been ill. She had had tuberculosis severe enough to precipitate hemorrhages. But she had never consistently taken to her bed before. Even when consumption threatened to overwhelm her in the spring of 1881, she had retreated to the Susquehanna Valley, rested a bit, slept late, gardened and climbed the easier surrounding hills. Now she was frequently in bed. George Palmer's fears for Alice's health were not unrealistic.

To further complicate the decision-making process the Freeman family needed considerable help and support from December of 1886 through the following fall. Alice's mother suffered an acute attack of "inflammatory rheumatism with neuralgia," was bedridden, in considerable pain, and needed constant nursing care.[69] Telegrams and letters flowed back and forth, and for weeks on end Alice did not know when she might be summoned to Saginaw. The expenses of nursing care fell on Alice.[70] Finally on March 10th Alice left for Saginaw and stayed nearly a month. She found her mother and father frail and old, her mother still bedridden, unable to walk, and in great pain, but continuing her interest in temperance and women's reform causes and every morning dictating letters that she could no longer write herself to carry on with her public work.[71] The family considered taking her to a sanitarium such as Battle Creek or Arkansas Hot Springs, but they felt they could not safely move her.[72] And all the Freemans were ailing with the usual assortment of winter colds and influenza.

The family's financial situation was also precarious. Despite her father's and Fred's flourishing practice much less had been done about freeing them from debt than Alice had hoped. They still owed six thousand dollars; expenses were high. They had built a new house the previous summer and had three extra servants to care for her mother.[73] George provided Alice with what emotional support he could from a distance, suggesting they would work out her family's money problems together "by a rigid campaign of economy and thoughtfulness."[74] Although the Freeman family may not yet have known Alice and George were betrothed, they were aware of the seriousness of Alice's attachment to George Palmer and that fact seems to have added to their insecurity. Undoubtedly everyone wondered how much longer they would be able to count on Alice's unstinting financial aid. However, when she returned to Saginaw for two weeks after commencement in June, she found Fred again in good health and her father no worse. As usual Ella and her husband were "not quite strong." Her mother was "much better than I feared" but not yet up to a long journey, and Fred predicted that she would not live long.[75] Of course both parents outlived Alice by many years. Now, however, the family's financial burdens were on Alice's shoulders, and on her return trip to Wellesley, it was Alice who became so ill she had to break her journey to recuperate.[76]

That fall Ella and Charlie Talmadge became a further drain on Alice. Charlie had decided to train for the ministry in Boston, and during Alice's hectic last months at Wellesley, Ella lived at Norumbega with her. George disapproved emphatically. He constantly urged Alice to have Ella make other living arrangements, and Alice promised, but nothing was ever done.[77]

Meanwhile the issue of George's previous marriage had to be resolved. Although preoccupation with a relationship long since terminated by death sounds strange to twentieth-century ears, Ellen, and

Alice's relationship to Ellen, was something with which both George and Alice felt they must deal. The first summer that they knew one another, George gave Alice the letters from his first courtship and marriage to read. He protested almost too much that Alice did not replace Ellen, but was a quite different attachment. However, both Alice and George seemed to need Ellen's approval. He wrote: "I only know that my honor for her and gratitude are not as a fact interfered with as you take possession of me. I used to tell her I should marry again if I could ever love anybody as I loved her, but I did not see how this could ever be possible. It has not been possible during these eight years, but how great you have made it so. I thank you and I believe in heaven Ellen herself does."[78] And Alice many times wrote to George in this vein, "how tenderly I think of her, always, or reverence her dear memory."[79] His family also felt compelled to meld Alice into Ellen. When Alice paid a first visit to Mary Palmer, wife of George's brother Fred, Mary wrote to George: "Of course Nell [Ellen] is strong in her. Neither I nor Nell could love her if she were not.... How Nell would have rejoiced in her, and she in Nell."[80] One way to explain this concern is to assume their belief in a literal resurrection when the three spirits would be compelled to face each other. Or perhaps they half believed, as did Susan B. Anthony, that marriage was so binding that second marriages after the death of one partner were sacrilegious and unacceptable.[81]

In all the courtship negotiations a crucial question, whether or not they should have children, was never mentioned. When Alice Freeman died many eulogists at her various memorial services suggested that the absence of children was a disappointment to the Palmers, and that they substituted attachments to Harvard and Radcliffe undergraduates, especially Lucy Sprague, who became a surrogate daughter. George Palmer in his memoir does not mention the absence of children, painting his idyllic portrait of their marriage, acknowledging no disappointments or lacks. Alice became sentimentally attached to Fred Palmer's small son and seemed always to have enjoyed children. When the Palmers married she was only thirty-two, hardly past child-bearing age. George was in his forties, but certainly not too old for parenting. However, in all their planning for the future the possibility of children is never mentioned. After they had been married several years George did allude in a letter to the absence of children. When commenting on the death of the son of a friend he wrote that

"I declare such a thing makes me glad we have no child," and Alice once wrote George from Saginaw: "Father pathetically asks me where his grandchildren are, and I tell him it isn't my fault.... When he comes East he may give you a scolding."[82] Perhaps George dared not jeopardize Alice's fragile health with a pregnancy. He had already lost one wife to consumption.

3

George Palmer wanted to announce the engagement as soon as Alice accepted his ring, but Alice insisted she must first tell her family, interview Margaret Evans of Carleton College as possible dean, and pick an auspicious time to tell Pauline Durant. Their differences over this question were strongly felt, and they came as close to quarreling as any time during their courtship. But George eventually capitulated, "Our sole thought must be Wellesley's interest."[83]

Alice conceived the happy thought that breaking the news to Pauline Durant around the time of Durant's own wedding anniversary on May 23rd would make Alice's marriage more palatable. She also made the announcement by letter to allow Durant time to react. Durant responded by letter, stunned, ambivalent, but unable on that "sacred day" of her own life to be completely negative. And she closed, "with warm love, your friend in trial."[84] Once Pauline had assimilated the news, she was "loving and sympathetic" in two long talks with Alice, but adamant that the trustees not be informed until the three, Palmer, Freeman and Durant, had made "definite plans for the college."[85] Pauline immediately suggested building the couple a house on campus, assuming Alice would stay on as Wellesley's president. To sweeten the shock and help Pauline feel she was being consulted in all the planning, she was invited to chaperone Alice for a Boxford visit and intimate consultations in early June.[86] The trustees were finally told in July.[87] Freeman did not resign and promised to guide the college until a successor could be found, and the trustees expressed the hope that she continue as president for the coming year if not longer. Meanwhile, George unsuccessfully pressed for an August wedding. He did not get his way. Freeman resigned, effective at the end of the fall term in December, at the September trustees meeting.[88]

Once their engagement was announced, the couple could do things openly that had previously been clandestine. In late September they again took the boat from Fall River to New York, this time for Augustus Palmer's wedding at Poughkeepsie.[89] They enjoyed supper alone in George's rooms in Cambridge after an October Saturday afternoon spent inspecting possible houses,[90] and a Boxford weekend together when the fall color was in its height.[91] But these happy interludes did not solve the problems of Wellesley's future.

Since April the possibility that George become president of Wellesley had engaged Alice's interest. By working together, none of her hopes, programs, and long-range plans would be in jeopardy. George was more than reluctant. Following a long discussion in his brother's office he wrote:

> I would do it if it were necessary for your health, or even if I believed your powers were to be paralyzed by change of duty. But I have been long in building up an influence here which I must not lightly abandon. I am sure you would find it somewhat humiliating to see me marry into a position. You would like to have me stand on my own two feet. I do that here, and you will stand by my side, my strong support. But I will not insist. Do with me as you see fit.[92]

Obviously George did not see it humiliating to Alice if she married into a position. However Alice did not abandon this solution to her dilemma. In September she relayed arguments of Trustee Willcox urging Palmer to accept the presidency, "that only thus can Wellesley be saved."[93] But George was now unequivocal in his rejection, declaring he would refuse the presidency on all terms.

Alice hoped to find a way she could marry and continue to live in Wellesley. During the summer when she had not yet consented to give up the presidency, she found a "pretty new cottage near the Station—just finished and, entrancingly convenient for perfect housekeeping." She would no longer have to live at Norumbega, she would not have to catch trains, and she was sure Harvard would not mind George's commuting to Cambridge.[94] But George intended to retain his Harvard base. He replied obliquely to her appeal with talk of possible Cambridge houses they might rent.[95] George Palmer eventually chose a house as close to the Yard as possible.

By the October trustees meeting, the basic decisions on the future governance of the college had been reached. Alice finally had relinquished the idea of continuing as president or installing George in that role. She had chosen Helen Shafer, professor of mathematics, as her successor.[96] Daughter of a Congregational clergyman, educated at Oberlin as were so many early women educators, gifted teacher and careful planner, she was to meet Wellesley's needs in a businesslike, if not inspiring incumbency.[97] Although not elected formally as a trustee until after her resignation took effect, Freeman fully intended to lend help and counsel from the board. It was agreed that the financial affairs of the college would be removed from Pauline Durant's supervision and placed in the hands of a bursar who valiantly tried during the following years to reduce the deficit and debt and sort out the tangled web of endowment and expenditure that he had inherited.[98] Although the problem of Wellesley's debts would not be solved for fifteen years, the beginning steps had been taken to put Wellesley on a firm financial footing.

4

By September Alice and George had decided to marry at the end of the term, and George was seriously looking for the temporary rental of a furnished house in Cambridge that would permit them to go abroad in June if his plans for a sabbatical year were realized. They began compiling a list of wedding guests and she started to plan her trousseau. At the end of October, he found a home, at 497 Broadway in Cambridge, "a pretty nearly perfect one, near the College Yard, of good size, and full of sunshine. It is exquisitely furnished, and we can have it at no great price until next summer. Will see it after Thursday's concert."[99]

Although they needed to economize, their economic outlook also seemed brighter. Instead of a combined income of $7,500, they would have to live on George's $3,500. For years Alice had lived in college and could spend freely on herself and her family. Now two would have to live on less than she did. However, George Palmer was promised a raise when senior philosophy professor, Francis Bowen, retired the next summer. George cautioned that "we are obliged to live snugly. But economics, when we are of one mind, are only an interesting game."[100] Certainly they lived very comfortably the rest of their lives. Generous wedding presents assisted with their immediate needs. Eben Horsford provided $5,000 toward the European journey, and Edwin Abbott presented them with $500, certainly princely gifts in the 1880s.[101] George's Aunt Hattie provided brass andirons, Carla Wenckebach sent a picture, and the Wellesley faculty spent over $200 on an expensive vase. Plates, spoons, and cut glass dishes arrived daily.[102]

As the wedding date drew near, Alice became increasingly aware of the finality of her decision. She queried George about second thoughts, but she was really thinking of herself. As she wondered if he was somewhat "disturbed in your mind," she confessed. "I am not ready to leave the College. I am not ready to be married, I have made no proper preparations, I have taken no training, and my work here is not done. But I walk as happily as a child to a holiday—or any happy girl to meet her lover."[103] However she spent her last days at the college in bed. She dared not go to chapel for fear of breaking down. She said her goodbyes to the students through one of her associates, and to George she uttered a cry from her heart: "The College life is all over! And I feel like an empty-handed, lonely creature. But I have you dearest! I say it over and over to quiet my heart."[104] Her decision was not easy. Her ambivalence showed to the very end.

Alice Freeman as a mature New Woman wished to continue to be someone who shaped her own life and her own goals, who took her own risks and was responsible for her own actions. This was the way she had governed her life since she was seventeen, for the fifteen years of her adulthood. But for the last five years, during her presidency, hers had been a lonely road. She found herself distanced from old friends like Lucy Andrews and Angie Chapin who were now on the faculty she led as well as her old friends. She increasingly needed to protect herself from her ever-demanding family. The normal women's networks on which she had relied for so long could no longer effectively provide her with emotional sustenance. Either women needed things of her or she needed things of them, and all her relationships were tuned to the needs of Wellesley College. George Palmer appeared at a crucial time in her life. She was alone and overextended. She needed support. Once more she saw marriage as an alternative. But neither did she wish to relinquish her long-cherished independence. She was confronted with the choice of her life, and making that choice was her most difficult decision. She

Alice Freeman in her wedding dress. (Courtesy of
Wellesley College Archives.)

wanted both worlds, but at her time and place in history she could not have them.

The reaction of friends and the public to Alice Freeman's decision had not made her choice easier. Mary Claflin was angry and "full of soreness," although like Pauline Durant, she soon became an enthusiastic supporter of the match.[105] The Wellesley faculty was stunned, apprehensive, and, of course, insecure. Anna Newman, superintendent of Norumbega Cottage, wrote Eben Horsford:

> For myself I am bitterly disappointed, and I believe I never faced the work of a year with such an utter lack of courage as I look forward to this. If I could see that it meant relief from care and rest from the already heavy burdens for the dear Princess I would try and not think of myself at Norumbega, but I cannot see that the contemplated change means anything but leaving a burden to which she is accustomed and taking up a greater of which she only knows the pleasant side.[106]

Despite initial sadness, the students eventually accepted their "princess's marriage" with girlish enthusiasm.

George Palmer later admitted that to pass their marriage by with a bare record, although he saw it as a very private matter, would be unfair because it presented certain problems of general public concern. "It excited much public debate at the time, and probably influenced more people for good or ill than any other event of her life." He also admitted that some trustees and faculty initially were unable to see "why marrying should break her career and leave mine intact."[107] He argued that by 1887 Freeman's task at Wellesley was essentially complete, but Freeman herself did not think so. The only sensible, realistic reason he ever advanced for cutting short her career was that had they lived in Wellesley with Freeman as president, her backbreaking schedule would have continued and her health been permanently impaired.[108] Her friend the educator and commentator Lyman Abbott thought many of her friends and the public saw her as "giving up a position of great influence and power for a minor position," despite her reassurances to the contrary.[109] As one supporter wrote in a letter to the editor, Freeman had "weighed the question of duty" and believed she could now do even more for education, that her coming marriage was in no way abandonment of her work as an educator.[110] But the feeling was widespread that she had betrayed a trust. As a woman she had accepted a position of influence and responsibility which she was now abdicating for purely selfish, personal reasons, thereby to many, not only women, she had betrayed her sex.[111]

Alice Freeman was not the only Wellesley academic to face the dilemma. In 1884 a colleague who married was invited to remain on the faculty and live outside the college. She chose instead to resign.[112] Young women academics frequently married in the late nineteenth century. In fact, the Wellesley *Annals* for 1883–84, commenting on the marital plans of instructors Parker, Jencks, and Foote, suggested that "there must be something in the atmosphere of the office which makes it incapable of supporting a life of single blessedness. One by one, faces to which we have turned in our anxieties, have gone to brighten less official places."[113] But Alice Freeman was no young novice teacher. By 1887, she was America's most visible and prestigious woman educator, and she was expected to devote her life to her chosen mission. Only about half the first generation of graduates of the women's colleges married, and they married later than the general population. As Jill Conway has pointed out, "They could not accept conventional marriage because their minds had been trained along lines which required discipline and independent effort, and they expected to put this training to a practical use which was not to be found within the narrow confines of domestic life."[114] Alice Freeman could accept marriage for herself, but many others saw betrayal in this acceptance.

And so George and Alice came together, the soon-to-be eminent philosopher and the lady college president, passionately but tentatively pursuing the path to matrimony. Alice Freeman truly wanted to marry. She expected thereby to find a fulfillment that serving the myriad needs of institution and individual could not provide. She loved George, and a sexuality that had always been close to the surface had been fully awakened by someone she could respect intellectually. The Cambridge milieu itself undoubtedly was attractive. As Charles Eliot Norton once told George (long before he knew of their attachment), Alice Freeman must find her life as president of Wellesley a lonely one. It was not lonely in the sense that loving, caring people were always around her, but it was lonely in that until George Palmer courted her she had no one with whom to share freely Wellesley's problems. She met his sympathetic concern with an avid hunger.

Who won at the bargaining table? One could certainly interpret it as a victory for George Palmer. He had captured a woman everyone loved, everyone respected, everyone (of any importance) knew, and who was undoubtedly the most prominent woman educator in the United States. He had given up nothing. And as he was committed to making a name for himself in higher education, she could only prove an asset. She had lost her position, her income, her mission and gained only a lover, a husband, and a companion. She was eventually to solve the dilemma, but the solution was inherent in her, not in the marriage.

The ceremony was performed at Governor and Mrs. Claflin's house on Mt. Vernon Street in Boston at 11:30 A.M. on the morning of December 23rd. The Reverend Doctor Herrick of Worcester was the chief officiant assisted by George's brother Fred and Alice's brother-in-law, Charles Talmadge. Although her family was present, the bride was attended not by her sister but by three small Claflin nieces. Six Harvard students acted as ushers. The bride wore a white moiré silk gown with a short train and a tulle veil fastened with lilies of the valley. It was a fashionable occasion. President Charles Eliot of Harvard, Oliver Wendell Holmes, and Phillip Brooks were among the guests, and the wedding breakfast table was "trimmed from head to foot with rare flowers in pretty designs."[115]

The Palmers caught the 4:15 train to Boxford where they spent the next ten days. Alice wrote to her parents the next day that George's farm tenants had a delicious supper on the table for them "which I was hungry enough to eat" and after supper she lay on the lounge and George read aloud Tennyson's *The Princess,* whose title the Wellesley girls had conferred on her years before. The Wellesley undergraduates' "Princess" had now been safely sequestered by George in his very own castle. The weather was fine, the sleighing enticing; moonlight and sunlight and walks in the woods competed with letter writing and sending out the 1,700 announcements.[116]

Both Harvard and Wellesley were eager to honor the bride and groom, and glittering receptions and dinners given by President Eliot, the Horsfords, and others would follow, but Alice insisted Wellesley must be granted the first reception on January 9th, soon

The atrium of College Hall, where the College's reception in honor of
George and Alice Palmer's marriage was held. (Courtesy of Wellesley
College Archives.)

after the students had returned from Christmas break. A student,
Emma Emerson, wrote home:

> Monday night's reception is the chief topic now. It is going to be a
> grand affair. All the faculty are having new dresses for it. There
> are to be refreshments (caterers from Boston, I suppose) in the
> parlor. The Beethoven Society are to have their refreshments in
> the dining room by themselves. There are 500 invitations sent out.
> We are lucky to get any at all we think.[117]

And after the gala event had occurred, the same undergraduate reported:

She looked very handsome and carried a handsome bouquet of flowers. Professor Palmer was simply dressed in black. He looked very nice, of course, but he wasn't the principal object of attention.[118]

Only seniors received invitations, and the students who were not invited lined the bannisters on all four floors of the great central atrium in College Hall. The bride acknowledged them by throwing kisses. The Palmers stayed the night in college and Alice led chapel the next morning.[119]

Although she was to be much on the Wellesley campus for the rest of her life, she was not to live there again. And the students sentimentalized in the *Annals* that

Only after she had gone did Wellesley realize what Miss Freeman had been to her—a guide and inspiration, a presence of light and courage, a law by whose standard we were wont to adjust ourselves, a gospel whose high aim for us we endeavored to make our own.[120]

Poor Helen Shafer, what a burden to assume. In her papers is a penciled fragment in her own hand: "not often is a new executive called to conditions more difficult on the personal side, the retiring president's magnetic qualities and brilliant career having engendered the belief that the college could not be carried on successfully without her."[121]

For Alice Freeman Palmer the options had narrowed considerably, but the dilemma was not yet resolved. She was George Palmer's wife and no longer president of Wellesley, but she would still find ways to occupy her position as the United States' foremost woman educator. The New Woman was still evolving.

NOTES

1. George Herbert Palmer said that he and Alice Freeman first met in 1884 at the home of Eben Horsford (Palmer, *Life,* 169). This may be correct, but their friendship and growing intimacy clearly dates from the spring of 1886.

2. Many of these courtship letters are available in published form. See Hazard, *Academic Courtship.* A complete file of the original letters including

those for the rest of their lives are deposited as part of George Palmer's papers in the Houghton Library, Harvard University. I have looked at these letters to compare them for completeness with the typescripts prepared for Caroline Hazard's use and deposited in the Wellesley College Archives. All citations in this book are to the Wellesley collection rather than the originals in the Houghton except for the period 1897–1900. No Wellesley typescripts exist for those years, and I have used the Houghton materials. A very few original letters between Alice and George are in the Alice Freeman Palmer Papers, Wellesley College Archives, and not part of the typescripts. The Freeman-Palmer correspondence is, of course, supplemented by other Freeman papers at Wellesley.

3. Hazard, *Academic Courtship,* ix.

4. For a comprehensive picture of courtship and marriage in the last decades of the nineteenth century see Ellen K. Rothman, *Hands and Hearts: A History of Courtship in America* (New York: Basic Books, 1984), pts. 2–3.

5. George Herbert Palmer to Alice Freeman, May 26, 1886. Wellesley Typescripts.

6. Alice Freeman to George Herbert Palmer, May 26,1886. Wellesley Typescripts.

7. George Herbert Palmer to Alice Freeman, June 2, 1886. Wellesley Typescripts.

8. Alice Freeman to George Herbert Palmer, June 7, 1886. Wellesley Typescripts.

9. Actually, she was being called on by a Harvard French professor during these months, but he did not interest her romantically.

10. Mitchell, *Two Lives,* 124; Palmer, *Life,* 280.

11. Alice Freeman to George Herbert Palmer, July 29, 1886. Wellesley Typescripts.

12. George Herbert Palmer to Alice Freeman, July 23, 1886. Wellesley Typescripts.

13. George Herbert Palmer to Alice Freeman, July 30, 1886. Wellesley Typescripts.

14. Ibid.

15. George Herbert Palmer to Alice Freemen, August 15, 1886. Wellesley Typescripts.

16. George Herbert Palmer to Alice Freemen, June 23, 1887. Wellesley Typescripts.

17. George Herbert Palmer to Alice Freemen, August 5, 1886. Wellesley Typescripts. In *Academic Courtship* Carolyn Hazard dated this July 1886.

18. The letters between George Palmer and Ellen Wellman, as well as many to his family, are part of the Alice Freeman Palmer Papers at Wellesley. He had given Alice the letters to read before their marriage. There are many similarities to the Freeman-Palmer correspondence. George wrote equally ardent letters to both women.

19. These paragraphs are based on George Herbert Palmer's biography by William Ernest Hocking in the *Dictionary of American Biography,* 7:180–82;

George Herbert Palmer, *The Autobiography of a Philosopher* (Boston: Houghton Mifflin Co., 1930), 3–40; and George Palmer's correspondence with his family and Ellen Wellman Palmer in the Wellesley College Archives.

20. Hocking, *Dictionary of American Biography*, 7:181.

21. Scudder, *On Journey*, 64–65; Mitchell, *Two Lives*, 121.

22. Scudder, *On Journey*, 64–65.

23. Mitchell, *Two Lives*, 123. Joyce Antler in her biography of Lucy Sprague Mitchell makes George Palmer, I believe unfairly, into a pompous, self-important, small-minded man (*Lucy Sprague Mitchell: The Making of a Modern Woman* [New Haven: Yale University Press, 1987]), chap. 5. Lucy herself certainly did not share Antler's assessment and viewed Palmer with affection and admiration.

24. George Herbert Palmer to Alice Freeman, March 19, 1887. Wellesley Typescripts.

25. Scudder, *On Journey*, 65.

26. Palmer, *Life*, 173.

27. George Herbert Palmer to Alice Freeman, January 30, 1887. Wellesley Typescripts.

28. Ibid.

29. Vesey, *Emergence*, 204.

30. George Herbert Palmer to Alice Freeman, April 21, 1887. Wellesley Typescripts.

31. George Herbert Palmer to Alice Freeman, September 5, 1886. Wellesley Typescripts.

32. Ibid.

33. Alice Freeman to George Herbert Palmer, October 22, 1886. Wellesley Typescripts.

34. Alice Freeman to George Herbert Palmer, September 1, 1886. This letter is found in Hazard, *Academic Courtship*, 41–43.

35. George Herbert Palmer to Alice Freeman, November 7, 1886, Wellesley Typescripts; Hazard, *Academic Courtship*, 61–62.

36. Alice Freeman to George Herbert Palmer, December 13, 1886. Wellesley Typescripts.

37. Ibid.

38. George Herbert Palmer to Alice Freeman, November 4, 1886. Wellesley Typescripts.

39. George Herbert Palmer to Alice Freeman, January 1887, Wellesley Typescripts; Hazard, *Academic Courtship*, 95–96.

40. George Herbert Palmer to Alice Freeman, December 3, 1886. Wellesley Typescripts. Hazard, *Academic Courtship*, 74.

41. Ibid.

42. George Herbert Palmer to Alice Freeman, December 4, 1886. Wellesley Typescripts.

43. George Herbert Palmer to Alice Freeman, December 3, 1886. Wellesley Typescripts. Hazard, *Academic Courtship*, 74.

44. George Herbert Palmer to Mary Palmer, undated [summer 1886]. Wellesley Typescripts.

45. George Herbert Palmer to Alice Freeman, August 30, 1886. Wellesley Typescripts.

46. George Herbert Palmer to Alice Freeman, September 17, 27; October 6, 1886; Alice Freeman to George Herbert Palmer, September 24, 1886. Wellesley Typescripts.

47. George Herbert Palmer to Alice Freeman, October 19, 1886. Wellesley Typescripts.

48. George Herbert Palmer to Alice Freeman, November 14, 15, 21, 1886. Wellesley Typescripts.

49. George Herbert Palmer to Alice Freeman, December 24, 25, 1886; Alice Freeman to George Herbert Palmer, December 26, 1886. Wellesley Typescripts.

50. George Herbert Palmer to Alice Freeman, January 19, 24, 1887. Wellesley Typescripts.

51. George Herbert Palmer to Alice Freeman, November 24, 1886. Wellesley Typescripts.

52. George Herbert Palmer to Alice Freeman, 21, November 15, 1886. Wellesley Typescripts. Karen Lystra's study, *Searching the Heart: Women, Men, and Romantic Love in Nineteenth Century America* (New York: Oxford University Press, 1989) lays to rest the myth of women's passionlessness as a characteristic of Victorian courtship and marriage. The Palmers' attitudes toward sex are reflected in a letter from George to Alice much later. He ridicules a new novel that he had just read, *The Heavenly Twins,* because "sexual desire is thought of as an incidental affair, having no necessary connection with life, but permitted by all bad men and possibly by good husbands on separable occasions." Somehow, he says, the novel makes sex about as important as a taste for sea bathing. (George Herbert Palmer to Alice Freeman, April 12, 1894. Wellesley Typescripts.) The Palmers knew better.

53. George Herbert Palmer to Alice Freeman, December 15, 1886. Wellesley Typescripts.

54. George Herbert Palmer to Alice Freeman, March 30, 1887. Wellesley Typescripts.

55. George Herbert Palmer to Alice Freeman, May 5, 1887. Wellesley Typescripts. Hazard, *Academic Courtship,* 162–64.

56. Alice Freeman to George Herbert Palmer, December 18, 1886. Wellesley Typescripts.

57. Minutes of the Board of Trustees, February 3, 1887. Wellesley College Archives.

58. Alice Freeman to George Herbert Palmer, January 3, 1887, Wellesley Typescripts.

59. Alice Freeman to George Herbert Palmer, January 18, 1887. Wellesley Typescripts. Hazard, *Academic Courtship,* 96–98. Only part of the letter is reproduced in Hazard.

60. Alice Freeman to George Herbert Palmer, January 18, 1887; George Herbert Palmer to Alice Freeman, January 19, 1887. Wellesley Typescripts.
61. George Herbert Palmer to Alice Freeman, January 24, 1887. Wellesley Typescripts.
62. Alice Freeman to George Herbert Palmer, January 25, 1887. Wellesley Typescripts. Hazard, *Academic Courtship*, 102.
63. Alice Freeman to George Herbert Palmer, February 3, 1887. George Herbert Palmer to Alice Freeman, February 7, 1887. Wellesley Typescripts.
64. Alice Freeman to George Herbert Palmer, June 4, 1887. Minutes of the Board of Trustees, June 21, 1887. Wellesley College Archives.
65. Alice Freeman to George Herbert Palmer, March 30, April 1, 2, 4, June 4, 1887. Wellesley Typescripts. H. C. Wilson, "Margaret Evans Huntington," a manuscript talk in Margaret Evans Papers, Carleton College Archives. Evans had a B.A. and M.A. from Lawrence College and had studied in Paris and Berlin in 1878–79.
66. George Herbert Palmer to Alice Freeman, August 6, 1886. Wellesley Typescripts.
67. George Herbert Palmer to Alice Freeman, May 22, 1887. Wellesley Typescripts. Hazard, *Academic Courtship*, 175–79.
68. Alice Freeman to George Herbert Palmer, July 2, 9, 10, 1887. Wellesley Typescripts. Hazard includes some of these letters, *Academic Courtship*, 196–97.
69. Alice Freeman to George Herbert Palmer, December 6, 16, 26, 1886. Wellesley Typescripts.
70. George Herbert Palmer to Mary Palmer, February 23, 1887. Alice Freeman Palmer Papers, Wellesley College Archives.
71. Alice Freeman to George Herbert Palmer, March 12, 13, 1887. Wellesley Typescripts.
72. Alice Freeman to George Herbert Palmer, March 27, 1887. Wellesley Typescripts.
73. Ibid.; Hazard, *Academic Courtship*, 149–53.
74. George Herbert Palmer to Alice Freeman, March 30, 1887. Wellesley Typescripts.
75. Alice Freeman to George Herbert Palmer, June 25, 1887. Wellesley Typescripts.
76. Alice Freeman to George Herbert Palmer, July 2, 1887. Wellesley Typescripts.
77. For example, see George Palmer to Alice Freeman, October 5, 1887; Alice Freeman to George Palmer, October 4, 1887. Wellesley Typescripts. The Talmadge's two babies had both died of diphtheria at Christmas 1881, Alice's first year as president (Alice Freeman to Eben Horsford, April 13, 1882. Photocopies, Eben Horsford Papers).
78. George Herbert Palmer to Alice Freeman, December 24, 1886. Wellesley Typescripts. Hazard, *Academic Courtship*, 86.
79. Alice Freeman to George Herbert Palmer, November 19, 1886. Wellesley Typescripts.

80. Mary Palmer to George Herbert Palmer, undated 1886. Alice Freeman Palmer Papers, Wellesley College Archives.

81. Kathleen Barry, *Susan B. Anthony: A Biography of a Singular Feminist* (New York: New York University Press, 1988), 231.

82. George Herbert Palmer to Alice Freeman Palmer, April 15, 1892; Alice Freeman Palmer to George Herbert Palmer, April 25, 1894. Wellesley Typescripts. George's grandniece was told by her grandmother, Eric Palmer's wife, that George did not want to have children because he felt they would interfere with the Palmers' intellectual lives but that a concern for her health was a factor in the decision (Helen Palmer Avery to Ruth Bordin, June 21, 1991).

83. George Herbert Palmer to Alice Freeman, March 1887; see also February 23, 26, 28, 1887; Alice Freeman to George Herbert Palmer, February 24, 1887. Wellesley Typescripts. These letters are in Hazard, *Academic Courtship*, 124, 108, 114, 118–19, 112.

84. Pauline Durant to Alice Freeman, May 23, 1887. Alice Freeman Palmer Papers, Wellesley College Archives.

85. Alice Freeman to George Herbert Palmer, May 24, 1887. Wellesley Typescripts. Hazard, *Academic Courtship*, 181–82.

86. George Herbert Palmer to Alice Freeman, June 5, 1887. Wellesley Typescripts.

87. Alice Freeman to George Herbert Palmer, July 9, 1887. Wellesley Typescripts. Hazard, *Academic Courtship*, 201–2. Minutes of the Executive Committee, July 11, 1887, Wellesley College Archives.

88. Minutes of the Executive Committee, September 14, 1887. Wellesley College Archives.

89. George Herbert Palmer to Alice Freeman, September 24, 1887. Wellesley Typescripts. Hazard, *Academic Courtship*, 235–36.

90. George Herbert Palmer to Alice Freeman, October 7, 1887. Wellesley Typescripts.

91. George Herbert Palmer to Alice Freeman, October 11, 1887. Wellesley Typescripts.

92. Alice Freeman to George Herbert Palmer, September 6, 1887. Wellesley Typescripts. Hazard, *Academic Courtship*, 227–29. Unlike Alice Freeman who had a fulfilling career that she could use to bargain with George Palmer, Helen Magill who received the first American Ph.D. given to a woman and who married Andrew Dickson White in 1890 failed to establish herself in academia. She had no such chips to use in her negotiations with White. Altschuler, *Better than Second Best*, 105.

93. Alice Freeman to George Herbert Palmer, September 6, 1887. Wellesley Typescripts. Hazard, *Academic Courtship*, 227–29.

94. Alice Freeman to George Herbert Palmer, July 20, 1887. Wellesley Typescripts. Hazard, *Academic Courtship*, 208–12.

95. George Herbert Palmer to Alice Freeman, July 20, 1887. Wellesley Typescripts.

96. Minutes of the Executive Committee, October 19, 1887. Minutes of the Board of Trustees. Wellesley College Archives.

97. Glasscock, *Wellesley*, 33–41.

98. Minutes of the Executive Committee, October 9, 1887; Alice Freeman to George Herbert Palmer, October 14, 1887. Wellesley Typescripts. Hazard, *Academic Courtship*, 242–43.

99. George Herbert Palmer to Alice Freeman, November 1, 1887. Wellesley Typescripts.

100. George Herbert Palmer to Alice Freeman, November 30, 1887. Wellesley Typescripts.

101. Diary, December 23, 1887. Horsford also gave them a dog, Rex, that was their beloved companion until 1902. Alice Freeman to Eben Horsford, June 1887. Photocopies, Eben Horsford Papers.

102. George Herbert Palmer to Alice Freeman, December 20, 1887; Alice Freeman to George Herbert Palmer, December 5, 20, 1887. Wellesley Typescripts.

103. Alice Freeman to George Herbert Palmer, November 7, 1887. Wellesley Typescripts. Hazard, *Academic Courtship*, 243–44.

104. Alice Freeman to George Herbert Palmer, November 7, December 21, 1887. Wellesley Typescripts. Hazard, *Academic Courtship*, 246–48.

105. Alice Freeman to George Herbert Palmer, July 15, 1887. Wellesley Typescripts.

106. Anna Newman to Eben Horsford, August 29, 1887. Photocopies, Eben Horsford Papers.

107. Palmer, *Life*, 173. Nonetheless combining marriage and career was not easily accepted. As late as 1936 at the time Mount Holyoke College was seeking a successor to Mary Wooley, Frances Perkins, then a Mount Holyoke trustee, wrote Rowena Keyes that she thought married women with children ought not to be excluded from consideration but suggested they might better look for a woman in middle age who had childbearing behind her. Frances Perkins as quoted in Anna May Wells, *Miss Marks and Miss Woolley*, 230.

108. Palmer, *Life*, 174–76.

109. Abbott, *Silhouettes*, 78–80. Jessie Bernard sees the academic monastic tradition, which was especially rigid in its application to women, as triggering the public debate that attended Freeman's resignation when she married. People felt that one who had championed the education of women should not abandon the cause for personal gratification. Bernard, *Academic Women*, 206–7.

110. Letter to the editor of the *Press* by J. R. Muller, unidentified clipping, October 13, 1887. Catherine McCamant Scrapbook, Class of 1887 Papers, Wellesley College Archives.

111. President Eliot himself saw her as entering a whole new career and giving "the whole force of her conspicuous example" to disprove the argument of those opposed to higher education for women that advanced training would prevent marriage (Palmer, *A Service*, 76–77).

112. Minutes of the Board of Trustees, February 2, 1884. Wellesley College Archives.

113. *Wellesley Annals*, 1883–84. Wellesley College Archives.

114. Jill Conway, "Perspectives on the History of Women's Education in the United States," *History of Education Quarterly* 14 (Spring 1974): 8; see also Solomon, *Educated Women*, 117–222; Bernard, *Academic Women*, especially 206–7; Mary E. Cookingham, "Blue Stockings, Spinsters, and Pedagogues: Women College Graduates, 1865–1919," *Population Studies* 38 (1984): 349–64; and Barbara Sicherman, "Colleges and Careers: Historical Perspectives on the Life and Work Patterns of Women College Graduates," manuscript, 1987.

115. Unidentified Clipping, December 1887, from Catherine McCamant Scrapbook, Class of 1887 Papers; Diary, December 1887; *Worcester Daily Spy*, December 24, 1887, Wellesley College Archives.

116. Alice Freeman Palmer to parents, December 24, 1887; Alice Freeman Palmer to Anna McCoy, December 24, 1887.

117. Emma Emerson [Dyer] to family, January 8, 1888. Emma Emerson Dyer Papers. Wellesley College Archives.

118. Emma Emerson [Dyer] to family, January 15, 1888. Emma Emerson Dyer Papers. Wellesley College Archives.

119. Ibid.

120. *Wellesley Annals*, 1887–88, 4–5.

121. Undated note. Helen Shafer Papers, Wellesley College Archives.

CHAPTER 8

Accommodation

In January of 1888 Alice Palmer opened a new chapter in her life. She was no longer a college president, nor was she ever again to be. But marriage did not change her position as the leading woman in American higher education, a position that was not to be challenged until late in the century by M. Carey Thomas, who became president of Bryn Mawr in 1894. Nor was her visibility dimmed in the world of the professions. Quite possibly Alice Freeman Palmer's stature as an educator was enhanced rather than diminished by her marriage.

Media attention to the wedding and the new aura that came with joining the Cambridge establishment contributed to her prestige. She was a well-known, attractive lady who was watched by the press. She did not disappear from view. As William Gardner Hale stated at her memorial service, "Alice Freeman Palmer was greater than Alice Freeman . . . no more perfect realization of the true accord of spirit, and of accordant aims in the service of others, can ever have been seen." And without marriage Wellesley's princess "would not have become all that she was."[1] She herself was not quite so certain of her position, especially in the early years of her marriage. The immediate reality of her life was that the priorities between marriage and professional interests posed serious questions.

1

For almost all middle-class women of Alice Freeman Palmer's generation, combining marriage and a career was an impossibility. Women could pursue careers as long as they were single. Once married, although their interests and contributions, as for Palmer, changed little, they could no longer accept a salary in exchange for their professional services because that implied unacceptable priorities in terms of obligations, that job rather than husband and home came first.[2] In theory the Palmers saw themselves as free of such hidebound Victorian constraints, and after her marriage Alice continued to exchange professional services for money with considerable consistency. What is more, her earnings provided an important component in the Palmers' standard of living. In this Palmer foreshadowed the next generation of professional women, several of whom, including her surrogate daughter, Lucy Sprague Mitchell, managed, with difficulty, to combine professional careers, marriage, and motherhood.[3] For the Palmers, however, the true determinant of Alice's priorities was psychological rather than financial. She needed a professional outlet, and George was unable to accept any arrangement other than that husband and home come first.

For Alice this ordering of her life at first was easy. She was exhausted. Her professional responsibilities had literally left her with no physical reserves, and she needed a rest. Also she had never before had a home of her own, and nest building had its attractions; putting together pretty new wedding presents and old favorites in an environment that she could control was a seductive process. A glamorous new social world, Cambridge and Boston at their most glittering, opened for her, and Alice was always a social animal. She and George also were planning his sabbatical year in Europe, her first trip to the continent and her first extended stay abroad. She was content with her new lot and was more than enough occupied.

The Palmer's first home was a small furnished house on the corner of Broadway and Prescott Streets in Cambridge just a block from the Harvard Yard. The rent was a princely $1,000 a year, nearly a third of their income, but apparently not considered high for Cambridge.[4] They kept a single servant who came with the house, and according to George, "Study was thrown to the winds; we devoted ourselves to resting, to becoming better acquainted with each other and with neighbors."[5] He described a busy social life of dinners and teas, inaugurated by President Eliot's gala faculty reception, afternoon calls (George recorded 341 in the course of a single season), and Monday open houses at which the Wellesley community was invited to join Alice Palmer's new Cambridge friends.[6] However, the details of their lives as chronicled in their letters, while confirming their rich social life, show that George continued to devote much of his time to professional duties, and that there was little time for "resting."

George Palmer avidly pursued his professional concerns, but he also shared management of the household. Although he described Alice as "the skillful mistress of her household," and credited her with finding servants, managing the budget, planning interesting delicious meals, and decorating their rooms, their correspondence belies him.[7] He was the one who more closely applied himself to these tasks. He was as capable as Alice of running their ménage, perhaps more so, and he probably had higher standards, at least when it came to food. Also she was absent a great deal, especially during the first years of their marriage. He filled the gap, but he also shared responsibility when she was home. He arranged for repair of the furnaces, had the double windows removed and put on, and managed to acquire a supply of fresh butter from the Boxford farm. He wrote on one occasion: "My domestic report today is 13 tumblers of grape jelly— with a very fair prospect of hardness—and five quart bottles of whole peaches.... You sometimes run a college and I a kitchen, and again I appear as a director of youth and you of servants. It makes our partnership a rich one that each can comprehend and even perform the other's tasks."[8]

Housekeeping chores cannot have been onerous for Alice, but the Palmers, not immune to the usual Boston prejudices, saw their Irish servant Annie as a trial, requiring constant vigilance to get her to listen carefully for the bell and "attend to the door in a tidy dress."[9] She more "steadily looked like a scarecrow" and "cooked in the middling manner that destroys appetite."[10] The Palmers eventually employed servants directly from Scotland, an arrangement they found much more satisfactory, although they also engaged an African-American couple in the late 1890s. But Irish Annie's shortcomings did not destroy Alice's new-found joy in housewifery. She referred constantly to our "pretty house." She seemed truly to enjoy being mistress in her own domain rather than trying to carve for herself a tiny semi-private niche while juggling the myriad demands of the Wellesley community.

George was busy with academic responsibilities and receiving increasing attention as a significant force on the larger academic scene. G. Stanley Hall, putting together his new and innovative Clark University at Worcester, Massachusetts, consulted him over staffing and programs. George was offered the chancellorship of Kansas State College, easily refused. And he was an influential voice at faculty meetings of Harvard College and frequently consulted by President Eliot. There were also disappointments. His new translation of the *Odyssey* failed to find a publisher that year. He confided in Alice about his work, and she felt that she shared it with him.

2

During the first six months of their marriage, Alice Palmer had few new professional responsibilities, but she observed and assisted the progress of the women's Annex (eventually to become Radcliffe College), then an anomalous adjunct to Harvard College where a few women struggled to obtain instruction.[11] George, who had always taken an interest in the Annex, taught there, and the welfare of Annex women became one of Alice's ongoing, self-assumed responsibilities. She continued active in Collegiate Alumnae circles, and she gave a great many informal talks before women's groups, mostly church-related.

But it was Wellesley that provided the greatest challenge to her new attachment to home and husband. She continued to watch over Wellesley and its progress with the attention and concern of a devoted mother. She was nominated to the board of trustees at the same meeting at which her resignation as president was accepted.[12] On February 21st when a member of the executive committee submitted his resignation, it was accepted immediately "in order to secure the services of Mrs. Palmer on that body."[13]

The trustees and their business were familiar territory. Ever since her elevation to the presidency in 1881, she had been attending their meetings, and the board was accustomed to her leadership and advice. President Shafer continued the practice President Freeman had initiated, participating in all board meetings. But no one, including Alice Palmer, seems to have been concerned that Alice Freeman Palmer's presence on the board presented any conflict of interest or possible interference with Shafer's prerogatives. Instead, Palmer saw it as her duty to be as active as possible. Although she would leave the country in a few months, she continued to shape the composition of the board itself, urging the election of Horace Scudder, one of her champions, as a trustee, and serving as a nominating committee member in the spring.[14] Against Pauline Durant's strong opposition, she favored a tuition increase to help combat the growing financial crisis.[15] Even routine matters like the recruitment of Wellesley graduates as teachers by secondary school administrators were carefully scrutinized by Alice Palmer.[16] And in June she was the speaker at the commencement dinner. Alice Palmer was a hands-on ex-president.

She kept in close touch with both her former faculty colleagues and with members of the board of trustees. Both Palmers eagerly solicited news of college affairs and assessments of the college, and they were not above making use of gossip and student informants. Both manipulated and used every influence they could garner to control Wellesley and propel it in the directions they felt it should develop.

3

Alice Palmer also had leisure. Perhaps for the first time in years she had time to read novels. Train journeys, formerly devoted to Wellesley business correspondence, now were enriched by careful attention to the works of Robert Lewis Stevenson, Jane Austen, and Charlotte Brontë. *Shirley* delighted her and inspired her to wish she could write.[17] But other than letters, Alice was not much for writing. That ladylike occupation could never for her be a substitute for the active life. Paying the price of past neglect, she also spent long hours with the dentist. Their dog, Rex, Eben Horsford's gift, was much a part of their lives, joining them at the fireside and accompanying them on walks. Even his depredations to the spring flowers were accepted with amused tolerance.

Despite the relaxed pace and the simple satisfactions brought by playing a new, less demanding role, Alice Palmer's health was slow to mend. Her cough would not go away, interrupting her sleep, making it almost impossible for her to read aloud, a favorite Palmer pastime, and probably contributing to her failure to gain weight. Months more would pass before she felt really well.

In the spring of 1888, when Alice went to Saginaw for an extended visit with her family, she and George were first parted for any length of time since their marriage. Once he was Alice's husband, George seldom went to Saginaw. Most of her family visits were combined with speaking trips and in any case undertaken alone. George Palmer always professed both affection and respect for Alice's parents and family. He wrote: "I do not specifically send my love to your father and mother . . . because they are so generally in my thoughts. I believe

Alice Palmer soon after her marriage. (Courtesy of
Wellesley College Archives.)

I have a very genuine fondness for them, quite apart from what I feel for you."[18] But George protested too much. The Freemans clearly tried his patience. Their enthusiasms and causes and her father's politics, their constant ill health, and especially their endless demands on Alice's affections and attentions (especially during the early years of their marriage) irritated George Palmer in spite of himself. The Freemans demanded and got from Alice services that he felt he could not ask for himself, and he resented this. In the spring of 1888, despite Alice's persistent cough, her mother repeatedly asked her to read aloud to her. George was clearly angry and forbade it.[19] During her Saginaw visits, Alice would plant flowers, groom the garden, and even wallpapered the house, tasks her mother was no longer able to do, and that George believed Alice had not the strength to do either.[20]

This 1888 visit, however, found the Freeman family prosperous and in better health than they had been in many years. Her father was working regularly and looking much better, and the two doctors Freeman had acquired new offices. "The practice," she reported "is consistently good, and money matters grow easier daily. If they keep well, they will soon have the mortgages off."[21] This new Freeman prosperity was important to both George and Alice. With only one salary, their own budget was tight. Expenses had been and were to be heavy, and they watched every penny. For example, Alice had her dental work done in Saginaw, rather than Cambridge or Boston, because it would be cheaper.[22] Nonetheless they continued to be generous with family members in real need, especially the two ministers, Fred Palmer and Charles Talmadge, who frequently received "luxury money" or help with insurance premiums.[23] George always felt himself fortunate to be able to live in a comfortable upper-class style and felt obligated to share his good fortune. As he once wrote to Alice, "I realize what joy wealth would bring me when I think how I could then put them, Fred and Mary and Ella, above want."[24]

Charles Talmadge, Ella's husband, was as restless as his father-in-law. His midlife decision to train for the ministry was followed later by a decision to pursue graduate studies and still later to transfer his denominational allegiance from the Methodists to the Congregationalists. This meant the Talmadges always needed money and frequently lived in the Palmer's Quincy Street house. They were not the only recipients of Palmer generosity. Several young relatives were educated by the Palmers, and as she left for Europe in 1888, Alice continued to worry about her family despite their being "much more contented and prosperous than in the old days. If only all will go well while we are so far away!"[25]

George's failure to accompany Alice to Saginaw was initially attributed to the tightness of money, and Alice's family felt bereft at his absence. "They all speak of you with so much affection and interest and longing that it quite goes to my heart to think we cannot come here together. We will, George, when we come home again [from Europe]."[26] They did not and the Freemans were never satisfied with the length of Alice's visits. "There is mourning every day in the family, because they [the remaining days] are so few. Poor father! I feel sorriest of all for him. He takes the absence very much to heart."[27] But her family had expressed similar feelings of deprivation when Alice was single and burdened with professional responsibilities. It was a continual tug, and one that no one, George or her family, made easier for her.

4

In many ways the relationship between George and Alice Palmer took shape during these first months of their marriage. George Palmer admired Alice Palmer in more than one way. He was much impressed with her reputation as an educator and certainly did not want marriage to jeopardize that reputation. He cherished her public position. He deeply appreciated her skills with people, even her oratorical gifts, which he shared, but rivalry over forensic talents was never at issue between them. And Alice admired George. He had read more widely, he was a better classical scholar by far, he was a Harvard professor, and most important, he was her protector. George looked after Alice, and Alice had never been looked after before. Her family, her students, and her trustees had all made demands on her. George made demands, but he cloaked them in tender concern for her welfare, and he saved her daily from one petty annoyance after another. George loved to manage, and in 1888 Alice had had managing up to the hilt. She was happy to relinquish decision-making for awhile.

Ever since the Palmers first met George had acted as Alice's protector, probably the first really adequate protector she had known in her life. Her father had often failed her. Her mother took more often than she gave. George looked after her, watched over her. This tells us much about why Alice was attracted to George, but it also tells us much about the expectations of the Victorian female. Myth had it that women and children lived in the secure, nurturing environment of the sacrosanct protective home. But real life was not always that way. Fathers died or went off to medical school. The ancestral farm was exchanged for a series of temporary rented houses, the income that had seemed unfailing suddenly evaporated. The nineteenth-century American economy, while generally expanding, was highly volatile, and social and political protections against its ravages almost nil. The secure Victorian home was often its victim. Nonetheless middle-class nineteenth-century American females believed in the safe harbor of domesticity. They expected to find this haven somewhere, and Alice eventually found it with George.

It was not that Alice was incapable of taking charge of her own life. She could and did. Nor was it that she failed to enjoy the independence and authority that being her own woman had given her. But like all Victorian women the expectation of a protected, protective sanctuary was embedded in her very being, however overlaid by the capabilities and expectations of the New Woman. George also supervised her intellectual concerns. Many of the books Alice read were selected by George. All her life he would feel that her general education had been somewhat spotty and in need of nourishment. While he respected her administrative talents and her skill at interpersonal relations, he saw himself as the imposer of culture, the man of learning, who could introduce her to the deeper riches of western civilization.

After their marriage, George Palmer was the primary force that shaped the course of Alice Freeman's life, but she too made subtle changes in his life, even in his work. When they returned from Europe in 1889, she was quick to discover Edward Bellamy's *Looking Backward*. When published in 1887 Bellamy's book was almost literally devoured by educated, concerned women who found in its utopian, if highly controlled, society an answer to the myriad and distressing problems of urbanization, industrialization, and rampant capitalism they saw growing uncontrolled around them.[28] Although usually she was not much concerned with politics, Alice read *Looking Backward* on a train trip to Saginaw and was much taken with it. Doubting a positive reaction from George, she wrote, "You will think the book a mere dreamer's fancy, but it is much more."[29]

George read it almost immediately, partly because he found his brother Fred and his wife also much impressed with the book. But as Alice had predicted, his initial reaction was contemptuous. "This is the form in which fairy stories still appeal to the people of our day. . . . I do not distrust the old order as much as this writer, nor have quite his confidence in the new. There seems to me too something cowardly in a novel's form as a method of appeal."[30] But he changed his mind as he read further, and he wrote the next day, "Perhaps my criticism of him for using the form of a novel was unjust," but, he added, "My fundamental doubts however about the whole system are not yet removed."[31] When he had finished the book, he willingly admitted, "It is a great book and will deservedly create quite a stir."[32] He gave Bellamy's ideas a prominent place in his ethics course that fall.

5

In late June 1888, the Palmers sailed for England on the *Ethiopia*. They spent the summer in England and the fall in Paris, where they lived simply, avoiding tourist resorts, staying in hotels only briefly before renting small furnished lodgings. Usually there were three bedrooms, parlor, dining room and kitchen, and they engaged a local, non-English speaking servant who did the cooking and marketing. George was the house hunter and arranger who tapped the concierge's connections to find domestic help.[33] This was a quiet, economical, non-stressful interlude, replete with the kind of comfortable leisure Alice had never experienced before. The Palmers walked a great deal, perfected their French, and spent many hours in museums, exploring the bookstalls, or taking brief excursions into the countryside, a pattern they were to follow on subsequent trips abroad.

Katharine Coman, one of Alice's young Wellesley colleagues, joined them for part of their Paris stay on December 10th, and the three set out together for Germany. They stopped first at Tübingen where George had been a student, and then spent Christmas in a Munich pension where their landlady had a "great, gorgeous Christmas tree" and "had baked Christmas cakes by the thousand literally, and gave us each great platefuls to carry to our rooms."[34] But Bavarian coziness could not banish the damp, dark German winter. Alice's health, still precarious, rapidly deteriorated, and George decided they must head south for Venice's milder climate.

Alice fell in love with Venice. She longed "to stay here in beautiful Venice so much that I hope the salt air will be warm enough, and that we may live here a couple of months."[35] They stayed in a palazzo with sunny windows overlooking the sea and "the curious careless life of the narrow streets."[36] She saw Venice as "a kind of dream."[37] She loved the gondolas, and she and George would "float and dream up and down in the warm sun."[38] They reviewed Italian, read Dante, and followed the poet in his wanderings about the Lombard plain, enjoying what she saw as "a lovely feast," and she found herself daily growing stronger in mind and body.[39] Despite her hope that they could stay in Venice a couple of months, after four weeks they moved on to Florence, Rome, and then Naples. In Rome, they met a Cornell Latin professor, William G. Hale, and his wife, also on sabbatical and traveling with their two small children and an English nurse. They arranged to accompany the Hales to Greece in the spring.[40] Thus began a friendship that was to last many years. But meanwhile they explored Naples where once more they lodged near the water "with the uproar of the rain and wind and sea just under our windows."[41] The southern metropolis proved too disorderly for them, however. Instead Alice was entranced with "wandering up and down the deserted streets" of Pompeii, "in and out of the pathetic empty houses with their pretty colors and graceful figures and the feeling everywhere of a recent disaster demanding fresh mourning."[42]

They sailed for Greece from Brindisi on April 14th, stopping at Patras for an excursion to Olympia, then on to Sparta, Argos, Mycenae, Corinth, and Delphi. On the Greek excursion Hale and Palmer took several strenuous side trips without the women and children. And in early May the Palmers headed north via Constantinople for Vienna and then to Berlin.[43] At this point, George pursued his professional studies more vigilantly. They also spent several days in Leipsig buying books for his library. Allowing themselves a month for further shopping and final sightseeing in London and Paris, they sailed on the Cunard Line's *Caphalonia* on August 15th.[44]

The glorious journey was over. Eben Horsford's generous wedding gift had been put to very good use indeed. George had relieved Alice of most responsibility while traveling and made all living and travel arrangements. They seldom went out in the evening and usually spent their mornings at home writing letters. It was a leisurely trip. Despite her exposure to a European wonderland, Alice had had time to rest, and her health had improved as the spring unfolded. She returned to Cambridge more robust than she had been since her early undergraduate days and she had gained weight at last. Her family was delighted. "Aunt Sarah said she never had expected to see me looking so strong in all my life, and Father thinks his highest ambitions are fulfilled. Mother laughs at me, and threatens me with enormous size when I am fifty. I am afraid she thinks this state less becoming than the former. Certainly, I cannot be said to 'look delicate.'"[45]

Years later George reminisced about the first European trip, as they planned a second continental tour.

Oh the luxury of the long days together on the Grand Canal, the Rue Galilee and Munich! We trained ourselves there in love, and the busy years since have shown that we learned our lesson well. That we might wake tomorrow at nine, in our parallel coffin beds, and hear the water slapping on the house and the gondoliers quarrelling! And then we would lie and talk of plans for the future and perhaps I would cross into your bed, and by and by the coffee and the little maid, and then the morning letters, the black book, and walk across the piazza, and perhaps the supper at Eumans in the Trinita. Golden days! which while surrounding us with outward splendors perpetually revealed the sufficiency of the twin life within. Some day we will renew them. Once more before we die we will buy nougat cones at the corner of the Rue Galilee.[46]

And they did!

This interlude between Alice Freeman Palmer's Wellesley presidency, and the Palmers' return from Europe was a happy period in Alice Freeman Palmer's life. George Palmer painted an idyllic picture: "whoever saw her ... remarked in her new buoyancy and her wider power."[47] And she certainly was content. Her daily cares and responsibilities had been substantially reduced, her health slowly improved, she was busy, but not too busy, with pleasant and interesting pursuits. And she was in love, deeply in love, with a man she found intellectually stimulating who shared his concerns, his work, his friends with her in a very real way and was equally eager to share her professional interests and tasks. Theirs was in every sense a shared, companionable life.

6

The Palmer marriage was going well, but the dilemma had not really been resolved, and tensions were inevitable. Not until their return from Europe, when they faced life in earnest as a married couple, would they seriously attempt to find a resolution.

The plan must have been devised during the European months or just after the Palmers' return to the United States. The solution was straightforward. Alice was to ensure her place in the wider educational world, not by returning to college administration, although very soon she did just that, but by continuing to expand her active contributions to Wellesley, Collegiate Alumnae, and other volunteer educational activities. She was to supplement this more or less normal pattern for married women through a paid lecture series and writing for popular consumption on educational policy.

Although the Palmers were not yet as prosperous as they would become a few years hence, George's salary was raised to $4,500 as of September of 1888, and they had returned from Europe with no debts.[48] Additional income, although welcome and frequently needed, was not the primary motive for what proved to be an exhausting undertaking. Instead the plan was clearly designed to ensure Alice Freeman Palmer's public position in the professional world, despite the loss of her institutional connection; in short, her career as a leading educator would continue.

George wrote to Alice at the end of her first year on the road: "I do not regret your year, though I believe since Oct. 1 just a quarter of it has been spent away from Cambridge, mostly without me.... It was of consequence to make a public place for yourself now that the old eminence of Wellesley is removed. This place has been won." And he added that "I do not approve of your becoming a mere housebody; only of making that first."[49]

A career plan for Alice was carefully laid out, a conscious strategy designed to preserve her presence on the national educational stage when she no longer retained an obvious institutional base. This was not the strategy of a reformer taking to the hustings to further her crusade. She was not simply lending her talents to a good cause, as her mother had always done. She was finding a proper paid niche for her professional skills, and pursuing her career in women's higher education. Although he continued to stipulate that home come first,

George Palmer had made a substantial concession, and I suspect it was George's strategy, designed and planned to disrupt his life as little as possible. She did not protest. Alice Palmer did not profess an ideology around which she could shape her life. Her commitments were to people and pragmatic goals rather than to abstract principles. Because she had not embraced feminist aims or clearly thought them through, it was easier for George to shape the pattern her life would take.

Alice Freeman Palmer was an old hand at speech-making, but she had never spoken for money before her spring lecture tour in 1890. In her diary she recorded that she was "to speak at Indianapolis and elsewhere for money. *First Time!*"[50] Rather than attach herself to a professional lecture bureau, she arranged her engagements herself. As she was to do frequently, she combined her first tour with a visit to her family in Saginaw, Michigan, and a stay of several days at her alma mater in Ann Arbor to attend the meetings of the Association of Collegiate Alumnae. At both places, just as she had been doing all her adult life, she spoke a number of times without charge.

Her Ann Arbor sojourn was a sentimental orgy, as well as a chance to practice one of her planned lectures. "Eight 'Wellesley girls' were at the station to meet me and brought me to this charming old house where old friends were standing on the wide porch to meet me. . . . How those blessed girls do wrap my world in with their thoughtful love!" She continued: "The Alumnae were in session all the morning with business relating to Fellowships, and College Endowments, I had to speak often, being appealed to at every turn."[51] In the afternoon she made the major address, "Social Life in Colleges." She "was glad to speak on a subject of so much importance, and I was received with the greatest warmth. . . . I do not take any two successive meals in the same house, but vibrate from one Professor's table to another."[52]

Adored, honored, feted, and she loved every minute of it, but she reassured George: "I love this place, but I keep thinking how poor I should be if I couldn't go away from it all to your arms. I am *so glad* that I wasn't persuaded to marry anybody until you asked me."[53] Throughout the tour Alice Palmer bounced back and forth between sheer joy at being the center of public attention, important again in her own right, and her loyalty to her marital commitments. One time when she was in Saginaw, she spoke at the opening exercises of the high school, and told George: "Though it would be great fun to try it all over again. I'd rather be your wife ... than any other dignitary I can think of."[54] And the previous September when she passed through Wellesley, she had written him:

I would not go back to the old days, sweetheart. As I passed along the familiar way last week, just when, ordinarily, I should have gone to the waiting work, and my train at last dashed by the station and the college towers in the distance, my sensations were too mixed for analysis. Yet there was no place in them for regret that my train did not leave me there. You are better dear than any college, to be your wife, a higher place than "The Princess" held in the days before you came, and made her a queen.[55]

All through the year that presumably produced a resolution to the dilemma, she was torn in two directions. She found the applause, the receptions, and being constantly asked for advice on substantive matters very heady stuff, but at the same time she had to believe that her marriage was more important to her. She eagerly reestablished ties with the women's network that had sustained her when she was single, the college friends, the Wellesley graduates, the former colleagues that warmly welcomed her wherever she went. Part of her resisted letting these journeys on her own come to an end. Part of her wished to be home in Massachusetts with her husband.

George Palmer experienced his own ambivalences. Part of the time he was fully cognizant of the sacrifices she had made. "How much you have given up for me! I vowed when I took you you should never regret it; but I don't keep my vows very well or at least not show that I meant to."[56] But on other occasions he thought the sacrifice he was making to permit her to realize herself professionally was too great. When informed she had accepted still another speaking engagement he complained: "You said you were to be at home on June 7. . . . Of course I have been calculating on a happy Sunday together after this barbaric absence. It cannot be you have agreed to prolong it three days in order that these persons may make money and renown out of you."[57]

Actually she did not return home until June 10th, prolonging her stay in the New York area.[58] She did not give in to his protests, but when the end of her tour was in sight, she wrote her husband: "One thing is certain—this year ends my public speaking career."[59] It did not. Both Palmers had speaking engagements at Chautauqua that summer, and she went off on another extended speaking tour the following winter. They quarreled occasionally about her obligations. George wrote: "You seem very near me today because I see now where I was wrong in our little clash—when I could have saved its beginning."[60] And he continued to complain: "You are very busy; and I am not unused to waiting for those fragments of you which others leave."[61] But at least twice a year she continued to set out on an extended lecture circuit and meanwhile took engagements closer to home.

Alice Freeman Palmer was very successful as a public speaker. She was much in demand for commencement addresses and other educational commemorations. By present day standards, the fees she received were not generous, but in June of 1891 she earned $150, "that important substance for which I came," for an address in St. Louis,[62] and ten speeches on her 1892 spring tour realized over $800.[63] A series of lectures at Chautauqua in the summer, where George also lectured, was usually one part of the year's work. Her addresses were always received enthusiastically. One observer suggested that only Phillip Brooks rivalled her as a speech maker. J. Laurence Laughlin commented on her "flexible, endearing voice," "her tactful, persuasive, brilliant" presentation.[64] Wherever she spoke on her lecture tours she was acclaimed. In Minneapolis, "eight different societies have sent me boxes of flowers today" and "the paper here had sketches of me in every morning's issue for a week."[65] While she usually spoke about women's education, for example "Phases of College Life" or "Why Go to College," she broadened her repertoire in the late 1890s. In 1901 she offered lectures on "The Education of Nature" and "Whittier's Homes and Haunts."[66]

The publications projected as another avenue of public exposure went less well. Alice Freeman Palmer managed during her lifetime to publish only a few articles and one brief educational pamphlet, *Why Go to College,* a distillation of her addresses on the education of women.[67] Published in 1897, it sold well enough, but sitting at a desk, putting her thoughts on paper, was not Alice Freeman Palmer's professional style, and she could never force herself to concentrate on producing the written word. Perhaps she liked applause too much.

Despite this failure, the campaign to retain Alice Freeman Palmer's position as a leader in higher education was a success. George Palmer believed that "the shelter of a home had enlarged her scope. From special labor in a particular field she advanced to general influence in the whole field of girls' education."[68] The "shelter of the home" was important in achieving this result only in that it undoubtedly was a major factor in restoring her health and may well have saved her life. But Palmer correctly assessed what happened to Alice Freeman Palmer's position in American education. Certainly it was enlarged and broadened after her marriage.

Perhaps symbolic of the end of one professional career for Alice Freeman and the beginning of another for Alice Palmer was the casting of a bronze bust and the commissioning of her portrait. Both Palmers took these commemorative efforts very seriously. Anne Whitney, prominent American sculptor and fellow Bostonian, was chosen to do the bust and everyone was pleased with the result, especially George who saw it as "a fresh and true impression of the face I love."[69] Abbott Henderson Thayer, born in Boston and trained in Paris and one of the foremost painters of women of his day, was chosen to execute the portrait, a gift of Eben Horsford to Wellesley College. The sittings were tedious and trying for Alice; the trips they required to Thayer's New York studio were a nuisance.

As the portrait took shape Alice was acutely disappointed. She wrote George, who had not seen it, that: "I hope that I have more strength of character and more moral purpose than anyone can infer from the picture . . . I am afraid he is going to present the college a pensively smiling young woman, rolling her eyes of light brown away from the audience in front of her, and leaving the spectators to surmise what she was like, or was interested in."[70] Her assessment was not far wrong. Abbott Henderson Thayer was true to his style in his portrait of Alice. His paintings invariably portrayed women in an idealized, ethereal, angelic, virginal mode. Lucy Sprague Mitchell reported that Thayer painted Alice's eyes blue. When George Palmer protested, he replied, "Her soul has blue eyes."[71] The portrait hangs in the Wellesley Library and does fail to convey the vigor with which she lived her life. Her disappointment sufficiently disturbed George that he came to New York to have a look for himself. He did not find the work displeasing, and Alice herself was eventually more satisfied. Eliza Mosher and Alice's cousin Electa saw it when nearly complete. They liked it and thought Wellesley would be pleased.[72]

Wellesley was pleased! In early June of 1890 a gala gathering was held in the new art building on campus for a "most agreeable pur-pose—the unveiling of the painting we had longed for months to see. Could Professor Horsford have pleased any college girl better than with this gift of the picture of Mrs. Palmer."[73] With her image now hanging on a wall, Alice Freeman's career as president of Wellesley College was firmly placed in the past tense.

7

Although lecturing for money established the continuity of Alice Palmer's professional career, volunteer service in the cause of women's education became an increasingly important part of her resolution to the ongoing dilemma. Palmer pioneered in a kind of accommodation that many married, educated, professionally trained women developed at the turn of the century and continued to use well past World War II: creative volunteering. These women used their professional skills in unpaid policy-making positions as mem-bers of boards and commissions, sometimes governmental and some-times private, but all having a visible effect on some part of the larger society. Unlike mid-nineteenth-century reformers these women had received a formal education preparing them for their careers. Fre-quently they had worked in those careers at least briefly, then mar-ried, but continued to use their skills as volunteers. When Palmer was in Cambridge her days were routinely filled with meetings, inter-views, appointments, and the business of the many groups in which she participated. She was a major participant in the Annex's struggle to acquire status within Harvard University. She was an advisor to the infant Barnard College. She accepted a position as a member of the Massachusetts State Board of Education in the fall of 1889 that she held the rest of her life. She played an active if informal role in placing women in academic positions in coeducational institutions as well as women's colleges all over the country. She served on the Board of the Corporation of the International Institute for Girls in Spain, was president of the Home Missionary Association, continued to be a mainstay of Collegiate Alumnae, and was Massachusetts's Lady Manager for the World's Columbian Exposition of 1893.

First and foremost came her devoted attention to Wellesley College. She had experienced no difficulty continuing her connection with the college as a recent president and key member of the board of trustees during the months immediately following her marriage, but she found it painful to reengage herself with Wellesley when she returned from Europe. She wrote George, "I find myself dreading the first going back." She thought it best she have as little to do with the college as possible and would make her first visit for the dedication of the Art Building or the occasion of George Palmer's fall lecture on Homer.[74] Whatever the reason for her reluctance (she probably feared feeling a true outsider after her long absence), it was not long before she was again comfortably and fully engaged with Wellesley affairs. Wellesley welcomed her back. "Mrs. Palmer will again be so near the college that she can grant it the happiness of frequent glimpses of her bright face, made brighter now by the months of rest and pleasure abroad."[75]

The most recent study of Wellesley College suggests that the Academic Council, the faculty governing body established by Alice Freeman, became the center of the college under President Shafer.[76] Certainly the Academic Council continued to gain in influence and power, and Alice Palmer consistently used her influence with its members to have an effect on its decisions, but the real center of power became the Executive Committee of the Board of Trustees. Much as Alice Freeman as president had used the board of trustees and its committees to increase her power as president and control the direction of policy, she now used the prestige and power of the board to continue this control. Earlier she had assumed this power, although never used when Henry Durant was alive, did exist and she carefully nourished and manipulated it during her presidency. The earlier precedent served her well now. In 1890–91, for example, it was she who presented the requests for faculty leaves, the report of the committee on faculty duties and rights, the policy concerning Bible study, and the status and role of the music school.

Alice Freeman chose Helen Shafer to be her successor, and she chose her because Shafer shared goals dear to the liberal and more progressive faculty that Alice Freeman had encouraged, supported, and hired. Shafer was also an able administrator, well organized, task oriented, and devoted to both the college and Alice Freeman Palmer. But during her tenure the executive committee exercised very detailed administrative functions, determining many purely administrative decisions on curriculum, class size, and faculty appointments. Alice Palmer's guiding hand was clearly evident in all of them.

Palmer consistently took the initiative on faculty appointments. At her first executive committee meeting after returning from Europe, Palmer reported she "had heard criticism of the management of the French department" that she was unable to ignore.[77] Both faculty and students served as her informants. As chairman of a subcommittee to investigate, by November Palmer had resolved the French department crisis. The general dissatisfaction had been documented, the need for change confirmed, and the offender removed but paid half salary until the end of the academic year when she would resign.[78] Palmer and Pauline Durant were appointed to a committee to seek a new head for the department of French.[79] Palmer was also a moving force in transferring Mary Calkins, who in 1891 was to establish one of the first psychology laboratories in the United States, from instructor in Greek to the new discipline of psychology which was, however, still part of the department of philosophy.[80]

Palmer did her best to resolve peaceably a nasty conflict in the Greek department. As she wrote George, "Miss Shafer must go on with the weeding process. It is by far the most pressing demand."[81] Alice's old friend, Angie Chapin, hired in the first years of the college by Henry Durant and who had since made no effort to acquire further training, was among those she felt needed to be weeded. Sensing her vulnerability, Chapin was reluctant even to go on leave. Although Angie Chapin remained on Wellesley's faculty until she retired in 1920, Palmer was successful in curbing Chapin's power over the Greek department, and she spent the rest of her career teaching Greek New Testament to freshmen.[82]

On occasion Alice Palmer ensured new appointments she wanted by raising the money herself. She first raised the funds and then maneuvered the appointment of Marion Talbot to a new chair of domestic economy.[83] Talbot had been Palmer's colleague in Collegiate Alumnae and had received early professional training at Massachusetts Institute of Technology in the new science of sanitation. Talbot's and Palmer's careers were to be interwoven for the rest of Palmer's life. Enlarging and properly staffing the inadequate gym was another of Palmer's projects. First she received the promise of a gift toward enlarging the gymnasium, then asked for board authorization to solicit further funds, and later raised money for increased instruction in gymnastics.[84]

New faculty appointments continued to be women. The pattern was threatened in the spring of 1891 when a Harvard man was strongly urged by several board members including Palmer as instructor of freshman composition. Despite Pauline Durant's opposition he was offered the post, but he declined when Harvard made a counteroffer.[85] Although of more concern to Durant, the conservative, than Palmer, women continued a monopoly on faculty positions.

Alice Palmer's active intervention in Wellesley's affairs was not confined to faculty appointments. It was she who took the lead in defining the duties and powers of various levels of faculty. When well-trained, ambitious women were added to Durant's original group, conflict over who was to teach what and how, and who was to make these decisions at the departmental level, was inevitable. In the fall of 1890 the executive committee adopted a formal statement proposed by Palmer defining the relationship and duties of the teaching staff. The senior professor was to be responsible for the content and methods of the work of the annually appointed instructors. The junior professors were to be solely responsible for the content, methods, and examinations and grades in their own courses. The distribution and assignment of courses was to be the joint responsibility of a department's junior and senior professors and the president.[86] Earlier department heads had exercised total control. Now it was shared with faculty. However, this decision did not solve all curricular problems, and a faculty committee was appointed to rethink the full program of course offerings. The result was a two-year struggle within the faculty including delays that frequently left the more "progressive" members frustrated and restless. In 1893 a new curriculum was finally adopted that broadened electives, increased program flexibility, and decreased the emphasis on classical languages.[87]

Alice Palmer played a crucial role in effecting an acceptable resolution to the many conflicting faculty interests. She met often and long with Helen Shafer and used her many faculty contacts to advantage.[88] By the end of 1893 new academic patterns had been firmly established. Not only had the curriculum been modernized, the faculty now moved through various levels: instructor, assistant professor, professor, in normal progression, and the practice of junior faculty leaves to pursue graduate training was well established.[89]

When Helen Shafer died in January of 1894 pressure was put on Alice Palmer to resume the presidency. She resisted even considering it seriously. She was so sure of her decision that it was unnecessary for George to raise his usual objections.[90] By the mid-1890s she was more than content to guide Wellesley in the directions she believed it must go without having to live on campus and face the myriad petty details of academic housekeeping.

Next to Alice Palmer's devotion to Wellesley College, the young women who struggled in the 1890s to obtain a sound education from a begrudging and uncommitted Harvard College made the largest claim on Alice Palmer's interest and energies. The Harvard Annex, as this group was informally called, had been organized in 1879–80, the year Alice Freeman came to Wellesley, to provide private collegiate instruction for women. Thirty-seven Harvard faculty repeated their courses of lectures to 27 women that first year and were paid small additional salaries by the women's group. In 1882 the Annex was incorporated as the Society for the Collegiate Instruction of Women, and slowly a few buildings, largely old houses, were added to its facilities. By 1893, 255 students were taught by sixty-nine Harvard faculty. The Annex was informally becoming a woman's college of some size, but it had no legal connections with Harvard College or the corporation despite the fact that almost all its instruction was provided by Harvard faculty. Annex women were denied use of Harvard's library, were barred from Harvard lectures, and were not awarded academic degrees, only certificates.[91]

George Palmer, having taught at the Annex from its beginning, was one of its most enthusiastic supporters, but Harvard alumni in general were scornful of the Annex and fearful of its potential for contaminating their sacred male bastion with bonnets and petticoats. Many members of the Harvard faculty and President Eliot were more sympathetic, although Eliot was always an uncertain friend. For some faculty it meant a welcome supplement to their incomes. Others, like Palmer, were genuinely committed to educating women. Before 1888 Alice was aware of and sympathetic to the Annex and its problems. Her good friend Lillian Horsford was on its board, but it was not until she moved to Cambridge in 1888 that she participated actively in its affairs. She spoke often to the Emmanuel Club, a student religious and social organization, invited Annex women to her home to tea, and as one student described interaction with her, brought to them "the radiance of her beautiful life."[92] Unlike Smith or Wellesley girls, Annex students had no women faculty with whom to identify. Their instructors were all Harvard men, and Alice provided a convenient role model. She had not only taught in but been president of a college. For Alice the Annex association worked much as George had promised her during their courtship: that helping Annex girls fulfill themselves would be one of the rewards of her life in Cambridge.

Although the Annex had been proposing legal affiliation with Harvard since 1880, it was not until 1892 that the possibility became a realistic hope. By then Columbia and Brown had accepted formal affiliation with their women's annexes. Eliot seemed sympathetic, promising, the Society for the Collegiate Instruction of Women thought, that if they raised a $250,000 endowment to prove their financial self-sufficiency the Corporation would take over responsibility for the women on its fringes and grant them the right to earn Harvard degrees. Alice Palmer had been active in fund-raising for the Annex as early as 1888, and when she visited her parents in Saginaw that year, she carried the account books with her so she could answer any queries the mail might bring.[93] Her involvement was to increase greatly when the big push came in 1892 and the Women's Education Association (WEA) was chosen as the fund-raising instrument. Founded in 1872 for the betterment of women's education, the Women's Education Association was particularly active in promoting opportunities for the scientific training of women.[94] At the time the association committed itself to secure an endowment for the Annex, Alice Palmer was its president. Although she accepted a position at the new University of Chicago that year, she stayed on as president of the Women's Education Association specifically to insure a successful outcome of the fund-raising drive.[95]

The endowment was raised, in large measure, under Alice Palmer's leadership. Although the women who subscribed did not want a separate college, the eventual agreement hammered out by the Annex leadership under Elizabeth Agassiz with President Eliot and the overseers provided otherwise. Radcliffe, separately incorporated, would grant its own degrees, although Harvard had agreed to countersign them. Harvard was also to oversee Radcliffe, approve its faculty, and describe its offerings in the Harvard catalog. This was not the incorporation of the Annex into Harvard that Alice Palmer and the women of the association had envisioned when the money was raised. Palmer protested that she could keep none of this money unless Harvard accepted women (albeit in a separate department) and granted their degrees.[96] Who was to control the subscribed money was also at issue. Did the Harvard establishment assume this responsibility? Or did the women retain control? Elizabeth Agassiz argued before the association that the compromise was acceptable. The donors to the fund and Palmer were unconvinced. All subscribed money was returned.[97]

During much of this struggle Alice Palmer was in Chicago, and George acted as her informal proxy in Cambridge. On at least two occasions during the negotiations, Eliot indicated to George that he wished for Alice's speedy return in order to "to talk of the Annex."[98] Although unsuccessful this time, both George and Alice continued to hope for a closer connection of Radcliffe with Harvard. For example, they were fearful of providing adequate but separate quarters for Radcliffe because they wished "eventually to see the [Harvard] College provide for its girls on the same terms as its boys."[99] Despite her long association with women's colleges, Alice never wavered in her belief that coeducation was the better way.

Alice Palmer consistently exerted her influence wherever she could in women's higher education. She was closely involved when Columbia's Collegiate Course for Women was transformed into Barnard College in 1889. When sitting for her portrait in New York, she was frequently consulted by the women leading the campaign, and she worked hard to convince them that their conception of a president as "a sort of upper housekeeper, a lady who will be nice with the girls," was hardly adequate.[100] She urged Marion Talbot for dean of Barnard in 1891 despite the fact that Palmer also wanted Talbot on the Wellesley faculty at that time.[101] In 1894 she aided the appointment of Emily James Smith, whom she knew well because of her University of Chicago connections, to head Barnard.[102] She acted as an advisor when the Women's College (later Pembroke) of Brown University was being planned and helped choose its first dean.[103] She kept a wary eye on President David Starr Jordan's appointment of women to Stanford and hoped unsuccessfully to see her old classmate, Lucy Maynard Salmon, on its faculty.[104]

In the fall of 1889, just after the Palmers' return from Europe,

Governor Ames appointed Alice to the Massachusetts State Board of Education. This board had been established in 1840 to care for the educational interests of the state and by 1889 had responsibility for the state normal schools, Boston Art Normal, the institutions for the deaf and blind, and supervised the district schools. In short, it controlled the education of teachers for the public schools, the training of the handicapped, and supervised the rural schools. At the first meeting Alice Palmer attended she was appointed visitor to Bridgewater Normal and Boston Art Normal and to the committee that was to consider establishing a higher grade of normal instruction for high schools.[105] Bridgewater continued to be her special responsibility throughout her tenure on the board, which ended only with her death. She also led the fight to raise admission standards and presided over a major revision in the teacher training curriculum in 1893.[106] On occasion she was chosen to prepare the board's annual reports, and she frequently lobbied for the normal school cause before the legislature, "showing such gifts as a pleader...that her colleagues on the board... spontaneously turned to her for service as a 'voice' more persistent and potent, perhaps than any other."[107] Although a moderate temperance advocate she fought successfully against a compulsory temperance education bill that placed onerous and unreasonable restrictions on teachers.[108]

She did good work for the state board. She had no axes, political or otherwise, to grind, and no doubt the training of teachers benefitted from her long service. Harvard's president, Charles Eliot, the Palmers' next door neighbor, would buttonhole George on Alice's absences from Cambridge to pass on his concerns with the education of secondary school teachers.[109] George would also relay to Alice in his letters concerns that Massachusetts governors had expressed to him as Alice's deputy about educational policy matters that were before the legislature.[110] Palmer herself was frequently distressed when she neglected her duties to the state board. "You can think how sorry I am to be away when this morning comes a note from Mr. Adams, chairman of the Ways and Means Committee...asking me to see him about the bills on education. Isn't it sad that I am away, for I might do some good if I could see him alone."[111] Nonetheless Alice Palmer missed many State Board of Education meetings. If she was in Cambridge, Boxford, or the Boston area and sufficiently well to travel by trolley or sit in a chair, she never missed a Wellesley appointment. Her record for the state board is less exemplary, but her influence for professionalism and excellence was there nonetheless.

Alice Palmer's other opportunity to work with and influence public education, occurred when she was dean at the University of Chicago. She was offered the position of supervisor of the Boston public schools. She seems to have considered the offer seriously for awhile. The salary was $4,000, she would no longer face frequent separations from George.[112] In the end, however, she refused the job. She wrote George when the offer was made that the board itself was hopeless, and that to fully rouse public opinion the "Boston schools will have to be worse before they are better. No one woman can do it alone."[113]

In the early 1890s Alice Freeman Palmer's watchful eye and willing advice were everywhere in women's education. But her focus moved more and more toward the expanding opportunities in coeducation provided by the new universities and coeducation's half sisters, the affiliate colleges at Brown, Columbia, and Harvard. Very soon the new University of Chicago was to provide her with a stunning opportunity to promote coeducation at what was designed from the beginning to be one of the world's great research universities. From 1892 to 1895 she divided her physical presence and her intellectual and organizational gifts between Chicago in the heartland of her beloved trans-Appalachian West and the Northeast corridor that had received most of her attention for the past fifteen years.

NOTES

1. William Gardner Hale's remarks at the Alice Freeman Palmer Memorial Service, University of Chicago, 1903, as printed in *A Memorial to Alice Freeman Palmer*, 19.

2. At about the same time that the Palmers were attempting to resolve their dilemma, Carrie Chapman Catt and her husband reached a different solution. Both were deeply concerned with reform causes, and agreed that George Catt would provide the couple's income, and Carrie would contribute her time and skills to reform. See Robert Booth Fowler, *Carrie Catt: Feminist Politician* (Boston: Northeastern University Press, 1986), 15–16. Of course this meant Catt had no status as a professional, only as a volunteer. Helen Magill, the first woman to receive a Ph.D. in the United States, was unable to continue her career after her marriage to Andrew Dickson White in 1890. See Altschuler, *Better than Second Best*. Magill White gave birth to three children in the early years of her marriage and White was much less tolerant than Palmer of any professional aspirations by his wife.

3. Mitchell, *Two Lives;* Antler, *Lucy Sprague Mitchell.* Dorothy Reed Mendenhall and Anne Walter Fearn, physicians who received their training in the 1890s and practiced in the early twentieth century also were able to combine marriage with professional careers. (Glazer and Slater, *Unequal Colleagues,* chap. 3).

4. Diary, December 23, 1887.

5. Palmer, *Life,* 190.

6. Ibid., 190–91.

7. Ibid., 224.

8. George Herbert Palmer to Alice Freeman Palmer, September 23, 1892. Wellesley Typescripts.

9. Alice Freeman Palmer to George Herbert Palmer, April 30, 1888. Wellesley Typescripts.

10. George Herbert Palmer to Alice Freeman Palmer, May 1, 1888. Wellesley Typescripts.

11. Alice Freeman Palmer to George Herbert Palmer, April 26, 1888. Wellesley Typescripts.

12. Minutes of the Board of Trustees, September 30, 1887, February 2, 1888. Wellesley College Archives.

13. Minutes of the Executive Committee, Board of Trustees, February 21, 1888. Wellesley College Archives.

14. Minutes of the Board of Trustees, February 2, and June 7, 1888. Wellesley College Archives.

15. Ibid.

16. Alice Freeman Palmer to George Herbert Palmer, April 26, 1888. Wellesley Typescripts.

17. Alice Freeman Palmer to George Herbert Palmer, April 26, 1888. Wellesley Typescripts.

18. George Herbert Palmer to Alice Freeman Palmer, May 2, 1889. Wellesley Typescripts.

19. Correspondence of Alice Freeman Palmer and George Herbert Palmer, April 1888. Wellesley Typescripts.

20. Alice Freeman Palmer to George Herbert Palmer, May 2, 1888. Wellesley Typescripts.

21. Alice Freeman Palmer to George Herbert Palmer, April 28, May 2, 1888. Wellesley Typescripts.

22. Alice Freeman Palmer to George Herbert Palmer, May 3, 1888. Wellesley Typescripts.

23. George Herbert Palmer to Alice Freeman Palmer, May 3, 1888. Wellesley Typescripts.

24. George Herbert Palmer to Alice Freeman Palmer, September 1, 1889. Wellesley Typescripts.

25. Alice Freeman Palmer to George Herbert Palmer, May 6, 1888. Wellesley Typescripts.

26. Alice Freeman Palmer to George Herbert Palmer, May 5, 1888. Wellesley Typescripts.

27. Ibid.

28. The most recent study of Bellamy's influence is to be found in *Looking Backward, 1988–1888: Essays on Edward Bellamy,* Daphne Patai, ed. (Amherst: University of Massachusetts Press, 1988).

29. Alice Freeman Palmer to George Herbert Palmer, September 1, 1889. Wellesley Typescripts.

30. George Herbert Palmer to Alice Freeman Palmer, September 2, 1889. Wellesley Typescripts.

31. George Herbert Palmer to Alice Freeman Palmer, September 3, 1889. Wellesley Typescripts.

32. George Herbert Palmer to Alice Freeman Palmer, September 4, 1889. Wellesley Typescripts.

33. Palmer, *Life,* 193–96.

34. Alice Freeman Palmer to Carla Wenckebach, January 6, 1889.

35. Ibid.

36. Ibid.

37. Alice Freeman Palmer to friend, January 27, 1889.

38. Alice Freeman Palmer to Carla Wenckebach, January 6, 1889.

39. Ibid.

40. Alice Freeman Palmer to Marion Talbot, April 9, 1889.

41. Ibid.

42. Ibid.

43. Ibid.

44. Alice Freeman Palmer to K. Coman, June 28, 1889.

45. Alice Freeman Palmer to George Herbert Palmer, September 4, 1889. Wellesley Typescripts.

46. George Herbert Palmer to Alice Freeman Palmer, April 17, 1894. Wellesley Typescripts.

47. Palmer, *Life,* 221.

48. Diary, 1888.

49. George Herbert Palmer to Alice Freeman Palmer, June 2, 1890. Wellesley Typescripts.

50. Diary, 1890.

51. Alice Freeman Palmer to George Herbert Palmer, May 30, 1890. Wellesley Typescripts.

52. Alice Freeman Palmer to George Herbert Palmer, May 31, 1890. Wellesley Typescripts.

53. Ibid.

54. Alice Freeman Palmer to George Herbert Palmer, May 27, 1890. Wellesley Typescripts.

55. Alice Freeman Palmer to George Herbert Palmer, September 7, 1889. Wellesley Typescripts.

56. George Herbert Palmer to Alice Freeman Palmer, May 24, 1890. Wellesley Typescripts.

57. George Herbert Palmer to Alice Freeman Palmer, May 30, 1890. Wellesley Typescripts.

58. Alice Freeman Palmer to George Herbert Palmer, June 4, 1890. Wellesley Typescripts.

59. Alice Freeman Palmer to George Herbert Palmer, June 5, 1890. Wellesley Typescripts.

60. George Herbert Palmer to Alice Freeman Palmer, June 17, 1891. Wellesley Typescripts.

61. George Herbert Palmer to Alice Freeman Palmer, February 11, 1892. Wellesley Typescripts.

62. Alice Freeman Palmer to George Herbert Palmer, June 3, 1891. Wellesley Typescripts.

63. Diary, 1892.

64. J. Laurence Laughlin's remarks at the Alice Freeman Palmer Memorial Service, University of Chicago, 1903, as printed in *A Memorial to Alice Freeman Palmer*, 7.

65. Alice Freeman Palmer to George Herbert Palmer, April 26, 27, 1892. Wellesley Typescripts.

66. George Herbert Palmer to Alice Freeman Palmer, June 20, 1901. Wellesley Typescripts.

67. A. F. Palmer, *Why Go to College,*

68. Palmer, *Life,* 221.

69. George Herbert Palmer to Anne Whitney, October 7, 1891. Alice Freeman Palmer Papers, Wellesley College Archives.

70. Alice Freeman Palmer to George Herbert Palmer, December 14, 1889. Wellesley Typescripts.

71. Mitchell, *Two Lives,* 122–23; for an assessment of Thayer see Ann Uhry Abrams, "Frozen Goddess: The Image of Woman in Turn of the Century American Art" in *Women's Being, Women's Place,* ed. Mary Kelley, 95–101. See also Banta, *Imaging American Women.*

72. Alice Freeman Palmer to George Herbert Palmer, February 25, 1890. Wellesley Typescripts.

73. *Wellesley Annals,* 1889–90, 5.

74. Alice Freeman Palmer to George Herbert Palmer, September 7, 1889. Wellesley Typescripts.

75. *Wellesley Annals,* 1889–90, 12.

76. Palmieri, "Adamless Eden," 147.

77. Minutes of the Executive Committee, October 3, 1889. Wellesley College Archives.

78. Minutes of the Executive Committee, November 16, 1889. Wellesley College Archives.

79. Minutes of the Board of Trustees, February 5, 1891. Wellesley College Archives.

80. Minutes of the Board of Trustees, February 6, 1890. Wellesley College Archives.

81. Alice Freeman Palmer to George Herbert Palmer, September 7, 1889. Wellesley Typescripts.

82. Alice Freeman Palmer to George Herbert Palmer, May 22, June 5, 1890; George Herbert Palmer to Alice Freeman Palmer, May 30, 1890. Wellesley Typescripts.

83. Alice Freeman Palmer to Marion Talbot, August 16, 1890 [misdated, really August 23]. Minutes of the Board of Trustees, June 2, 1892, Wellesley College Archives.

84. Minutes of the Board of Trustees, November 6, 1890, June 2, 1892. Wellesley College Archives.

85. Minutes of the Executive Committee, May 8, 1891. Wellesley College Archives.

86. Minutes of the Executive Committee, November 13, 1890. Wellesley College Archives.

87. Alice Freeman Palmer to Marion Talbot, November 15, 1892. Marion Talbot Papers, University of Chicago Archives. Glasscock, *Wellesley,* 137–38.

88. See especially her correspondence with George Herbert Palmer for the period, and Alice Freeman Palmer to Marion Talbot, November 15, 1892. Marion Talbot Papers, University of Chicago Archives.

89. President's Report, 1893, Wellesley College Archives.

90. Alice Freeman Palmer to George Herbert Palmer, April 2, 1894. Wellesley Typescripts.

91. For the origins of Radcliffe College and its relationship to Harvard University see Solomon, *Educated Women,* 54–55; Horowitz, *Alma Mater,* 95–104; Sally Schwager, "Harvard Women" (Ph.D. diss., Harvard School of Education, 1982); *Report of the Special Committee of the Board of Overseers,* June 1898; Barrett Wendell, "The Relations of Radcliffe College with Harvard," *Harvard Monthly* 29 (October 1899): 1–9.

92. Nadine Crump as quoted in Schwager, "Harvard Women," 266–67; Diary, 1888–92.

93. Alice Freeman Palmer to George Herbert Palmer, April 26, 1888. Wellesley Typescripts.

94. Final Report, 1929, Women's Education Association Papers, Radcliffe College Archives.

95. Report, 1893. Women's Education Association Papers, Radcliffe College Archives.

96. Schwager, "Harvard Women," 332; Alice Freeman Palmer to friend, Thanksgiving, 1892. Alice Freeman Palmer to George Herbert Palmer, April 3, 1893. Wellesley Typescripts.

97. Alice Freeman Palmer to George Herbert Palmer, April 3, 1893. Wellesley Typescripts; Schwager, "Harvard Women," 341–48.

98. George Herbert Palmer to Alice Freeman Palmer, January 12, 16, 1894. Wellesley Typescripts.

99. George Herbert Palmer to Alice Freeman Palmer, January 6, 1895. Wellesley Typescripts.

100. Alice Freeman Palmer to George Herbert Palmer, December 16, 1889. Wellesley Typescripts.

101. Alice Freeman Palmer to Marion Talbot, August 16, 1890; Alice Freeman Palmer to George Herbert Palmer, March 1891. Wellesley Typescripts.

102. Marian Churchill White, *A History of Barnard College* (New York: Columbia University Press, 1954), 26.

103. *Alice Freeman Palmer: In Memoriam*, 37. Pamphlet in the Alice Freeman Palmer Papers, Bentley Historical Library.

104. Alice Freeman Palmer to George Herbert Palmer, undated 1892. Wellesley Typescripts.

105. Minutes of the State Board of Education, November 7, 1889. Massachusetts State Archives.

106. Minutes of the State Board of Education, March 2,; May 4, 18,; June 1, 1893. Massachusetts State Archives.

107. George Perry Morris, "Alice Freeman Palmer," *American Monthly Review of Reviews*, February 1903, 170.

108. Alice Freeman Palmer to George Herbert Palmer, February 1900. George Herbert Palmer Papers. Houghton Library, Harvard University. George Herbert Palmer discusses Alice Freeman Palmer's Board of Education service in his *Life*, 243-48.

109. See George Herbert Palmer to Alice Freeman Palmer, May 22, 23, 1890. Wellesley Typescripts.

110. George Herbert Palmer to Alice Freeman Palmer, June 7, 1891. Wellesley Typescripts.

111. Alice Freeman Palmer to George Herbert Palmer, April 19, 1902. Wellesley Typescripts.

112. George Herbert Palmer to William Rainey Harper, May 11, 1894. William Rainey Harper Papers, University of Chicago Archives. Hereafter cited as Harper Papers.

113. Alice Freeman Palmer to George Herbert Palmer, April 2, 1894. Wellesley Typescripts.

CHAPTER 9

Challenge

In 1892 the Palmers, both Alice and George, were offered the chance to pursue a joint academic career at the University of Chicago. For Alice this opportunity offered a happy solution that went beyond her most optimistic dreams to the unresolved dilemma. Here was the perfect alternative to arduous lecture tours and lengthy separations. It was as well the professional challenge of the century. William Rainey Harper and the University of Chicago were providing American academia with a stirring new model.

1

Two great private universities, destined to challenge the old Ivy League establishment, took shape at the turn of the decade. In the Far West, Stanford University, endowed by California railroad magnate Leland Stanford, opened its doors in 1891, and its newly assembled faculty, presided over by President David Starr Jordan, began instruction on a complete and opulent campus. But it was the University of Chicago, despite its makeshift physical plant and constant scrambling for funds in the first years, that posed the deepest challenge to old established ways. Although the new fortune of John D. Rockefeller was to make possible Chicago's realization, Chicago's genesis, unlike Stanford's, was not the product of a benevolent millionaire's imagination. William Rainey Harper, professional educator, Yale professor and Yale Ph.D., had his own dream and his own sense of mission.[1] Pudgy, ebullient, persuasive, Harper left a distinguished and well-paid chair at Yale to put together a new university that emphasized graduate studies and attracted a faculty so distinguished that it could welcome its first students with a reputation for academic excellence already in place.

Harper was a spectacular recruiter, competing in a world where academic talent was both socially valued and financially rewarded. He was unable to lure any stars from Johns Hopkins or Harvard, but he did attract William I. Knapp of Yale, almost half the staff of poorly funded Clark University, and top talent from the state universities, including John Dewey from Michigan. Eight of his original professors were former college presidents. His goal was to create a faculty composed of men and women with established reputations, not young promising unknowns, and he was prepared to offer spectacular salaries and great freedom to build auxiliary staff to those scholars he saw as essential to his enterprise.

The existing academic community viewed Harper and Chicago with ambivalence. Sometimes they saw the University of Chicago as "Harper's Three Ring Circus," an adjunct to the city's famous Midway amusement district. John D. Rockefeller was at the height of his unpopularity in the 1890s, and many of the eastern intelligentsia were skeptical of linking education with "tainted" money.[2] Chicago was dubbed the "gas trust university" or "Standard University" by easterners scornful of Harper's grandiose plans and contempt for tradition.[3]

However, many less traditional academicians viewed Chicago with excited approval. When G. Stanley Hall, psychologist and founder of Clark University, visited the Palmers, Alice reported, "You should have seen his enthusiasm—his conclusion that in the new university lay the leadership of the future."[4] Harper's innovations were myriad. For example, businessmen, rather than clergy, dominated the board of trustees. A university press dedicated to the dissemination of research and scholarship was to function as a full department of the university. An extension division modeled after the British experiment pioneered by the University of London was to provide outreach to the larger community, coeducation on all levels was to be the norm, and women were to be included on the faculty. Harper also offered high salaries and promised opportunities for his faculty to pioneer in new scholarly directions.

While innovations in higher education in the 1880s at Clark and Johns Hopkins had emphasized graduate study, specialization, research, and scholarship, Harper encompassed and enlarged these goals. He was prepared to pay for this emphasis on research and scholarship by providing fellowships for graduate students and light teaching loads for senior faculty.[5] But the University of Chicago also consciously attempted to avoid elitism. Harper's vision combined scholarly goals with a democratic commitment to the larger society, a populist appeal that found its embodiment in correspondence courses open to almost everyone, an extension division, a summer session that attracted many practicing teachers, and popular lecture series. As Chicago's historian has said, one way or another the University of Chicago "was a presence, a new but somehow ageless being actively at work in the land, to be watched sometimes with admiration and sometimes warily, as if it might prove to be other than it seemed."[6] Chicago was a force that could not be ignored.

Chicago and Stanford between them had created an upheaval in staid academic circles. What is more they had created a sellers' market for academicians who were suddenly blessed with job mobility they had never expected and monetary rewards to match.

Harper's planning was well underway by 1890 when the university was incorporated. He was formally named president in February, 1891, and began actively recruiting that year. Since he envisioned a coeducational institution from the beginning, as his administrative officer with responsibility for women he was eager to persuade Alice Freeman Palmer to join his staff. Also he had his eye on George Palmer. Harper's initial intention was to concentrate on building three great departments: Semitics, classics, and philosophy, and for philosophy George Herbert Palmer would make an eminently suitable head.

The Palmers were curious about Chicago as were most prominent academicians long before Harper first approached them. Alice was in New York City sitting for her Wellesley portrait when Harper first was expected to visit Cambridge, and she was truly afraid she would miss him.[7] Fortunately for her Harper did not arrive in Cambridge until about March 12, when he made a joint offer to the Palmers. He proposed that George become professor of philosophy and head of the department at the princely salary of $7,000 a year, and Alice come as dean of the Woman's Department and professor of history at a salary that could range from $2,000 to $5,000.[8] The flexibility in Alice's salary no doubt reflected uncertainty over whether she would work full or part time. If she was paid $5,000, she would be making more than George's Harvard salary at the time, no small sum.

Harper's offer to the Palmers is quite probably the first time a major university attempted to attract an academic couple to its professoriate, a practice that was not to be much repeated for nearly a century. It is also likely that Harper was more intent on capturing Alice than George. True, George's professional star was rising rapidly at this time. Less than two weeks before Harper made his move, President Eliot called George into his office and asked him if he could suggest his name as president of the young University of California at Berkeley.[9] George Palmer's books were being well received and his organizational talents widely recognized. It would have been a great coup for Chicago to have acquired him at the height of his career, but there were other promising philosophers to be had. Alice Freeman Palmer was unique. If Harper wanted an academic woman of real stature on the staff of his coeducational university, Alice was at that time the only woman with broad experience in educational administration who had a national reputation, to say nothing of a charismatic personality that attracted media attention. If Harper was to share administrative duties with a notable woman, he had no choice but to lure Alice Freeman Palmer to his windy campus at the hub of the continent.

Alice was more than willing to oblige. George Palmer was at first also tempted by Harper's offer, but for him Cambridge had strong competing attractions. For Alice, the opportunity for the Palmers to work as a couple in an exciting new educational venture could provide the ultimate in happy solutions to her problems.

2

The decision was agonizing. The Palmers spent nearly three weeks in Chicago in late March and early April, talking with Harper and his trustees and advisors, inspecting the Gothic quadrangle slowly taking shape on the marshy land at the northern edge of the city, attending concerts in Richardson's magnificent new Chicago Auditorium, and reviewing the progress of the Columbian Exposition of which Alice was one of the Lady Managers. George returned to Cambridge on April 11th, and Alice left the next day for a visit with her family to be followed by her spring lecture tour and a second Chicago stay on World's Fair business. The Palmers were not together again until May 5th, and the decision hung fire until Alice's return as they discussed the pros and cons back and forth in their letters. Alice Palmer was enthusiastic, full of plans, large and small, more and more convinced that they should accept Harper's offer. Almost immediately she advised George: "You'd better begin a file of applicants and other correspondence relating to your work here [University of Chicago]."[10] She passed on rumors she heard about men whom George might consider for the Chicago philosophy department. "Mr. Pond says that Mr. Dewey [John Dewey] has the reputation in Ann Arbor of being too much the dreamer."[11] She forwarded enthusiastic local publicity to George: "I send you a *Graphic*, full of the University, and a morning's paper. I was introduced to the Friday Club today as 'the most talked of woman in Chicago.'"[12] And she reported at length on a conversation in Minneapolis with Harry Pratt Judson, who was to join the Chicago faculty. "All his reasons for going are good. I must say I long to get my hands on the Woman's College," and then protected herself against disappointment by adding, "but the next moment I long to stay in our own pleasant place."[13] When Alice Palmer returned to Chicago to attend to her World's Fair responsibilities, Harper was away, but she continued to consult with and advise university officials.[14]

Letters from women eager for Chicago jobs poured in. Wellesley alumnae urged Alice Palmer to take the Chicago position. "Old Wellesley girls ... long to see me take this untrammeled leadership and do something far greater before I die than I could ever have done at Wellesley." One graduate reported that "all the women of the Northwest will gather about my work if I will come. It does surprise me very much to see the strong feeling among my old friends everywhere about it. Mary Roberts ... wants me to take all the Wellesley teachers whom we have talked of for their sakes. She thinks I could do so much in making a way for them in a broader place."[15] Once again women put pressure on Alice Freeman Palmer to pursue her career above all else. Duty to womanhood demanded that her position as an educator be exploited for the general benefit of her sex. She had gone too far to be allowed to retreat into domesticity.

Alice Palmer herself was thinking of the good she could do. She wrote her young friend and Collegiate Alumnae colleague, Marion Talbot, whom she had just installed at Wellesley, that if the Chicago offer was accepted she would "have the nomination of the other professors and I hope you know what that means and will begin to get your trunk ready."[16] She saw it as so splendid a chance for women "as makes one gasp for breath."[17]

Actually Harper was not as sympathetic to the aspirations of women as eager Wellesley alumnae or others believed. One historian argues that if Harper had followed his own preference, Chicago would have admitted no women students or had any women on its faculty. But western colleges were under considerable pressure to admit women at this time, partly because the shortage of teachers in the West was acute, and Harper could not ignore this populist demand. Also, if Chicago was to attract sufficient students to make Harper's dream come true, he must open Chicago's doors to women.[18] Forty percent of Chicago's student body when it opened were women, and by 1902 it enrolled more women than men. Women were a financial necessity. But the University of Chicago was not to prove as supportive of women faculty as Palmer and the Wellesley alumnae had hoped. Although he appointed women, pioneers like Marion Talbot and Elizabeth Wallace who spent their careers at Chicago were often given short shift and had to fight long and hard for proper status. However in 1891–92 women perceived Chicago as opening new educational doors and providing opportunities for academic women that they would not have in the East. And Alice Freeman Palmer agreed with them. Here she could do more, she thought, for women's education than she had ever been able to do at Wellesley.

Her choice of career course was clear. She unreservedly wished the Palmers to accept Chicago's call. She wrote George toward the end of her lecture tour, "Let's come to Chicago where we know nobody, and everyone is too busy to get acquainted, and where we may be together all the time after morning office hours and have the same kind of work."[19] This was the ploy she used most consistently. As George had played endlessly on the theme of Alice's poor health to convince her to marry him, Alice now played on his loneliness during their long separations. If they went together to Chicago they would never have to be apart again. Both George and Alice hated the long weeks apart that her lecture tours required. Chicago would permit them to work together, rather than forcing her out of Cambridge to perform on the national scene.

Their letters show clearly how their working partnership had developed. When they were apart Alice shared her professional concerns with George, but she also worried about an article he had written on college vices, the final draft of which she had not been able to see because she was away. He took considerable trouble over professional responsibilities she had left behind in Cambridge, Wellesley affairs and concerns of the State Board of Education, as well as answering some of her correspondence. Their working lives were intertwined and yet of necessity separated because without an institutional base she must operate on the national stage. Both complained frequently about separations. She wrote: "But, dear George, this must be stopped. There is no fun in it."[20]

Alice also saw Chicago and its opportunities as putting an end to the nagging discontent and bouts of increasing irritability that had plagued her since their return from Europe and caused stresses and strains between them. When they were apart, Alice always apologized to George for her behavior when they were together. "If only I could change myself! That is what is needed, I know, and I always fancy it will come—but it does not. Perhaps less than ever this year, when I haven't been quite well!"[21] Although she was busy and doing useful things, her life lacked focus and challenge and the monetary rewards for her efforts were slim. In the last analysis, George was the family's breadwinner and on some level this left her feeling less useful than she knew she could be. She wanted real control of her professional destiny. In desperation, probably at her own irritable behavior, she once proposed that if they must stay at Harvard, they live in Boxford during the academic year as well as in summer. "All the heavy expenses would be stopped. I could devote myself to reading and writing—the distance would be ample excuse for resigning everything except Wellesley."[22] George would have more quiet writing time. The implication was that the fatigue caused by her heavy schedule interfered with the even tenor of his days. However, she must have known that the reclusive life was not for her. Despite her protests, she enjoyed the traveling, the receptions at the homes of wealthy alumnae, the applause and bouquets of roses that greeted her speeches, the press reports of her triumphs. But the nineteenth-century dual career marriage was no easier to achieve without stress than it was to be a century later.

Lending weight to Alice's desire to accept the Chicago offer was the fact that the Palmers' financial resources were strained. At one point in April of 1892 George was down to his last five dollars, and Alice had borrowed from her brother Fred to meet tour expenses.[23] In a few days her checks began to come in, he received his salary for his Annex teaching, and they once more were solvent. But clearly they had difficulty maintaining the standard of living to which they aspired on George's salary and her incidental earnings.

Nonetheless, as Alice's enthusiasm for the new challenge from Chicago increased, George, back in Cambridge, found more and more reasons for staying at Harvard. Occasionally he was strongly tempted. William James agreed with him that "the Chicago staff would be a weightier one than we have here," and Phillip Abbott "was aghast at its splendor. He thought we should be perfectly justified in going on such terms." But George also cautioned Alice, "discourage Harper when you see him. I don't want to go."[24] Also his colleagues almost uniformly discouraged the move. William Jewett Tucker, president of Dartmouth, was "very earnest against Chicago. He considered it very wrong for persons of our years and position to enter into missionary work. . . . He thought another generation would pass before the West would have students fitted for a University of our sort, and believed the work of bringing them up to this point could be exactly as well performed by teachers of another grade than ourselves."[25] A few days later George "sent to Harper the half dozen conditions I had previously read to him, and accompanied them with a letter advising him once more to drop the entire matter for a year."[26] George's doubts multiplied. "The whole scheme seems to me more and more improbable, especially improbable that it can be launched at present."[27] A week later he wrote: "The more I think of it, the more thoroughly distasteful the abandonment of Harvard for Chicago becomes. Perhaps on monied grounds we have no right to refuse. I half incline to believe we have not. But it will certainly break the power of our lives and unite us to something which we can never heartily approve."[28] For George, Cambridge's secure charms exerted themselves with increasing power as Alice dreamed enthusiastically of solving the dilemma with a new challenge.

George Herbert Palmer eventually found his rationale for staying in Cambridge through the connection of William Rainey Harper and the University of Chicago with the American Baptist churches. By the 1890s Palmer was very wary of evangelical protestant fundamentalism. He still attended Congregational church services regularly and professed a deeply held Christian faith, but his was an intellectual Christianity. Sentimental Jesus lovers repelled him, and he found a literal belief in hellfire and damnation as repugnant as clinging to the Savior's breast. He was also a firm believer in nonsectarian education.

He had used Wellesley's and the Durants' evangelical associations as a deciding factor in his refusal to join Alice at Wellesley as co-president or in any other capacity. He was equally suspicious of Harper's Baptist antecedents and connections.

William Rainey Harper was not trained as a clergyman as were many of the older generation of college presidents, and he had not become a Baptist himself until he joined the faculty of Dennison University in 1876. He assiduously avoided clergymen as members of his board of trustees, and religious tests for faculty or students (unlike early Wellesley) were specifically banned, but Chicago's Baptist connections were very real. Original sponsorship of the university was by the American Baptist Educational Society. The president of the university and two-thirds of the trustees were required to be members of the Baptist churches, and Rockefeller, Chicago's chief benefactor, was a prominent Baptist layman.[29] George Palmer was aware of these religious ties as he considered Harper's offer. In late April the occasion of the transference of the Baptist Theological School to the University of Chicago to serve as its divinity school reinforced Palmer's apprehensions. At the ceremony of the transfer itself speeches by the prominent Baptist clergymen strengthened these suspicions. George wrote Alice that they were

> by utterly fourth rate men; and apart from the cheap theological stuff of which they mostly consist, they occupy themselves largely with exultation of the University which now is theirs. Harper himself says, "This union makes possible one thing which otherwise would have been impossible—it gives the university a divinity school. As a Baptist university its divinity school must be Baptist. It will accordingly bind the University to our own churches and to all churches as nothing else could."[30]

These words were a red flag to George. He saw the divinity school infiltrating every department of the university. He dismissed Harper's promises of non-sectarianism. "The idea of any such genuine separation of Church and College as we intend . . . never enters their heads."[31] He reminded her of her troubles with evangelicalism at Wellesley and questioned "bending our necks to that yoke again."[32] Clearly Harper had given him the rationale he had been waiting for to stay at Harvard.

George Palmer also consulted with Arthur Marsh, whom he hoped would join him in Chicago if he made the move, and with William G. Hale, his Cornell friend, who had already accepted a Chicago chair, and Hale discussed Palmer's position with Harper and tried to reassure George without much success.[33] Alice also tried to reassure George. She quoted Harry Judson, who was himself a Baptist, and later to be a president of the University of Chicago, as saying that the

> foolish and miserable speech making in Chicago at the Theological Anniversary the other night was the last wail of the dead party of their Church, . . . so the old party were allowed their wail, but that it means absolutely nothing to any man who understands the denomination today.[34]

George Palmer wrote William Rainey Harper on May 5th that he would publicly announce his refusal of the Chicago offer on Saturday and urged Harper "to drop all thoughts of us."[35] Poor Alice! She tried and tried, but she did not really have a chance. George Palmer could not be persuaded to go to Chicago, and the joint career would never become a reality.[36]

3

But Alice Palmer had not given up. She still campaigned to be allowed to play some role in the creation of the new university. In late May she herself wrote Harper that although she was not yet ready to make a commitment, "how gladly" she would assist him if some way could be worked out. And she laid down conditions for acceptance of a call, that "it would be understood that I was responsible . . . for the policy, the administration of the life, the management of the details, of the Woman's Department whether I was in Chicago or in Cambridge." She must be "Dean all the time," despite the fact that she would need to be absent two-thirds of the time, and that she would need the assistance of "an able woman on the grounds."[37] By late June Alice Palmer suggested to Harper that she was available for a flexible appointment and could arrange to spend October (when the university would first open its doors) in Chicago despite her reluctance "to break upon our home life so seriously."[38] Clearly she could not give up Chicago.

On July 6th she told Harper that if Marion Talbot would come to Chicago (and of course she had been trying to recruit her since April) she would "try some guidance from a distance."[39] And ten days later she laid out her proposition in detail. She must be (1) temporary dean or advisory dean, assisting only in the organization of the Woman's Department; (2) she would be in residence no more than twelve weeks, divided into two longer periods in September-October and January-February and two shorter periods as needed; (3) all matters that pertained to the Woman's Department would be referred to her whether in residence or not; and (4) that she would expect $3,000 in salary plus traveling expenses for her trips to Chicago and be provided with her living while there.[40]

These were stiff conditions for Harper to meet. And one can imagine the intense discussions at the Palmers' Boxford home that preceded them. No doubt George Palmer helped frame these terms, hoping Harper could not possibly accept them. Harper would have to employ Marion Talbot at the junior salary level and then pay Alice a salary whose full-time equivalent would be $9,000, an extremely high academic salary indeed. Certainly no other members of his faculty were demanding traveling expenses. If Alice was to go, George must have decided it must be worth the Palmers' while financially. Alice confessed to Harper that George was most reluctant to have her make any commitment, but "would not utterly refuse consent."[41] Nonetheless George Palmer wrote in his bold emphatic script in the margin of Alice's letter to Harper, "I hope you will return an emphatic 'no' to my wife's proposition!"[42]

She and George had been married less than five years, and once again she was pursuing an independent career. George Palmer must have found her decision almost intolerable. In his biography of Alice, although he discusses every other phase of her professional career with pride and caring, he mentions her work at Chicago only briefly and minimizes her substantial contributions there.[43] It was an interval that he obviously preferred to forget.

Although the appointment had been made, she and Harper had to unravel some minor misunderstandings that summer. She resisted being called dean rather than acting or advisory dean in official announcements and especially professor of history, a title that inspired letters from numerous women eager to take the courses that she obviously would not offer. She was alarmed that college bulletins gave no indication that she would not be in continuous residence. She protested that Harper's use of her name without these revisions would hurt both the university and her, that she might be accused "of having deserted my home and my husband or of being utterly unscrupulous toward the University."[44]

Harper briefly equivocated but soon completely agreed to Marion Talbot's appointment. Both Alice Palmer and Talbot had fully accepted appointments by August 12th, and the ambiguities concerning Talbot had been resolved. Talbot had received her release from Wellesley, and the two women not only conferred eagerly about their new shared responsibilities but embarked on a large correspondence concerning Chicago affairs.[45]

Marion Talbot was not only a colleague of Alice Palmer but friend and confidant.[46] Long before Talbot joined the Wellesley faculty in 1890 she and the Palmers were intimate partners in furthering the cause of women's higher education. George was as admiring of her talents as Alice. One of the roles they envisioned for Talbot at Wellesley was to be, according to George, at the center of "real college government," and they were about to see her installed as head of Waban cottage when the Chicago offer matured.[47] George was equally determined that she accompany Alice to Chicago. In fact Alice warned Harper during the negotiations that "Mr. Palmer says I shall not undertake this work unless she will go too!"[48] Talbot wanted a chair, hopefully as head of a Department of Sanitary Science for which she had trained at the Massachusetts Institute of Technology (MIT). Sanitary science (although later transformed into home economics) was envisioned by Talbot as a social science that could train experts to deal with the problems of urbanization. Since many of these problems were seen as a kind of municipal housekeeping, both women students and faculty were attracted to the discipline.[49] Its research focused on women, children, and communities, a kind of combination of urban sociology and public health. Sanitary science resembled, according to one historian, today's women's studies programs, but in the beginning it was also much more.[50] Talbot did not get her own department until 1904 and then it was called the Department of Household Administration (more akin to home economics), but she was appointed in 1892 as assistant professor of sociology, her courses were taught in that department, and she found in its head, Albion Small, a supportive colleague. Her early publications appeared in the *American Journal of Sociology*.[51] She remained on the Chicago faculty, becoming a full professor in 1904, until her retirement in 1925. When Talbot became a serious contender to head Barnard College in 1893 Alice Palmer both urged her to stay at Chicago and used the offer to impress Harper of Talbot's importance to the university.[52] Her appointment made possible Alice Palmer's flexible, commuting relationship to the university for she had a competent surrogate always in residence.

4

On September 18, 1892, Alice Freeman Palmer said goodbye to bucolic Boxford, the Palmer's summer home, leaving George to preserve the last fruits of the season and move their household back to Cambridge. Accompanied by Marion Talbot, Alice left Boston the next day by train for Chicago, a long journey she was to repeat many times in the next three and one-half years. Both travelers were enthusiastic, as was William Gardiner Hale whom they picked up along the way. However, Talbot's New England friends were less sanguine and saw her departing civilization for the great unknown. They presented her with a chip off Plymouth Rock to tuck in her luggage.[53]

She needed her talisman, for the physical prospect that met this trio of venturesome academics at the end of their journey was not very promising. Women students, Palmer, Talbot, and assorted other faculty were all to be housed in the Hotel Beatrice, an unfinished six-story apartment building two blocks from the University of Chicago campus. The Beatrice still bore a sign, "World Fair Rooms to Let," that indicated its original purpose—to supply accommodations for visitors to Daniel Burnham's White City that was rising on the lakeshore nearby. Adjoining streets were unpaved, former farm buildings vainly attempted to fit an urban landscape, and plank walks provided access to the swampy campus where unfinished quadrangles had begun to show themselves amidst the mud.[54]

Inside the Beatrice conditions were not much better. Much of the furniture was still not assembled, no servants were on hand, and the electricity was not yet turned on. Candles in beer bottles provided the only illumination in this abstinent Baptist setting. Palmer and Talbot themselves cooked the first breakfasts for the arriving students. Soon ninety people occupied this makeshift dormitory.[55] The weather was damp and sticky and Alice found it particularly onerous in the unfinished university buildings "where we are stepping over shavings and piles of lumber and carpenter tools all the time."[56] Even at the Beatrice, which was to have been finished by September 1st, and which the university would have to vacate in April to accommodate the fair, carpenters were continually at work.[57]

But within two days of her arrival Alice Palmer had moved into her "Deanery," an office near the president's, with brick floors and oak woodwork, and opulently furnished with a "beautiful desk, sumptuous furniture." She was busy supervising student entrance examinations, buying chests of drawers, carpets, and bedding for the Beatrice, and offering copious advice to William Rainey Harper, whether solicited or not, on such matters as inviting women to serve on the board of trustees.[58] She was enthusiastic, exultant. She toured the campus with Harper the night she arrived and pronounced it "*noble.*"[59] Even George responded to her excitement and the depth of the challenge. "Few are the people who have been present at the birth of a University; and this is one which all the country watches and no part of it more than that which you superintend. A proud position indeed!"[60]

The city of Chicago's women were already organized and active on a half-dozen fronts when the University of Chicago opened its doors.[61] Chicago itself in the 1890s was a very exciting place where a plethora of innovations were welcome ranging from the new architecture of Louis Sullivan and Daniel Burnham to Marshall Field's consumer-pleasing department store. And women were showing the way. The Chicago Woman's League and the Illinois Woman's Alliance were in the forefront of progressive reforms. Hull House was the leading star in a growing settlement movement. The city was a center of militant trade unionism, some of whose leaders were women.[62] The Chicago Woman's Club, including among its members such social denizens as Bertha Palmer but also middle-class reformers like Frances Willard, was the motivating force behind several philanthropies, among them a legal aid service for the poor and an Industrial Art Association which provided Saturday vocational classes for working-class boys.[63] Now women were also to play a part in Chicago's new university.

No challenge was ever sweeter to Alice Freeman Palmer than her opportunity to help shape the University of Chicago. In a sense

Wellesley had been thrust upon her, as had been the dozen volunteer tasks she had since undertaken for women's education. Her earlier teaching positions were an economic necessity. But Chicago opened up a new range of opportunities. Women were to be appointed to the faculty, admitted to graduate school, awarded fellowships on equal terms with men, and all as part of a coeducational institution of major scale. When Chicago opened it had more than 120 people on its faculty, more than Johns Hopkins had students in its early years, and twice as many graduate students as undergraduates.[64] In 1894 nearly a quarter (25 out of 110) of the students registered for graduate study were women. In its first decade Chicago trained more women than any other institution.[65] Alice Palmer understood from the beginning the implications of Chicago for women in higher education and was aware of her role as expediter. If she was vigilant and persistent, women would be able to pursue the Ph.D. untrammeled by the petty restrictions of Harvard and Yale, they could hold teaching and re-search chairs on a prestigious graduate faculty, and they could help to open wide the doors for women. And her own instincts about the role she could play were constantly reinforced by the expectations of other women. Not all of Palmer's hopes were realized at Chicago, but she knew the opportunity was there.[66]

Alice Palmer's role at Chicago was very complex. She was much more than a dean of women. Her function was to act as what we would now call a vice-president or assistant president (she was called a dean), although one whose administrative responsibilities were somewhat limited because she was not always in residence. Harper consulted her about everything from faculty positions to the style of caps and gowns. She had much to say concerning the physical facili-ties at Chicago, especially dormitories and eating commons, and was a major contributor to the university's stance on student life. At first glance her contributions to institutional housekeeping seem to over-whelm her truly academic roles. However, she also served, as did the whole faculty, as an admissions evaluator. More importantly she was an arbiter of faculty appointments, an active participant in faculty meetings, a skillful controller of trustees, and a faithful solicitor of special funds, especially for women's concerns. In short she did everything (except teach) at Chicago that she had done at Wellesley with the added chore of manipulating Harper himself. At Wellesley she had been the president, now she had to carefully guide the president. Fortunately the president was eager for guidance. He hungered for her counsel, disliked her absences, and continued, long after George Palmer had made clear he would never leave Cambridge, to attempt to seduce him to Chicago so that Harper could have Alice full time.

The relationship between Harper and Palmer was complicated. She had his complete trust, certainly at the beginning. He confided in her as he may have in few other people. He depended on her and quite rightly felt he would have been hard-pressed to translate his elaborate academic dream into a functioning university community without her guidance and incredibly efficient hard work. He told her his own plans, was honest about financial matters, and heeded her advice in many substantive decisions. But he also saddled her with what he undoubtedly saw as essentially female chores. She ran all over Chicago finding bargains in linens for the dormitories, she trained cooks and housekeepers, she checked bathroom facilities. She bought the plates, the soup tureens, and the bed sheets for the University of Chicago. But if the university was to open and continue to operate these matters required attention. No university president today would hesitate for a moment to entrust these chores (seen as business matters) to a man. That is what the current vice president for financial affairs and his or her myriad bureaucrats are for. Men have done these tasks for countless institutions and not felt such jobs feminized them. Palmer wore the hats of at least three contemporary vice presidents: academic affairs, student affairs, and financial affairs, all rolled into one. Faculty appointments, graduate fellowships, student aid, and dormitory eating arrangements were all her concern.

Despite their long separations the lives of Alice and George Palmer continued to be closely interwoven. He asked her advice about candidates for Harvard's philosophy faculty and checked what she knew against his own information. Some of George's favorite students were placed in Chicago with Alice's help, and George provided a constant flow of information about Cambridge administrative practices. Her first letter home asked that he "send me the Harvard Calendar and some other Harvard documents showing the organization, resources, etc., and also the Wellesley statistics which you will find in the desk in the parlor."[67] Many such requests followed, and George always answered them promptly. But he also assisted Alice with such mundane matters as to see that the University of Chicago's china, bought in Boston, was delivered on time.

He seemed reconciled to being alone in Cambridge and basked in others' admiration of Alice. "Everybody warmly approves of your connection with Chicago."[68] However, he continued to complain about how her Chicago appointment was described in the university's publicity. "You have never accepted a position there for longer than a year; yet the implication is distinct that this is but the first year of a series.... You told them you were not competent for a Professor of History and could perform no such duties. But they think this title a good thing for them and do not hesitate to put you in a false position."[69] George could never accept any scholarly pretensions on Alice's part. She resisted being listed as a professor not because she felt incompetent, but because her interrupted periods of residence could not accommodate a teaching schedule.

Alice missed George and could not quite relinquish her vision of their joint career. She reported that both Harper and the senior professors frequently lamented: "If only Mr. Palmer were here he would know and have the power to bring it about." She added: "That is true, dear, and sometimes my heart cried out to take you one year—this troubled, struggling year—away from Harvard to shape this great, crude, eager life.... I only fumble at trying to do what you would have been expert at."[70] Harper proposed various devices such as a lecture series to attract George to Chicago at least for a few weeks, and during his vacations George did sometimes go to Chicago with Alice. Certainly he was more than generous with epistolary advice.

No doubt George Palmer's academic know-how contributed substantially to Alice Palmer's usefulness at Chicago. Her own administrative experience had been confined to an undergraduate residential women's college, but as George Palmer's wife, Alice had been exposed intimately to the inner workings of Harvard, everything from academic politics and power struggles to the new university emphasis on laboratories and advanced study. She personally knew almost every academician of any stature in the United States and some from abroad. She had entertained many of them in her home. They had to answer her letters and take her requests seriously. Wellesley and Harvard replaced the Michigan network she had relied on in the

1880s. Wellesley students came to Chicago for graduate work. Chicago-trained women like Edith Abbott were hired at Wellesley as faculty. Promising Harvard junior faculty launched their careers at Chicago.

5

Alice Palmer's most immediate task during the fall of 1892 was, as she saw it, "to produce decent results out of the most impossibly vulgar plans for [campus] life," to somehow create suitable and comfortable "arrangements for the life of a hundred young lady students," to replace what she saw as a "cheap and inadequate" scale of living as planned by Harper and the trustees.[71] And she performed this task superbly. After a few weeks the Beatrice was providing gracious quarters and food of sufficient quality that most of the faculty wanted to board there, and she managed this miracle without alienating either Harper or the trustees. Her strategy with Harper was to "tell him as little as I can, and take every bit of responsibility I dare to assume."[72] The trustees were forced to tour the Beatrice and view firsthand the squalid conditions fostered by their parsimony. Afterwards "there was a very serious hour" in her office when she "explained what I meant by suitable arrangements . . . everything inexpensive but exquisitely kept and in good taste."[73] And their wives were enlisted to aid in the improvements.

She shamelessly made use of every connection she had in both the Boston area and Chicago to expedite her plans for comfortable well-run dormitories. She had been in Chicago only a week when:

I went into the city in the morning after breakfast and bought linen and cutlery. Mrs. A. A. Sprague [wife of the partner of a major wholesale grocery firm] took me in her carriage [Palmer was to become a close friend of the whole Sprague family], and we asked merchants whom she knew to give the University what I needed. Mr. Barlett, at whose home we parted, promises to give the cutlery we need, and at Marshall Field's we got about a hundred dollars worth of linen for $40.00! Dr. Goodspeed [secretary of the board of trustees] is so pleased with the way I have been bamboozling furniture, etc., out of the merchants that he is like a summer morning, and I mean to paint the rooms out of the University money before I am through.[74]

This vignette is repeated many times in her letters. And this particular effort I have quoted here was only to make the temporary quarters at the Beatrice habitable.

At the same time she was planning the new dormitories, the first of which was to be ready in the spring. The day before Snell Hall opened in April, she wrote George: "Have gone all over Snell with the plasterers, carpenters, and plumbers still at work . . . I have seen the head janitor, the head plumber, and now have a talk with President Harper."[75] When she would return to Cambridge from Chicago she would check plans with knowledgeable people on the Harvard staff and enlisted the aid of Ellen Richards, MIT's pioneering professor of sanitary science with whom Talbot had trained, to plan the common kitchens that would feed all the residential students.[76]

But her main task, as she saw it, was not to set Chicago's campus style and living standards, although that was important to her, but to assure women an equal place in the university community. Her initial achievements were substantial. Eight women were on the first Chicago faculty and six of the forty-three graduate fellows in 1892–93 were women.[77] She lobbied Harper relentlessly for both women faculty and fellows. Almost as soon as she had accepted her appointment she wrote that "some splendidly equipped women are writing me about work for a Ph.D.," and mentioned Mary Calkins the psychologist whom Charles Eliot had prevented from being admitted as a formal candidate for a Ph.D. at Harvard and who was now on the Wellesley faculty.[78] Ten days later she was making a case for Alice E. Pratt and continuing to argue the importance of women Ph.D. candidates at Chicago.[79] Palmer herself and Talbot were, of course, the first female appointments to the faculty, but both Martha Foote Crowe (English) and Alice Bertha Foster (physical culture) were essentially Palmer's appointments.[80] In appointing women Chicago was far ahead of other universities of similar stature. Not until 1898 did the University of California get so much as a part-time woman physician as professor of hygiene, and she had to be funded privately by Regent Phoebe Hearst. With over a third of its students women, only one graduate fellowship was held by a woman.[81] Despite the fact that it had admitted women since 1870 and trained perhaps half the women faculty of the women's colleges, the University of Michigan did not acquire its first woman faculty member until 1896 when Eliza Mosher was appointed dean of women and professor of a nonexistent department of hygiene because no existing department would accept her.[82] Although women played a lesser role than she had hoped, Alice Palmer's relentless lobbying produced concrete results immediately at Chicago.

Palmer demanded academic excellence of the women she championed for the Chicago faculty. Martha Crowe proved invaluable in her role as residence hall manager and counselor but a failure in the English department. Palmer encouraged Harper to transfer her teaching duties, to Crowe's distress, from the university proper to the extension division.[83] Palmer respected and needed Crowe's administrative skills in the dormitories, and she would find a suitable place for her, but she would not pretend that Crowe met Chicago's high academic standards when the evidence pointed the other way. Excellence in the English department was more important than smooth-running women's residences.

But securing faculty appointments and fellowships for women was only part of Alice Palmer's vision for Chicago. Precisely how did Alice Freeman Palmer see her role in furthering the status of women at this new university? Palmer wrote many letters but few formal pieces, and letters are rarely careful expositions of position. Marion Talbot did write about her aims at Chicago. Certainly Palmer and Talbot shared many of the same goals, although Talbot had many more years of actively implementing them. Talbot defined what they were trying to do as liberty, equality, unity, and social responsibility, a vague, amorphous set of goals to be sure.[84] Although their ideas might differ from those of modern feminists, I am quite certain that equality was a goal that both women championed. Palmer's lobbying for women faculty and women's access to graduate fellowships fits under this rhetoric and never ceased as long as she had a platform at Chicago. She was responsible for the hiring of women as senior fellows in English and history in 1893.[85] She tried to hire the poet Harriet Monroe as at least an occasional lecturer in 1894.[86] Palmer also supported the Chicago club women who unsuccessfully agitated for representation on the board of trustees.[87] She was both incensed and amused when the Presbyterian Union gave a banquet to the

faculty and invited only the men.[88] Talbot and Palmer expected
women to perform in faculty governance and administration as the
equals of their male peers. They also espoused the hope that all
women on campus would be equal and opposed sororities among the
students as elitist and divisive.

Their concept of liberty is more difficult to understand. Both
women had experienced coeducation early in their lives without rules
and without special protection for women, Palmer at the University
of Michigan, Talbot at Boston University and MIT. Nonetheless at
Chicago they aimed to create a protective environment for women.
Their later experience in Wellesley's carefully nurtured College Hall
and cottages, where responsibility rather than liberty was the watch-
word, seemed to have shaped the way they envisioned women in a
university setting. Chicago approached its women students in the
protective manner of the eastern women's colleges rather than the
free benign neglect that midwestern state universities employed when
women first joined their student bodies. But this protective atmosphere was to be administered and enforced through self-government in which the whole community of women undergraduates,
graduates, and faculty was to participate, rather than imposed from
above. For example, strongly as Palmer felt about sororities she endeavored to persuade the students of her point of view rather than
make an arbitrary ruling. She fought successfully with Harper when
the university opened in 1892 to ward off a tangle of petty meddlesome rules designed to regulate social intercourse between men and
women students. He wanted no coeducational rooming houses, no
male students or unmarried instructors taking meals at the Beatrice,
only purely official relations between instructors and their students.
Alice commented, "I don't think he knows what to make of such
sentiments as mine . . . he is good to me, and says, 'Have your way,'
and adds, 'you know, I can't help it.'"[89] And she had to fight repeatedly against inappropriate rules. Three years later Harper was proposing that students who marry be dismissed. She moaned to George,
"Oh dear!—the childishness."[90]

The house system of dormitory living was designed to implement
self-government and the sense of community as well as provide a
protective residential setting. In the early years, when women faculty
and graduate students almost invariably lived in the residence halls,
progress was made toward achieving this goal. It was the prospect of

developing this feeling of community that made all the tedious hours spent on housekeeping chores worthwhile. But the unity of a single women's community was not easily achieved. For one thing many Chicago students were commuters who lived at home and did not share in residence hall life. Palmer hoped to integrate non-resident students into the life of the campus through a Woman's Building for which she assiduously raised money throughout her Chicago tenure.[91] But it was a wish not realized during her Chicago years. The Chicago Women's Union was installed finally in Livingston Hall in 1904 and not until 1915 was a real women's building, Ida Noyes Hall, dedicated.[92]

Secondly, despite Palmer's and Talbot's attempts to avoid it, elitism and cliques were inevitable. In 1894 the possibility of sororities threatened the idea of a unitary, residence-based community of women at Chicago. Although Harper was opposed to fraternities, fearing they would exacerbate class differences and the early faculty agreed with him, fraternities were reluctantly permitted on campus in 1892 and eventually incorporated within the house system.[93]

Alice Palmer opposed secret societies from the beginning. Although fraternities did not control University of Michigan campus life when she was a student as they did by the 1890s, her Michigan experience, where the literary societies and Student Christian Association dominated the campus scene and fraternities were often disruptive, predisposed her against Greek societies. She wrote George more than once that she did not "want the boyish foolishness of it," but she also did not wish to begin by forbidding something.[94] In the end Harper took that decision out of her hands. Chicago had fraternities.

By 1894 women demanded similar club privileges. As Alice Palmer wrote George, "the girls have been stirred up to form 'sororities' . . . I want to prevent it, without forbidding it, and it takes time and strength."[95] Harper left this decision to Palmer and Talbot. Alice thought she won. She wrote ten days after the women had first requested sororities that "this morning our great anxiety is done away. The girls came in today to say they will not start sororities, and they seem intelligently to accept my reasons for not wishing it, as well as to very sweetly wish to follow my inclination."[96] National sororities never did find a place on campus, but secret "clubs" with all the trappings of sororities soon appeared. However, they did not possess their own houses and in that sense Palmer was successful.[97]

Social responsibility was another goal of Palmer and Talbot. From the beginning Harper had seen his university influencing public policy in the community and helping society achieve the reforms that would create a decent society for all. He had enthusiastically espoused the ideals of service and reform so dear to turn-of-the-century progressives. Major universities and their officers were quick to concern themselves with public questions in the 1890s. Palmer and Talbot saw women on the campuses as supplying much of the idealism that would make this concern effective. Women would set the tone of life and morals at Chicago.

Talbot undoubtedly had the broader social vision. Perhaps Alice Palmer had been overexposed to zealous reformism by her mother and father. In any case she often took a slightly amused view of "causes" and strong convictions (other than women's education). Palmer knew Jane Addams and was close to the reform-minded, public-spirited women of the Chicago Woman's Club, but her primary interaction with them was to secure money for her own purposes. However, as early as 1894 University of Chicago women were involved in settlement house work in the city's stockyard district. Jane Addams herself addressed the original committee of the Christian Union that initiated the project. Although a building was not erected for several years, five rooms were rented, five residents installed and additional professors and students assisted in the work.[98] Addams's connection to the university was close. She served on the university's extension staff, and at one time Hull House was used as one of the university's extension centers.[99] The Chicago uplift community and the university interacted constantly, but the interaction was not really of Palmer's doing. It was Talbot, not Palmer, who engaged in reform commitments that influenced the larger Chicago society.

However, if one credits Alice Palmer with being a major force in creating the opportunity for women to obtain specialized university training, she must have indirectly contributed to women's major reform role in the Progressive Era.[100] For example, at Wellesley Palmer at least passively facilitated the exploration of social movements by Vida Scudder, her close friend and colleague. She ensured the success of Scudder's Wellesley career, providing her with a secure base from which to expound her radical ideas and launch her settlement house schemes. Women were trained at Chicago in part because of Palmer. They were not only exposed to liberal professors like Albion Small, but also formed a tightly knit community of academic women who consistently contributed their expertise to the building of the early twentieth century's "better world." They also made use of their relationships with each other formed in this community that Alice Palmer had so consciously created.

Marion Talbot did participate in the interests and goals of these progressive reformers. But there is virtually no mention, for example, in Palmer's correspondence of the social upheaval in Chicago brought on by the Panic of 1893, the hordes of unemployed wandering the streets, the scores of homeless sleeping in the parks. The university community was not unconcerned. The Chicago Woman's Club was active in philanthropic work. Palmer played a key role in creating the setting that activated women's political and reform impulses, but she eschewed this route herself. Why? Perhaps her relationship to her parents provides the answer. She may have associated her father's deep political commitments with his tendency toward irresponsibility, and her mother's reform causes with her exhausting demands on Alice's time and energy. During much of Palmer's early life, politics represented a restless quest for change, and a strong drive for reform was associated with intolerable burdens thrust on her. Nonetheless her parents' legacy was not easily escaped. Palmer may have made fun of the suffragists and stayed clear of most reform causes, but she worked indefatigably to create an environment where women could make a social contribution.

Although Marion Talbot's social vision may have been more all-encompassing than Palmer's, Palmer nonetheless joined her in one radical vision, a campus where women were slightly more than equal. In a sense Palmer and Talbot were invoking the last vestiges of the nearly century-old spheres doctrine, that in a large area of life that involved nurturance and morals, women were better governors than men. Palmer demanded equality for women in faculty status and governance and in access to academic disciplines, but she wanted more than simple equality in the social sphere. Women were to set the tone, define the social patterns of campus life. Men's values, especially if they did not conform to the ideal, were to be subordinate to women's. Women had always aggressed in this sphere, and almost always men had fought back. Palmer and Talbot at Chicago pioneered in this concept of women's role on coeducational campuses. The concept was tried with less success at other coeducational universities. Sometimes it failed even to get a real hearing, as at Palmer's alma mater, the University of Michigan.

During Alice Palmer's tenure at Chicago, women's influence on campus was pervasive, reflecting the pervasiveness of her own influence and power. Social, if not academic, control of the campus was in the hands of women, but women also made their presence felt in the classroom, the faculty meeting, and the president's office. Alice Palmer's ideal of a women's community within a large university came very close to realization. Women flocked to educational institutions in unprecedented numbers. By the turn of the century so many women filled Chicago's classrooms that they threatened to overwhelm the men whom they already outnumbered in the junior college. Women received over 56 percent of the Phi Beta Kappa keys in 1902. Because women came so close to dominating the University of Chicago campus, a frightened Harper, with considerable male faculty support, proposed in late 1901 to limit their influence by confining them to segregated classes.[101] Palmer had long since departed the quadrangles and was to die before the end of 1902, but Marion Talbot led the opposition, which was sizable and vocal and included all the women faculty, staff, and students, several male faculty, like John Dewey, and a large group of alumnae. Women all over the United States responded with alarm and petitioned the trustees and Harper to desist. Nonetheless separation was adopted by the faculty in principle and partially implemented in some junior college classes for several years after 1903 before it was quietly allowed to die. Women were no longer a threat, men by that time greatly outnumbered women on campus and clearly controlled campus life.[102] It can be argued that the issue of separatism at Chicago was a direct reaction to Palmer and Talbot's success in putting women at the center of university life.[103] The measure of their success inevitably bred their failure. Many decades were to pass before women again occupied the position in Chicago's quadrangles that they had achieved during their first years.

Palmer also concerned herself with preventing two aspects of student life rampant at other universities from gaining a foothold on the Chicago campus: a sexist male milieu in which hazing and rowdyism could flourish and narrow evangelical sectarianism. And she expected a strong women's community to be the most effective means of negating these undesirable aspects of student life. She had Harper's full support in the first. The sometimes violent pranksterism that marred student life at most nineteenth-century colleges and universities never flourished at Chicago. For example, Harper refused to tolerate boisterous celebration of football victories.

Alice Palmer also met head-on any attempt at Chicago to introduce rowdy, sexist patterns. The first months after Chicago opened were probably too chaotic to provoke much undergraduate mischief, but by midwinter of 1893 normal adolescent rebelliousness and an understandable need for fun and games showed itself in the Chicago male undergraduate community. Palmer was not in residence when the first outbreak occurred, and Marion Talbot had to cope alone with only Alice's advice and sympathy to aid her. Palmer wondered why the men "can't wait when their main business should be study and when Chicago has no place for parties. In another year we'll show them what good times can be."[104] But the trouble did not subside, and when she returned in April she had to spend "every other minute over the trouble in Drexel—the undergraduate hall for men, where boorishness of every sort has been going on and a small knot of men going into vice. Two dozen of them came to the Snell Tuesday night and gave the girls a very rough serenade, and so I got my hands on them, and they will discover before I leave that bar-room behavior here must be put down."[105] She blamed the difficulty on Harper's failure to provide proctors for the men's residence halls. But she would not tolerate this kind of behavior. Essentially Harper agreed with her and made his own contributions to requiring an adult atmosphere on campus. But Alice saw herself as the real arbiter of "social and domestic matters" at the university and told Harper so.[106]

Harper had to be convinced of the dangers of narrow evangelical sectarianism. She fought that battle early in her Chicago career. The struggle focused on whether the Young Men's Christian Association should be permitted on campus. Both Alice and George, like many intellectuals in the 1890s, became increasingly liberal in religion and were adamant against the "Y." They saw it as narrow, bigoted, and antagonistic to the ecumenical, tolerant, eclectic Protestantism they espoused. For example in the 1890s, the YMCA could not tolerate Unitarians, a position that was anathema to the Palmers. To Alice "the rampant Y.M.C.A. man is wild lest 'skeptics' get any influence" on campus.[107] She and her friends, Professor Hale, Laughlin, and Judson, spent hours with Harper arguing the wisdom of a locally controlled non-sectarian student religious association such as the Student Christian Association she had known at Michigan and fostered at Wellesley. All four told Harper that they could not in conscience join a "Y," and he agreed that if "we could not conscientiously join it . . . the influence would be disastrous." She hoped "a spirit was introduced which may prevail."[108] And they did succeed in having a broadly-based Christian Union accepted.[109] Eventually Chicago did have a YMCA but it was always more liberal than most.

6

Although Alice Palmer may have seen her primary mission at Chicago as assuring full equality for women in the new university, she did not limit her concerns to issues of gender. For example, she played as active a role in choosing male faculty as she did in selecting women. One of her main concerns was building a strong English department dedicated to teaching writing to underclassmen. Chicago was not successful at attracting Harvard senior professors, but both the Palmers knew the young "comers" in Cambridge, still unrewarded and unknown but likely to acquire enviable reputations with time. Her first candidate was young Robert Herrick, their friend and protégé and a distant cousin of George. The English department was in the midst of a conflict over whether extension teachers should be used to instruct undergraduates in the university proper, a practice Alice strongly opposed. She began her campaign in February of 1893, argued her views strongly to Harper, and planned strategy with Palmer friends like William Hale and J. Laurence Laughlin who held the senior positions in the department. By April she had convinced Harper to offer Herrick an instructorship in rhetoric at a salary of $1,500 for the next academic year with the promise of an assistant professorship in two years if all went well. She herself was authorized to make this offer to Herrick.[110] Herrick, later a popular turn-of-the-century novelist, came to Chicago in the fall of 1893.

To further strengthen the English department, Alice Palmer played a major role in bringing Robert Morss Lovett to Chicago despite the fact that Harvard was actively trying to keep him.[111] In order to ensure Lovett's prompt appointment before Harvard could convince him to stay, she promised Harper that three friends of the university would guarantee his $1,200 salary at least for the first year. Although the trustees were not to know their identity, the three friends were Alice, George, and J. Laurence Laughlin. However, she hoped actually to raise the money elsewhere.[112] Lovett came to Chicago, funds were raised elsewhere, and the Palmer's usually strained exchequer remained intact.

Her efforts to control and strengthen the English department did not cease with these two crucial appointments. When another senior professor of English was to be appointed in the fall of 1894, she wrote Harper that it seemed impossible that George Lyman Kittridge could be lured to Chicago, and of the other candidates she believed Francis Gummere of Haverford would be "a better man for us, altogether the strongest in the country [of those] who could be moved, more balanced than Cook of Yale, a man of thorough scientific training who has kept his charm as a teacher."[113]

She also politely but firmly vetoed the appointment of her Cambridge neighbor, Arthur Gilman, to the history faculty, writing Harper, "It would never have occurred to me to think of him as a candidate for any professorship," and negatively assessing his qualifications. "Many know far more of American history than he does."[114]

Along with faculty appointments Alice Freeman Palmer's fine hand appeared in other major academic policy decisions. She was involved in the planning for graduate study and used George's knowledge of Harvard's graduate department to help shape the one at Chicago. George shared private departmental communications with her to assist in the planning.[115] She worked hard to achieve full faculty governance of the university and spent hours with Harper and key faculty members before the crucial faculty meeting in February of 1893 when standing committees were to be appointed with authority over admissions, fellowships, honors, and advanced standing.[116] It was difficult for Harper to share formal power, and he preferred to settle controversial issues with a fait accompli by making a speech announcing a policy, but Alice did her best to convince him of the necessity for permitting the faculty to play a part in decision-making. Harper was not always tractable. It took much hard work to convince him to appoint Lovett. They disagreed on money-raising for the Student Fund Society.[117] But she continued to give him advice, whether he wanted it or not.

Her wide acquaintance in academic circles meant that she was privy to all academic gossip. She reported to Harper, but also refuted, charges that the "Chicago faculty were materialists, agnostics, godless men in great numbers."[118] When the Panic of 1893 resulted in a severe cash shortage for the university that left no money to pay some ten faculty salaries including Alice's, rumors became rampant in the East that the new university was doomed and would have to close its doors.[119] She discussed the rumors with Harper and told him he should make a statement at convocation to counteract the damaging effects. Harper did, but failed to do it to her satisfaction.[120]

Although they did not always agree Harper continued to confide in Palmer and make her one of his major consultants during her first two years at Chicago. When he conceived his plan of bringing E. Benjamin Andrews, president of Brown University, to serve as a resident president or co-president at Chicago for six months of each year while Harper was away raising money, Alice was his primary confidant. Andrews was also to serve as dean of the graduate school and head of the philosophy department. She wrote George: "you can imagine what difficulties I foresee and how anxious I am. As far as I know no one knows it but me."[121] Actually when the appointment became known the faculty were much upset. The senate reprimanded Harper for presenting them with an accomplished fact, an appointment made. Alice agreed with them that the faculty should have been consulted, but supported Harper, believing "this is as good as any arrangement that could be made."[122] Andrews's tenure was short-lived, and Alice's friend Harry Judson eventually took over his duties and became Harper's successor.

Another administrative area in which Palmer worked tirelessly was money-raising. She seems to have been somewhat more successful than she had been at Wellesley. Much of this fund-raising focused on a women's building and student aid funds, but she did not confine her efforts to money for women's activities. For example, she also found donors to fund Robert Morss Lovett's original salary. Her money-raising efforts with the Chicago Woman's Club were particularly successful. During 1892 and 1893 they were responsible for raising more than a million dollars for women students.[123] Palmer attended their every meeting when she was in the city, sometimes with less than satisfactory results, as in the fall of 1894 when she went to the opening meeting of the season, and "as I feared, the Chairman and Secretary of the Committee simply did nothing."[124] The student aid fund-raising had not been started. She constantly chased after Bertha Palmer, wife of hotel baron Potter Palmer, luring her to the campus, dining at the Palmer mansion, writing her many letters, and eliciting many promises but with few concrete results.[125] Sometimes her efforts bordered on the frenetic.

> Monday the Committee on the Building, Tuesday the Loan Fund at Mrs. Wilmarth's . . . Mrs. Ela invited north side ladies to hear me tell about the Woman's Building Thursday at 1:30, and Mrs. Sprague Friday. Yesterday I went to the Fortnightly Club . . . and saw scores of women several of whom I got a chance to ask to help, and they promised to talk to their husbands and to tell their friends. Two ladies subscribed $100 each on the spot. . . . I feel like a pick pocket. . . . However I shut my teeth and go ahead.[126]

Nor were her efforts confined to her Chicago sojourns. She and Marion Talbot called on a Beecher niece in Massachusetts during the summer holidays of 1893 hoping for a gift toward Beecher Hall, a new woman's dormitory.[127]

Whether in Chicago, at home in Cambridge, or on the road (for Alice Palmer frequently combined speaking trips and visits to her family with her Chicago stays), she had the university on her mind, and she was at work promoting its interests in one way or another. When she was not in Chicago she wrote frequently to Talbot and Harper and occasionally to Laughlin, Hale, and other close friends. After Robert Herrick joined the faculty in 1893, he was her constant informant, sometimes messenger, and occasional confidant. She read the Chicago newspapers when away to help keep informed. When she returned to Cambridge after nearly six weeks in Chicago in the fall of 1892, she wrote Marion Talbot that when Talbot's letters came her inclination was to start back immediately to Chicago herself.[128] Talbot received detailed almost daily instructions on personnel and dormitory matters. Palmer's correspondence with Harper during 1892–93 shows how hard it was for her to entrust the crucial decisions of those early months to others and how she longed to be in Chicago attending to problems herself. "I long to be in the midst of it," she lamented. "At least give me more to do for you."[129]

7

During those years Alice Palmer was indeed a busy lady. Her Wellesley responsibilities did not cease. She continued as an active member of the State Board of Education. She had other Cambridge obligations including a husband whose family lived nearby, and two homes, one of which had just become the Palmers' Cambridge residence. She was also a member of the Lady Board of Managers of the Columbian Exposition of 1893. George and Wellesley were the most demanding.

She could not abandon Wellesley. She was still both a trustee and a member of the executive committee. She did not consider relinquishing either post. Her interventions were probably less frequent, but she struggled to make board meetings. Eben Horsford's death in 1893 did not make things easier. She had lost a powerful surrogate who kept an eye on Wellesley affairs. As commencement approached in 1893 she was busy winding up the academic year in Chicago. She wrote George, "I must of course go to Wellesley for the Trustees' meeting next Tuesday morning, and that means Commencement in the afternoon and no way of reaching Boxford that night. . . . I wish you could go over for the public exercises. They are so unhappy, and feel so sore at my 'leaving them to raise money for the Annex, and to spend my time in Chicago' that I long to either go or have you there."[130] A number of major policy decisions were made at Wellesley during those years. It is surprising because of the strong stand she took on sororities at Chicago, but she seems to have participated minimally in the decision to allow society houses on the Wellesley campus.[131] Bible study was further curtailed in 1893, but Palmer was not present at the meeting.[132] The Academic Council received formal recognition by the trustees in 1894 and Palmer played an active role.[133] Helen Shafer, her successor, was often ill and died early in 1894. Again Alice Palmer was deeply concerned in the problem of finding a new president. Fortunately Palmer was in Cambridge for the many crucial meetings in January and February, and the board finally settled on one of Alice Freeman's recruits when she was president, Julia Irvine, a classical scholar who had trained in Leipsig.[134] Irvine consulted Palmer frequently on policy.[135]

Midway through her second year at Chicago the Palmers moved into the house on Quincy Street that was to remain their home for the rest of their lives. Alice's larger income undoubtedly helped make this move possible. Fortunately, George as usual attended to the details of an extensive remodeling and the move itself. However, Alice's family continued to make demands. Her father appeared unannounced in Chicago during the hectic opening week of the fall term in 1893. Of course, he wanted to see the fair and expected her to show it to him. Her always helpful friends, the Spragues, took him in. Alice tried to find a little time for him.[136] George's family gathered at the Palmers for Thanksgiving.[137] George's older brother Julius was dying and needed additional succor. She accompanied George to the concert and drama series in Cambridge.

The World's Fair continued to demand some of her attention although her responsibilities had peaked earlier, and she had severed her official ties as a Lady Manager when she accepted the Chicago job. Although George was crushed that it kept her away from Cambridge for a few extra days, she participated in the opening ceremonies in October of 1892. She participated in all the festivities, sat on all the platforms.[138] It was a great moment, 150,000 people under one roof, "grand bands playing the Star Spangled Banner, everybody is shouting wildly. . . . It is so superb that my heart is in my throat."[139] Alice loved pageants. But there was World's Fair business too. Space for education was below that allotted in 1876, and she enlisted President Harper's help in getting it increased.[140] The pageantry thrilled her but she was keenly aware of the exposition's importance to women—enlarging their outlook and "proving they could organize independently toward a complex end."[141]

With this kind of schedule of responsibilities, it is no wonder Alice Palmer got sick. Halfway through her first year a severe cold put her to bed at the Beatrice for a week, but she worked on, receiving a succession of callers with whom she dealt with everything from dormitory charges to faculty appointments.[142] In an attempt to better protect her time she stayed with the Otho Spragues the next year, but again illness harassed her. In addition to her usual colds, she developed hemorrhoids. As she often did, she looked to her old classmate Eliza Mosher for help. Probably Mosher operated on her in November in New York.[143] Although Mosher's treatment did not eliminate the problem permanently, she seemed to get relief. A wicked tooth tormented her in the fall of 1894, but her first serious illness in several years struck her in the spring of 1894. She returned to Cambridge in May seriously ill after a Herculean fund-raising marathon that left her completely exhausted. One of her severe colds developed into peritonitis and in mid-June, a month later, although she was out of danger, she was still too weak to sit up for more than brief periods. Harper had been told she was ill and unable to travel. Nonetheless she saw him as angry that she did not return to Chicago and the money-raising circuit. She wrote plaintively to Laurence Laughlin that the women's committee to raise money for a women's building did not respond to her letters. Could he get information for her, had any money been raised?[144] Her interest in women and Chicago did not flag, but once more her body was telling her she had done enough.

However, halfway through her second year of commuting Alice Palmer's enthusiasm for Chicago's new academic challenge began to wane slightly. Harper, mercurial, impetuous, and sometimes petty, was not the easiest person with whom to get along. He was beginning to rely on Palmer less as his academic enterprise was more solidly underway and increasingly used her as a convenient handmaiden rather than as a trusted advisor. He consulted her less and less about academic appointments and university policy. He continued to draw on her talents as an administrator of residential institutions (and she was less and less interested in housekeeping), but essentially he converted her into a fund-raiser. Finding donors had never been one of her Wellesley successes. She tried hard for Chicago with some success, but the job only made her sick and reactivated all her old physical weaknesses: the debilitating colds, the cough, the fatigue. Cambridge and the Quincy Street house began to beckon alluringly.

When Palmer returned to Chicago after Christmas in January of 1894 she found President Harper furious because she had recommended Elizabeth Wallace, a Chicago instructor, for a position at Knox College. Harper thought her "disloyal." She in turn was critical of Harper because everything was in the hands of a few with "the sad results of centralization."[145] George suggested she discuss with Harper ending her connection with Chicago at the end of that year.[146] But what he really had in mind was only a ploy to stimulate Harper's positive assessment of Alice. It was that spring that Palmer was offered the supervisorship of the Boston Board of Education. She considered it seriously, but George was negative. "I have never supposed that place could compare in power and dignity of work with the one you have now." He argued further, "I do not know an occupation for you which presents so little hardship as this . . . I do not want you to sit about the house at the absolute mercy of committees, callers and alpaca women. . . . Don't give up a place which offers tolerably good work until you see your way to something better."[147] About that time Harry P. Judson, an old friend and ally, was made dean of the graduate school at Chicago instead of Andrews, and Judson was someone with whom Palmer had always worked easily. Faculty governance in policy matters was again in the ascendency. She had agreed to stay at Chicago for another year, but it would be her last.[148] In May she so advised Harper, although she did not formally resign until December, effective the end of the academic year.[149] Harper forwarded her resignation to the board of trustees but took no personal notice of it. He greeted it with absolute silence. This was the unkindest cut of all.

Palmer was convinced that Harper no longer wanted her at Chicago, that she was too quick to organize faculty against schemes of his which she opposed. She always favored faculty over administrative decisions at Chicago. Also she fought him bitterly over Wallace's release which he opposed to the end.[150] Palmer felt "the value and influence of work such as mine here, coming and going as I do, depends very much upon mutual confidence between the president and myself."[151] Confidence in Harper she could no longer feel, and she believed this lack to be mutual. Nonetheless she wrote Harper an affectionate note as she sailed for Europe in August and a congratulatory letter from Paris when the university received a new Rockefeller gift.[152] With time the bitter memories faded. She remembered instead the exultant sense of creation that marked Chicago's early months. She wrote Laurence Laughlin: "Here I sit and the buildings of old Harvard vanish, and turn into the new University a thousand miles away. And I live it all over again, even the old Beatrice days . . . and laugh over the toothpicks, and faculty meetings, and all the rest of the mad, merry, desperate, friendly time."[153]

Alice Palmer had one more formal relationship with Chicago. She was invited to make a major address at the dicennial celebration in 1901 and participate in the dedication of Foster Hall.[154] Harper's invitation came very late, barely five weeks before the event. She was insulted at its tardiness. Her busy schedule was already set. She at

Alice Palmer in the formal portrait made for the
University of Chicago's dicennial celebration.
(Courtesy of Wellesley College Archives.)

first refused and then shuffled her many June speaking engagements to accept. She wanted the accolades and she cared about Chicago. She sat on the platform with Harper and John D. Rockefeller. Rockefeller, whom she had never met, grasped both her hands and thanked her for what she had done.[155] The occasion was bittersweet. Harper did not use the occasion to confer on her the honorary LL.D. that was appropriate. Nor did the University of Michigan a few days later where she went to speak and participate in the twenty-fifth anniversary of her class. Neither of the universities that meant the most to her saw fit to give her what George knew she most wanted. By this time she had several LL.D. degrees, but honors from Chicago and Michigan would have capped her career.

What honors Chicago chose to bestow came after her death and that of President Harper. A campanile in her memory was dedicated on the University of Chicago campus in 1908. Her neighbor Charles Eliot wrote on that occasion, "I have never known a woman who better deserved to have her name and work recalled at a seat of learning in insistent and serviceable harmonies."[156] Alice Palmer would have liked those adjectives. She saw herself as both serviceable and insistent and as untiring as a set of bells.

What did Alice Palmer give to the infant University of Chicago? Her friend, William Gardner Hale, thought he summarized her contribution at her memorial service. First of all, he said, her name—she was known. In 1892 the University of Chicago was not. That is only partly true. Second, she "established the standards of refined and hospitable living which still prevail," a worthy goal that she certainly aspired to; third, she collected and institutionalized the interest-free student loan fund which enabled many impecunious students to attend the university.[157] Hale was Palmer's friend. He had often followed her guidance when both were on campus, but he had forgotten Palmer's most important contributions: insistence on an equal place for women at all university levels, her fight for faculty governance against an arbitrary administration, for self-governing student life free of petty rules.

Alice Palmer's influence and performance during the University of Chicago's early years is impressive. Until very recently few women have exerted the kind of power that she exercised over academic policy decisions of fundamental importance. Undoubtedly she thought she had made a breakthrough, that women henceforth would be privy to the highest councils of academia, equal to men in shaping American universities. Actually she was participating in a fluke of history. Personality in juxtaposition with opportunity had provided her a unique occasion. She was an experienced, knowledgeable administrator with a dozen hands-on skills useful to a president beleaguered with problems. William Rainey Harper needed Alice Freeman Palmer's talent for solving practical affairs and her ability to make decisions expeditiously. In a modest way Alice Palmer did provide women with a stronger place in coeducational universities in the 1890s, but that foothold proved ephemeral and it was not until the 1970s that her hopes were realized. Chicago women like Marion Talbot and Elizabeth Wallace had a toehold and by persistent vigilance parlayed the toehold into a permanent place for women in the university, but hardly more than their sisters were able to secure in other institutions (especially state universities) which had not benefited by the pioneering zeal of Alice Palmer.

Alice Palmer was full of energy, willing to expedite practical problems, well connected in the academic establishment, and basically free economically of the job she had undertaken. All this gave her true independence from academic bureaucracy and free rein for her practical, eclectic way of approaching problems, but it did not provide women with a pattern for subduing male bastions of power. She herself experienced the negative implications of her approach as Chicago and Harper became more confident and needed her less. The great expectations to which she had responded in 1892, her own expectations and those of the women who had urged her to encompass their destiny, did not come to pass. Women neither took their places with men as scholars and scientists and academic administrators, nor did they control the social spaces of campuses, set the style, as Alice would have had it, or establish higher behavioral standards than those at male universities. Her goal would have made universities not only exemplary oases of scholarship but incubators of progressive reforms and bastions of a new morality. She failed. Perhaps knowing intuitively that she had failed, she gradually withdrew into Cambridge's safe, still waters, where she was who she was—an educator valued, respected, and loved, and George Palmer's equally respected wife—and lived out her short life as a mover rather than a shaker.

NOTES

1. Richard J. Storr, *Harper's University: The Beginnings* (Chicago: University of Chicago Press, 1966), is still the best account of Chicago's early days.

2. Darnell Rucker, *The Chicago Pragmatists* (Minneapolis: University of Minnesota Press, 1969), 14–15.

3. See ibid., 16; and Rosenberg, *Beyond Separate Spheres*, 1. For a critical and analytical contemporary account of the Chicago experiment, see the *Nation*, 55 (September 22, 1892): 216–17.

4. Alice Freeman Palmer to J. Laurence Laughlin, December 21, 1892.

5. W. Carson Ryan, *Studies in Early Graduate Education* (New York: Arno Press, 1971), 93–115.

6. Storr, *Harper's University*, 211. The University of Chicago's outreach was not bound by class or social status. Hilda Polacheck, a bright Polish immigrant who worked in a shirt factory attended for one term in 1904 on a scholarship arranged by Jane Addams (Hilda Satt Polacheck, *I Came a Stranger: The Story of a Hull House Girl*, ed. Dena Polacheck Epstein [Urbana: University of Illinois Press, 1989], 86).

7. Alice Freeman Palmer to George Herbert Palmer, January 18, 1892. Wellesley Typescripts.

8. Diary, March 12, 1892. Alice Freeman Palmer to Marion Talbot. Marion Talbot Papers, University of Chicago Archives. Two women, Elsa Lovina Ames and Ellen Louise Lowell, were on the faculty of Stanford University when it opened in 1891, but both were in junior positions. One taught drawing and the other physical education (Orrin L. Elliott, *Stanford University: The First Twenty-Five Years* [Stanford: Stanford University Press, 1937]), 61–63). However, the next year Mary Sheldon Barnes, a University of Michigan graduate who taught at Wellesley in the 1870s, became assistant professor of history at Stanford and taught and published there until 1897. She had come to Stanford without an appointment the previous year with her husband Earl Barnes, head of the department of education. (Robert E. Keohane, "Mary Sheldon Barnes," in Edward T. James, ed., *Notable American Women, 1607–1950* [Cambridge: Harvard University Press, 1971], 1:92–93.) The Barneses were certainly an academic couple, sometimes publishing together, but they were not hired together. It was his career, not hers, that sparked Stanford's interest and brought them there.

9. Diary, February 29, 1892.

10. Alice Freeman Palmer to George Herbert Palmer, April 11, 1892. Wellesley Typescripts.

11. Ibid.

12. Alice Freeman Palmer to George Herbert Palmer, April 22, 1892. Wellesley Typescripts.

13. Alice Freeman Palmer to George Herbert Palmer, April 29, 1892. Wellesley Typescripts.

14. Alice Freeman Palmer to George Herbert Palmer, April 22, 1892. Wellesley Typescripts.

15. Alice Freeman Palmer to George Herbert Palmer, April 26, 1892. Wellesley Typescripts.

16. Alice Freeman Palmer to Marion Talbot, March 16, 1892. Marion Talbot Papers, University of Chicago Archives.

17. Ibid.

18. See Rosenberg, *Beyond Separate Spheres,* 30–31.

19. Alice Freeman Palmer to George Herbert Palmer, April 26, 1892. Wellesley Typescripts.

20. Alice Freeman Palmer to George Herbert Palmer, April 22, 1892. Wellesley Typescripts.

21. Alice Freeman Palmer to George Herbert Palmer, April 30, 1889. Wellesley Typescripts.

22. Alice Freeman Palmer to George Herbert Palmer, April 30, 1892. Wellesley Typescripts.

23. George Herbert Palmer to Alice Freeman Palmer, April 17, 1892; Alice Freeman Palmer to George Herbert Palmer, April 22, 1892. Wellesley Typescripts.

24. George Herbert Palmer to Alice Freeman Palmer, April 14, 1892. Wellesley Typescripts.

25. George Herbert Palmer to Alice Freeman Palmer, April 16, 1892. Wellesley Typescripts.

26. George Herbert Palmer to Alice Freeman Palmer, April 19, 1892. Wellesley Typescripts.

27. George Herbert Palmer to Alice Freeman Palmer, April 17, 1892. Wellesley Typescripts.

28. George Herbert Palmer to Alice Freeman Palmer, April 24, 1892. Wellesley Typescripts.

29. Rucker, *Chicago Pragmatists,* 10–11; Storr, *Harper's University,* 18, 43.

30. George Herbert Palmer to Alice Freeman Palmer, April 24, 1892. Wellesley Typescripts.

31. Ibid.

32. Ibid.

33. George Herbert Palmer to Alice Freeman Palmer, April 29, 1892. Wellesley Typescripts.

34. Alice Freeman Palmer to George Herbert Palmer, April 29, 1892. Wellesley Typescripts.

35. George Herbert Palmer to William Rainey Harper, May 5, 1892. Harper Papers.

36. George Herbert Palmer's brief account in his *Life* of the Chicago offer and Alice's reaction to it is almost pure fiction. He wrote that she was "from the first against accepting the calls" because "she loved her home" and thought his roots "were too deep in Harvard soil for removal to be quite honorable" (Palmer, *Life,* 233).

37. Alice Freeman Palmer to William Rainey Harper, May 28, 1892. Harper Papers.

38. Alice Freeman Palmer to William Rainey Harper, June 25, 1892. Harper Papers.

39. Alice Freeman Palmer to William Rainey Harper, July 6, 1892. Harper Papers.

40. Alice Freeman Palmer to William Rainey Harper, July 16, 1892. Harper Papers.

41. Ibid.

42. Ibid.

43. Palmer, *Life*, 242–45.

44. Alice Freeman Palmer to William Rainey Harper, August 13, 1892. Harper Papers.

45. Alice Freeman Palmer to William Rainey Harper, August 22, 1892, Harper Papers; and Correspondence of Marion Talbot and Alice Freeman Palmer, 1892. University of Chicago Archives.

46. See Marion Talbot, *More than Lore: The Reminiscences of Marion Talbot* (Chicago: University of Chicago Press, 1936); Geraldine Joncich Clifford, *Lone Voyagers: Academic Women in Coeducational Universities, 1870–1937* (New York: Feminist Press, 1989); and Correspondence of Alice Freeman Palmer and Marion Talbot, Wellesley College Archives and University of Chicago Archives.

47. Alice Freeman Palmer to Marion Talbot, July 5, 1892. Marion Talbot Papers, University of Chicago Archives.

48. Alice Freeman Palmer to William Rainey Harper, August 6, 1892. Harper Papers.

49. See Virginia Kemp Fish, "'More than Lore': Marion Talbot and Her Role in the Founding Years of the University of Chicago," *International Journal of Women's Studies* 8 (May/June 1985): 228–49; Rosalind Rosenberg in Faragher and Howe, *Women and Higher Education*, 119–20.

50. Gordon, *Higher Education*, 35.

51. Fish, "More than Lore," 234.

52. Alice Freeman Palmer to Marion Talbot, May 23, 1893. Marion Talbot Papers, University of Chicago Archives; Alice Freeman Palmer to William Rainey Harper, May 23, 1893. Harper Papers.

53. Talbot, *More than Lore*, 6.

54. Ibid., chap. 2.

55. Ibid., chap. 6.

56. Alice Freeman Palmer to George Herbert Palmer, September 25, 1892. Wellesley Typescripts.

57. Ibid.; Talbot, *More than Lore*, chap. 6.

58. Alice Freeman Palmer to George Herbert Palmer, September 22, 1892. Wellesley Typescripts.

59. Alice Freeman Palmer to George Herbert Palmer, September 20, 27, 1892. Wellesley Typescripts.

60. George Herbert Palmer to Alice Freeman Palmer, September 23, 1892. Wellesley Typescripts.

61. For a discussion of Chicago's women's network in the 1890s see Bordin, *Frances Willard*, 149–52.

62. Mary Jo Buhle, *Women and American Socialism, 1870–1920* (Urbana: University of Illinois Press, 1981), 71– 73; Louise C. Wade, *Graham Taylor: Pioneer for Social Justice, 1851–1930* (Chicago: University of Chicago Press, 1964) chap. 3; and David F. Burg, *Chicago's White City of 1893* (Lexington: University Press of Kentucky, 1976), chap. 4 all contain good accounts of the Chicago ambience in the 1890s.

63. Lena Ruegamer, "Chicago Women Reformers, 1863–1893: The Development of an Elite Network." Paper presented at the Conference on Female Spheres, New Harmony, Indiana, October 1981.

64. See Ryan, *Early Graduate Education*, 119–20.

65. Ellen Fitzpatrick, *Endless Crusade: Women Social Scientists and Progressive Reform* (New York: Oxford University Press, 1990), 29–30; Rosenberg, "Academic Prism," 326; Catherine Clinton, *The Other Civil War: American Women in the Nineteenth Century* (New York: Hill and Wang, 1984), 138.

66. Chicago's promise to open up all of academia to women was better than its performance. Of the nine women who received Ph.D.'s in the social sciences in its first decade and a half not one received an appointment at a coeducational university while two-thirds of the males did, and the percentage of males on the Chicago faculty steadily increased rather than decreased (Fitzpatrick, *Endless Crusade*, 72–73).

67. Alice Freeman Palmer to George Herbert Palmer, September 20, 1892. Wellesley Typescripts.

68. George Herbert Palmer to Alice Freeman Palmer, October 19, 1892. Wellesley Typescripts.

69. George Herbert Palmer to Alice Freeman Palmer, September 25, 1893. Wellesley Typescripts.

70. Alice Freeman Palmer to George Herbert Palmer, October 21, 1892. Wellesley Typescripts.

71. Alice Freeman Palmer to George Herbert Palmer, September 25, 1892. Wellesley Typescripts.

72. Ibid.

73. Alice Freeman Palmer to George Herbert Palmer, September 27, 29, 1892. Wellesley Typescripts.

74. Alice Freeman Palmer to George Herbert Palmer, September 26, 1893. Wellesley Typescripts.

75. Alice Freeman Palmer to George Herbert Palmer, April 14, 1893. Wellesley Typescripts.

76. Alice Freeman Palmer to William Rainey Harper, March 16, 1893. Harper Papers.

77. Gordon, *Higher Education*, 87–88. Gordon's book is the first major study of the role of women at the University of Chicago and the pioneering role played by Palmer and Talbot. Interestingly, more attention previously has been paid by historians of women's education to Alice Freeman Palmer's

career at Wellesley than to her truly pioneering work at the University of Chicago.

78. George Herbert Palmer to Alice Freeman Palmer, June 3, 1890. Wellesley Typescripts, Alice Freeman Palmer to William Rainey Harper, August 13, 1892. Harper Papers.

79. Alice Freeman Palmer to William Rainey Harper, August 24, 1892. Harper Papers.

80. Alice Freeman Palmer to William Rainey Harper, Fall 1892. Harper Papers. Gordon, *Higher Education*, 87.

81. Gordon, *Higher Education*, 58–62; Rosenberg, *Beyond Separate Spheres* stresses the importance of women's access to graduate work at Chicago, chap. 3.

82. Peckham, *The Making of the University of Michigan*, 94.

83. Alice Freeman Palmer to William Rainey Harper, May 1, 23, 1893. Harper Papers.

84. Talbot, *More than Lore*, 90.

85. Alice Freeman Palmer to George Herbert Palmer, June 13, 1893. Wellesley Typescripts.

86. Alice Freeman Palmer to William Rainey Harper, November 30, 1894. Harper Papers.

87. Alice Freeman Palmer to George Herbert Palmer, September 20, 1892. Wellesley Typescripts.

88. Alice Freeman Palmer to George Herbert Palmer, October 12, 1892. Wellesley Typescripts.

89. Alice Freeman Palmer to George Herbert Palmer, October 10, 1892. Wellesley Typescripts.

90. Alice Freeman Palmer to George Herbert Palmer, January 15, 1895. Wellesley Typescripts.

91. Alice Freeman Palmer to George Herbert Palmer, April 18, 1893; October 6, 18, 23, 1894. Wellesley Typescripts.

92. Gordon, *Higher Education*, 98–99.

93. Storr, *Harper's University*, 168–70; Thomas Wakefield Goodspeed, *A History of the University of Chicago: The First Quarter Century* (Chicago: University of Chicago Press, 1972), 252–53.

94. Alice Freeman Palmer to George Herbert Palmer, October 2, 10, 11, 1892. Wellesley Typescripts.

95. Alice Freeman Palmer to George Herbert Palmer, October 9, 1894. Wellesley Typescripts.

96. Alice Freeman Palmer to George Herbert Palmer, October 18, 1984. Wellesley Typescripts.

97. Gordon, *Higher Education*, 105–6.

98. Goodspeed, *University of Chicago*, 447–48; Steven J. Diner, *A City and Its Universities: Public Policy in Chicago, 1892–1919* (Chapel Hill: University of North Carolina Press, 1980), 123ff.

99. Jane Addams, *Twenty Years at Hull House* (New York: New American Library, 1961), 108.

100. For a discussion of the role played in progressive reform by University of Chicago women see Dorothy Brown, *Setting A Course: American Women in the 1920s* (Boston: Twayne, 1987), 34–5; and especially Ellen Fitzpatrick, *Endless Crusade*, chap. 3.

101. Gordon, *Higher Education*, 112–20. Charles Van Hise, president of the University of Wisconsin, also favored sex segregation. Leland Stanford's founding grant had stipulated that the trustees provide equal advantages to men and women, and Mrs. Stanford was especially welcoming to them. But the increasing percentage of women among the students was soon perceived as a threat not only by Stanford men but also by Mrs. Stanford who herself stipulated a quota of 500 by charter amendment (Elliott, *Stanford University*, 132). By 1907 women outnumbered men in seven of the thirteen state university colleges of arts and sciences. Men feared the so-called "culture" courses like literature would become the preserve of women and drive out the men (Geraldine Clifford in Faragher and Howe, *Higher Education*, 169). See Rosenberg, *Beyond Separate Spheres*, 43–45 for a discussion of the fear of feminization at coeducational universities.

102. Goodspeed, *University of Chicago*, 405–8; Talbot, *More than Lore*, chap. 10; Gordon, *Higher Education*, 112–20.

103. Gordon, *Higher Education*, 190.

104. Alice Freeman Palmer to Marion Talbot, February 26, 1893. Marion Talbot Papers. University of Chicago Archives.

105. Alice Freeman Palmer to George Herbert Palmer, April 20, 1893. Wellesley Typescripts.

106. Alice Freeman Palmer to George Herbert Palmer, February 14, 1893. Wellesley Typescripts.

107. Alice Freeman Palmer to George Herbert Palmer, October 21, 1892. Wellesley Typescripts.

108. Alice Freeman Palmer to George Herbert Palmer, October 11, 1892. Wellesley Typescripts.

109. The tolerance of the Christian Union is documented in a student memoir "First Impressions of the University of Chicago" by Madelin Wallin (Madelin Wallin Papers, University of Chicago Archives), who arrived on campus in 1893.

110. Alice Freeman Palmer to George Herbert Palmer, February 14, April 14, 18, 20, 1893. Wellesley Typescripts. Alice Freeman Palmer to Robert Herrick, June 8, 1892. Robert Herrick Papers, University of Chicago Archives.

111. Alice Freeman Palmer to William Rainey Harper, May 3, 1893. Harper Papers.

112. Alice Freeman Palmer to J. Laurence Laughlin, August 31, 1893.

113. Alice Freeman Palmer to William Rainey Harper, November 3, 1894. Harper Papers. Gummere, a long respected scholar, stayed at Haverford despite many attractive offers. Interestingly he was the one man M. Carey Thomas might have married (Dobkin, *Making of a Feminist*, 129).

114. Alice Freeman Palmer to William Rainey Harper, March 16, 1893. Harper Papers.

115. Alice Freeman Palmer to George Herbert Palmer, April 20, 1893. Wellesley Typescripts.

116. Alice Freeman Palmer to George Herbert Palmer, February 2, 10, 1893. Wellesley Typescripts.

117. Alice Freeman Palmer to George Herbert Palmer, June 19, 1893. Wellesley Typescripts.

118. Alice Freeman Palmer to William Rainey Harper, May 1, 1893. Harper Papers.

119. George Herbert Palmer to Alice Freeman Palmer, September 25, 1893. Wellesley Typescripts. Storr, *Harper's University*, 249ff.

120. Alice Freeman Palmer to George Herbert Palmer, April 18, 1893. Wellesley Typescripts.

121. Alice Freeman Palmer to George Herbert Palmer, October 10, 1893. Wellesley Typescripts.

122. Alice Freeman Palmer to George Herbert Palmer, January 5, 10, 1894. Wellesley Typescripts; Storr, *Harper's University*, 90.

123. Gordon, *Higher Education*, 89.

124. Alice Freeman Palmer to George Herbert Palmer, October 4, 1894. Wellesley Typescripts.

125. Alice Freeman Palmer to George Herbert Palmer, January 22, October 4, 10, 23, 1894. Wellesley Typescripts.

126. Alice Freeman Palmer to George Herbert Palmer, October 6, 1894. Wellesley Typescripts.

127. Alice Freeman Palmer to William Rainey Harper, August 31, 1893. Harper Papers.

128. Alice Freeman Palmer to Marion Talbot, October 30, 1892. Marion Talbot Papers, University of Chicago Archives.

129. Alice Freeman Palmer to William Rainey Harper, December 1, 1892. Harper Papers.

130. Alice Freeman Palmer to George Herbert Palmer, June 15, 1893. Wellesley Typescripts.

131. Minutes of the Board of Trustees, June 20, 1893, November 2, 1893. Wellesley College Archives.

132. Minutes of the Board of Trustees, June 1, 1893. Wellesley College Archives.

133. Minutes of the Executive Committee, February 1, 10, 1894. Wellesley College Archives.

134. Alice Freeman Palmer to Robert Herrick, January 31, 1894. Glasscock, *Wellesley*, 42–55.

135. George Herbert Palmer to Alice Freeman Palmer, October 15, 1894. Wellesley Typescripts.

136. Alice Freeman Palmer to George Herbert Palmer, April 18, 1893. Wellesley Typescripts.

137. Alice Freeman Palmer to J. Laurence Laughlin, Thanksgiving Eve, 1892.

138. Alice Freeman Palmer to George Herbert Palmer, October 13, 18, 1892. Wellesley Typescripts.

139. Alice Freeman Palmer to George Herbert Palmer, October 21, 1892. Wellesley Typescripts.

140. Alice Freeman Palmer to William Rainey Harper, December 1, 1892. Harper Papers.

141. Palmer and Palmer, *The Teacher*, 362.

142. Alice Freeman Palmer to George Herbert Palmer, February 14, 1893. Wellesley Typescripts.

143. George Herbert Palmer to Alice Freeman Palmer, November 25, 26, 27, 1893. Wellesley Typescripts.

144. Alice Freeman Palmer to J. Laurence Laughlin, June 13, 1894. Alice Freeman Palmer to William Rainey Harper, June 13, 1894. Harper Papers. Alice Freeman Palmer to George Herbert Palmer, June 5, 1894. Wellesley Typescripts.

145. Alice Freeman Palmer to George Herbert Palmer, January 4, 5, 1894. Wellesley Typescripts.

146. George Herbert Palmer to Alice Freeman Palmer, January 13, 1894. Wellesley Typescripts.

147. George Herbert Palmer to Alice Freeman Palmer, April 4, 1894. Wellesley Typescripts.

148. Alice Freeman Palmer to George Herbert Palmer, April 6, 7, 11, 18, 1894. Wellesley Typescripts.

149. Alice Freeman Palmer to William Rainey Harper, May 9, December 14, 1894. Harper Papers. In fact, both Palmers were offered chairs at the University of Michigan in the spring of 1895; George promptly refused for both of them. Michigan was about to embark on creating a Dean of Women and Alice was first choice. See George Palmer to James B. Angell, March 31, 1895. Angell Papers, Bentley Historical Library.

150. Alice Freeman Palmer to George Herbert Palmer, January 8, 9, 1895. Wellesley Typescripts. Wallace returned to Chicago after a year and a half at Knox and a year studying at the Sorbonne to a distinguished Chicago career that ended only with her retirement. Her autobiography, *The Unending Journey* (Minneapolis: University of Minnesota Press, 1952), is a delightful, beautifully written account of Chicago's early decades.

151. Alice Freeman Palmer to George Herbert Palmer, January 15, 1895. Wellesley Typescripts.

152. Alice Freeman Palmer to William Rainey Harper, August 17, November 18, 1895. Harper Papers.

153. Alice Freeman Palmer to J. Laurence Laughlin, Christmas Day, 1898.

154. William Rainey Harper to Alice Freeman Palmer, May 2, 1901. Harper Papers.

155. Alice Freeman Palmer to George Herbert Palmer, June 16, 1901. Wellesley Typescripts.

156. Charles Eliot to Harry Pratt Judson, June 6, 1908. Harry Pratt Judson Papers, University of Chicago Archives.

157. William Gardner Hale's remarks at the Alice Freeman Palmer Memorial Service, University of Chicago, 1903, as printed in *A Memorial to Alice Freeman Palmer*, 20–21.

CHAPTER 10

Resolution

1

During Alice Freeman Palmer's last months at the University of Chicago, the Palmers found themselves thinking of their coming European sabbatical. George wrote on one occasion: "And to Europe I find myself looking forward more and more. . . . Can you and I only lie once more in a Venetian chamber alone and hear the water lapping, Harper's smiles or frowns will count for little."[1] And before long they were doing just that. With Chicago finally behind her, the Palmers sailed August 17, 1895, for Boulogne on the *Maasdam*, which they thought cheaper and cleaner than the Cunard liners.[2] Both were weary. The last few years had been strenuous and demanding.

They rode bicycles through the countryside of Normandy and Brittany during the fine September weather.[3] The bicycle as a form of transportation truly liberated its users. It did not, like a horse, have to be fed, housed, or harnessed and was always ready to go. George had succumbed to the bicycle craze in 1892 and had used his wheel as his major transport for two years. Alice was a novice who had sat on a bicycle only three times when they set out on this ambitious adventure. Her legs were stiff the first days and they made way slowly, taking time to inspect Norman churches, ruins, and old villages.[4]

When they reached Paris and met up with their trunks which they had sent on ahead, they began housekeeping in the same apartment where they had lived seven years before. As Alice said, "It is all like a fairy story."[5] They read and wrote mornings, visited churches, museums, and galleries in the afternoons. They had three bedrooms so the Herricks, who were also in Europe and whose traveling was partly financed by the Palmers, joined them for awhile in Paris. In December they sought the sun in the south of France. They spent part of March in Florence, then went on for six weeks to their beloved Venice, "the one spot in Europe which best met Mrs. Palmer's ideas of Paradise."[6] During the late spring and early summer they visited Vienna, Germany, and England before returning to Cambridge for the fall term.[7]

All this time the bicycles went with them. They not only bicycled in Normandy and Brittany, but in Picardy and Provence. They rode the Corniche Road from Frejus to Alassio and over 300 miles between Venice and Vienna, most of it mountainous. Their bicycles took them through the Black Forest from Tübingen to Freiburg and for shorter excursions in the Midlands. At the end of the year their cyclometers registered 1,500 miles, quite a feat for a middle-aged academic couple.[8] George wrote of Alice on a bicycle.

At the call of the white road she felt all ties to be cut. . . . She could turn to the right or left, could feel the down-pressed pedal and the rushing air, could lie in the shade by the roadside, visit a castle, dally long at luncheon, gather grapes or blackberries from the field, stop at whatever small inn might attract at night, and for days together commune rather with nature than with man."[9]

No better description of the 1890s New Woman could be found anywhere.

2

After this joyous vacation, Alice Freeman Palmer settled more comfortably into a routine of influence "without portfolio" in the arena of women's education. Everyone expected her to have time for new chores. As she wrote Robert Herrick, "'Being a person of leisure, now that you do not go to Chicago—you can surely do this,' comes several times a day."[10] The women's colleges, especially Wellesley, continued to need her careful attention. Four more years would pass before she could turn Wellesley College over to a leader that she really trusted. Meanwhile her guiding hand was needed on campus and in the board room. The affiliated colleges, Radcliffe and Barnard, experienced their most acute need for attention during this period. The problems confronting the State Board of Education and Massachusetts facilities for training teachers were as challenging as ever. She resumed a demanding lecture schedule.

When she returned from Europe in 1896, Alice Freeman Palmer's role as Wellesley College's powerful, guiding trustee became central to her life. She lent strong encouragement to President Irvine who was engaged in a fierce battle with the old guard to further professionalize the faculty, upgrade the curriculum, and soften the sharp evangelical edge of college life. Pauline Durant wanted none of these changes, and her vote and that of Alice Palmer in trustees meetings usually fell on opposite sides of any question.

For one thing, the old religious taboos began to crumble. The library was opened on Sundays. A Roman Catholic was hired to teach French. Palmer supported both innovations. Predictably Mrs. Durant was opposed.[11] In 1897 the fight focused on hiring a Catholic to train the choral class in the Beethoven Society. This time Mrs. Durant brought up her heavy artillery. The evangelist Dwight Moody was a perennial member, but seldom attender, of the trustees. Alice wrote George: "Mrs. Durant sent for Mr. Moody. He came and gave us nothing less than a blowing up—he called it a protest, said we were drifting and would turn the whole college over to the Catholics."[12] Julia Irvine was angry and said some unwise and bitter things. This time the vote went against those committed to change.

However, change was inevitable. Domestic work was abolished and tuition raised over Mrs. Durant's objections.[13] The purge of faculty continued with Palmer's support, reflecting the generally improved standards in women's higher education in the last decade of the nineteenth century. Culling and weeding poorly trained teachers was not accomplished without bitter fights in which Palmer, although advocating and sometimes initiating the changes, usually tried to play a conciliatory role. It was she who worked out the terms of Frances Lord's particularly acrimonious termination to permit her to retire with dignity on a reasonable pension,[14] as well as the easing of Anne Morgan from philosophy.[15] Palmer also took the lead in eliminating from the college's offerings unnecessary departments like philology and nonfunctioning programs like a Ph.D. which had never been a realistic possibility.[16] She also sponsored the new course offerings proposed by the faculty, the adjusting of faculty salaries upward, and the elimination of the requirement that faculty live in college.[17] She was fully behind the faculty's drive for autonomy and professionalization.

Palmer's greatest gift to Wellesley, however, was persuading Caroline Hazard to succeed Julia Irvine as president in 1899. Irvine had made attempts to resign as early as 1897. The constant conflict that accompanied change exhausted her physical and emotional resources. More importantly, she seemed unable to put the college on a firm financial footing. By 1896 the college debt was over $100,000, and the college continued to experience an annual net loss of about $10,000 throughout the decade.[18] Irvine did not see herself as a money-raiser and Pauline Durant's capital was long since depleted. Faculty salaries needed adjustment. Raising tuition was only a partial solution. Irvine felt she could no longer continue, and a search committee for a new president was appointed in February of 1898 with Palmer a member.[19]

It is possible Palmer at first favored calling a man, but Mrs. Durant argued, probably rightly, that appointing a man at this juncture would forever close the post to women.[20] Mary E. Woolley, the young woman shortly to become president of Mount Holyoke College but then on the Wellesley faculty, was high on Palmer's list of suitable candidates. However, Caroline Hazard was Palmer's final choice and accepted the appointment in the spring of 1899.[21] No longer was Alice Freeman Palmer to guide the college. Wellesley again had an autonomous policy-maker at its head.

Hazard was the daughter of a wealthy Rhode Island mill owner with a fortune of her own. This contrasted with the middle-class professionals who had headed the college since 1881.[22] She had been educated privately, had no college degrees, and no administrative experience, but she took charge, obviously with Alice Palmer's blessing, from the beginning. Under Irvine the executive committee had dealt in great detail with faculty appointments and salaries, curriculum and graduation requirements. When Hazard became president meetings were less frequent, shorter, and largely concerned with business and financial matters.[23]

Hazard knew well the nineteenth century's millionaire entrepreneurs who found in educational philanthropy a worthy use for their expanding fortunes. She made use of her acquaintance to solve Wellesley's financial problems. Her brother, Rowland G. Hazard, joined the trustees in 1899, and it was his good offices that resulted the next year in John D. Rockefeller offering the college an endowment of $100,000 if the existing indebtedness could be retired by commencement 1900.[24] Several younger faculty, including the Palmers' old friend and protégé Vida Scudder, strongly opposed accepting "tainted" Standard Oil money. The source of the money bothered Alice Palmer not at all. If money was used in good cause, it was good money despite its origins. She wrote Scudder that the trustees would act with "conscientious care, and their decision will be on moral grounds," reminding Vida that Palmer herself "seven years ago had to decide whether I would take a responsible office in the organization of a college founded by Mr. Rockefeller."[25] Palmer voted to accept the gift and so urged the trustees and suggested she and Vida agree to disagree and yet respect each other.[26] In fact she rejoiced in the gift and gave Caroline Hazard full credit for it. To her old secretary, Anna McCoy, Palmer wrote: "Miss Hazard grows better everyday!.... How good for Wellesley."[27] Moreover she personally made sure the endowment would be forthcoming. When nearly $10,000 of the funds needed to pay the college's debts was yet to be raised and commencement was only four days away, she, George, and their faithful friend Edwin Abbott pledged their personal savings, if necessary, to complete the fund.[28] Fortunately the money was raised elsewhere.

Since 1881, when Alice Freeman assumed the presidency, Wellesley had gradually been transformed from Henry Durant's ideal, a haven where hard-working, deserving, "calico girls" could be trained for Christian womanhood, into a well-financed liberal arts college with a faculty of professional scholars and scientists that exercised considerable curricular autonomy. This was a far cry from the mid-1870s when Durant governed and financed his own private fiefdom. Much of the credit for the change is attributable to Alice Palmer.

However, Alice Freeman's careful monitoring of the higher education of women was not confined to Wellesley. In the spring of 1902 she made two speeches in New York, but also consulted at Barnard College and the Veltin School.[29] She accepted a post on the board of Bradford Academy and worked hard to bring the problem-laden school up to twentieth-century standards.[30] She devoted many days to the work of the State Board of Education. She earlier had participated on the committee that raised the money to ensure the Johns

Hopkins Medical School would be open to women.[31] During nine days in January of 1902 she had meetings or conferences for some board or other every day except one.[32]

By the 1890s Alice Freeman Palmer's ideas on higher education were as carefully formulated as they would ever be. Her 1891 *Forum* article was republished in Anna Brackett's *Woman and the Higher Education* in 1893. She made no changes in the text. Perhaps none were asked. Her much-delivered lecture, *Why Go to College*, was published in pamphlet form by Thomas Crowell and Co. in 1897. These two articles are the only formal statements of Alice Palmer's educational philosophy from her own pen.

Why Go to College was a straightforward if hortatory answer to the question posed in its title. Palmer asserted that higher education for women provided an insurance policy in case of economic need. It also brought many larger benefits. It stimulated occupation, the appreciation of diversity, a hospitality to new ideas, an ability to serve society, and of course the capacity to be a better wife and mother.[33]

The "Higher Education of Women" article was largely descriptive. She cataloged the profound changes the previous quarter century had brought to higher education overall, changes on which there was still no general agreement, such as the elective system, age of admission, and degree requirements. However, Palmer had been an ardent supporter of the changes. She then discussed the three types of higher education available to women: coeducation, the affiliated college, and the women's college. She saw coeducation as the least expensive way to provide for women and also the most widespread. However, she credited coeducation with much more than frugality and accessibility. She affirmed that only the best-equipped universities could provide training in advanced research. Many were in Europe. Some were in the United States. All were now closed or had once been closed to women. They must all be made coeducational if women's scholarship was to thrive. She wrote of her own experience at the University of Michigan where men and women were treated exactly alike and saw this equality as developing strength and independent balance. She believed that "in a large tract of her character— is it the largest tract?—[a young woman's] needs and those of the young man are identical."[34]

She saw as coeducation's only disadvantage that, "refining home influences and social oversight are largely lacking."[35] It was, of course, this lack that she had tried to remedy at Chicago. She admitted that the women's college did provide students with "a home within its own walls" and helped "develop other powers than the merely intellectual," necessitating a faculty that must be more than specialists and scholars.[36] She admitted the importance of women's colleges in building "character, inspiring service to others, cultivating manners, developing taste...."[37] But the upshot of her argument was that the women's college could not provide adequate research training.

The affiliated college or annex "lives by favor not by right," and that was its greatest disadvantage. The uncertainly of faculty (who at the Harvard Annex, for example, were all paid volunteers from the Harvard faculty) made orderly pursuit of science and laboratory courses difficult.[38] Annie Nathan Meyer, one of Barnard's founders, disagreed with Palmer in a lively debate in the periodical press about the disadvantages of the annex, especially Barnard.[39] To Palmer, however, coeducation was the wave of the future, as it was of course to be.[40] She foresaw in *Why Go to College*, even before she went to Chicago, what she would pioneer on that campus—coeducational universities solving the problem of "home influences" by taking more responsibility for their "girls," a commitment to in loco parentis that was to prevail for better or for worse until the 1970s.

3

Meanwhile Alice Palmer returned to her demanding lecture schedule. She promised eight commencement addresses for June of 1897.[41] The following June, except for a brief respite when she returned home for the Wellesley commencement, she lectured almost every day, and complained to George, "How shall I keep it up?"[42] Not only did she deliver her platform lectures but she was expected to give informal advice and counseling, attend teas and dinners, and meet with influential citizens everywhere she went. From Western College for Women in Ohio she sent George a clipping of her schedule as outlined in the local newspaper and commented, "You can see I am expected to earn my hundred dollars in the next two days."[43] As was true earlier in their marriage, part of the motivation for this demanding schedule seems to have been economic. As she began another tour she wrote in the spring of 1898, "If I can only make good speeches and come back with money to pay the month's bills I shall be perfectly happy."[44] The Palmers missed her Chicago salary, and she attempted to partly compensate for its loss by her lectures. However, almost always her subject was "The New Education" or "Why Should Girls Go To College?" She was also doing her bit for the higher education of women.

Hers was a grueling schedule especially on tour, but her general health was much better after 1895 than it had been in previous years. Her major physical catastrophe was a serious accident in November of 1898. She was returning to Cambridge by trolley from doing errands in Boston, stepped off the car, and was hit by a bicyclist riding on the wrong side of the street. She was unconscious nearly twenty-four hours. Undoubtedly she suffered a concussion, possibly a skull fracture, because nausea, heavy hemorrhaging, violent headache, and amnesia plagued her for several days. She was in bed for weeks, and months passed before she made a full recovery.[45] Her only other debilitating bout with ill health was an operation for hemorrhoids at the New England Hospital For Women and Children in the late summer of 1901.[46] Her surgeon, for at the time women typically looked to women for treatment, was Emma L. Call who taught hygiene at Wellesley in the 1890s.[47] However her lungs, the scourge of her earlier years, never bothered her seriously after the Palmers' second European sabbatical.

Perhaps more important to her well-being, Alice Palmer had finally made her peace with being George's wife. She had found a new and satisfying form of usefulness. George's family became increasingly important to her, especially his cousin, Robert Herrick, and his wife Harriet. Their bonds to Alice had been cemented in Chicago when Herrick became a faculty member sponsored by both the Palmers. Although Harriet was Robert's first cousin, Alice had encouraged their marriage. George reluctantly agreed but counseled, as a late-nineteenth-century eugenics enthusiast, that they have no children. They ignored George's advice, and Alice Palmer Herrick was born to them in 1896. Unfortunately she was severely retarded and physically handicapped, but Alice always referred to her during the child's short life as her granddaughter, and was marvelously supportive to the beleaguered Herricks. Fred Palmer's son Eric, always a favorite, lived with them while he attended Harvard. The Palmer family celebrated Thanksgiving, New England fashion, as the year's major holiday, and the ritual gathering of the clan most often took place around Alice and George's dining table in Cambridge. George was close to his family, especially his brothers and the Herricks, and Alice embraced them with him.

Alice's family was also much in evidence, especially her sister Ella and her husband Charles Talmadge, who continued to be in and out of Cambridge throughout the 1890s. Charles received a Harvard M.A. in 1900 which required a year in residence. He had abandoned Methodism for Congregationalism a year or two earlier. The result was that he was not permanently settled in a parish until the fall of 1901.[48] Fred Freeman married in 1895, and at long last Alice's sister Stella was replaced after a fashion by her namesake, Fred's infant daughter, another Estella, born in 1901. Alice found her bewitching. "Her eyes shine like stars, and she laughs and flirts, and makes herself fascinating at every turn."[49]

The Freemans' prosperity was now assured. Alice's parents owned seven houses and lots in Saginaw, and "Fred is very prosperous if he chooses to save."[50] Her mother's health improved as she grew older, and she was able to join Alice at a family reunion at Osborn Hollow in 1899 followed by a visit to the Palmer's Boxford farm.[51] The Susquehanna family reunion was repeated the next year with her father present. She and her father visited the old farm where she was born and the country school she had attended until she was seven. It was a nostalgic occasion, and she wrote George, "If you could only see this heavenly valley and the lovely chestnut crowned hills."[52] But George never accompanied her to Broome County. Father Freeman suffered a severe bout with what was called heart failure in 1902, but rallied and outlived his daughter by many years.[53]

Although they still suffered from acute cash crises on occasion, the Palmers found themselves in comfortable circumstances. Their joint income which had been $6,000 in 1892 had risen to $9,300 in 1893, largely because of Alice's position at Chicago, but also because both had lucrative speaking engagements that year. For example, George gave ten lectures at Chautauqua and Alice six.[54] In 1897 George's Harvard salary was raised to $5,000; also stock they owned and thought worthless suddenly acquired considerable value. Edwin Abbott had given George 100 shares of railroad stock in 1885 that they believed without value, but the company was now assumed by the Wisconsin Central Railroad as part of a reorganization. They were paid $1,200 in back interest and the stock itself was redeemed for over $10,000. George calculated that with their other savings, they now had a nest egg of $20,000 at 5 percent.[55] Also Robert Herrick repaid them a loan of $1,500 they had made to help him finance his European journey in 1895. George protested repayment, insisting that the loan was really a gift because he thought of Herrick as a son. Although refusing interest, he accepted the money, and deposited it in an endowment fund for Alice.[56]

The Palmers had extravagant tastes, but they also were very generous. They paid half the expenses of George's niece by his first marriage at Hyannis Normal School and supported another needy distant relative at the University of Iowa.[57] For many years Alice contributed to the support and work of Charlotte Hawkins Brown, a young black woman who worked as a nursemaid and whom Alice encountered on a Boston street corner reading Virgil. Palmer subsidized Brown's education at normal school and sometimes single-handedly supported a struggling school for poor blacks that Hawkins Brown later founded in the South.[58] Year after year the Palmers gave away a large proportion of their income. Alice calculated that by the end of January of 1900 their gifts since the previous September totalled over $800.[59] George's Harvard salary was still $5,000, and this generosity was made possible at the considerable personal sacrifice of their killing schedule on the lecture circuit.

The Palmers were generous with their personal income but also with their other resources. In 1900, 1,200 Cuban teachers were guests of Harvard to help Cuba prepare for its new role as a United States possession. The Palmers were active in helping raise the $70,000 necessary to finance their stay. They also opened their Cambridge home to Alice Gordon Gulick, who had been forced, because of the Spanish-American War, to leave Spain and evacuate the International Institute for Girls which she headed.[60]

4

The Palmers' two houses became increasingly important in both their lives as they grew older. During the first years of their marriage they had rented Cambridge houses, small and furnished, that required a single servant, but by 1890 they felt a strong need for a permanent home of their own. They considered building on land owned by and

Alice and George in the library of the house on Quincy Street.
(Courtesy of Wellesley College Archives.)

adjacent to the home of Edwin Abbott, their benefactor and good
friend, but Alice was reluctant. As she saw it, they dared not risk any
near-neighbor strains; "nothing at all of our pleasant relations must
be so much as touched." Abbott was also on the Wellesley Board of
Visitors which no doubt fed her reluctance. Instead she suggested
they borrow "$5,000 of Professor Horsford and buy the Craigie
Street house at once, and settle the building problem."[61] They had
building plans drawn that they liked very much, but abandoned the
idea of a new house designed for them as financially imprudent. Alice
wanted something permanent that they could furnish and feel at
home in, but like George she feared financial overcommitment.[62]
Finally they agreed to take the great botanist Asa Gray's house at 3

Mason Street, Cambridge, unfurnished, at $1,200 a year. They furnished it over the summer and agreed they would help make ends meet by renting rooms to students, a practice they followed the rest of their lives.[63]

The Palmers lived very comfortably on Mason Street until 1894 when the Peabody house on Quincy Street became available, and Alice's Chicago salary placed it almost within their means. George leapt at the chance of installing himself next door to President Eliot in one of the three houses within Harvard Yard. Alice was busy in Chicago during most of the remodeling and refurbishment. It was George's project, and he wrote her in January: "I am all aglow to be settled there and am confident we shall feel more at home than we have ever felt anywhere except in Boxford. The Library, and parlor, and yes your study, will be beautiful rooms."[64] The Quincy Street house still stands, a handsome classic early Federal house with high ceilings, square rooms, and marble mantels. The thirty-six foot library with hard pine floors (eventually covered with two oriental rugs) and large windows looking out on the trees and lawns of Harvard Yard was a new addition created by George. He also designed and had built a convenient pantry and first-floor lavatory.

The Palmers moved to Quincy Street during March of 1894 soon after Alice returned from one of her Chicago stints. The remodeling had cost them nearly $3,000 and the long-term lease from Harvard Corporation another $7,500.[65] Their financial resources were strained, but as usual they worried a little, and then did what they wanted. And their open hospitality only increased. A stream of visitors, from college students to college presidents was always welcome. The great philosophers of the era, as Lucy Sprague reminisced, George Santayana, William James, Josiah Royce, and Hugo Munsterberg, were all intimates of the household.[66] Wellesley's hard-working princess had been handsomely installed in her own palace created by George.

For Christmas and spring vacations and in the long hot Boston summers the Palmers retired to Boxford, the property that had been in the Palmer family for generations and where various relatives maintained summer quarters. The family seems to have owned the property communally at first, but in 1896 Alice and George acquired outright the house George had occupied for years by buying the shares of two other family members.[67] They began to repair and refurbish this house in 1891, adding a large piazza and a study-library, and brought their own servants with them for the summer rather than depending on the tenants in the farm house for domestic help.[68]

They saw life at Boxford as brief excursions into a bucolic paradise. They walked in the woods, birded in the meadows, bathed in the pond, and cherished the moonlight from the piazza. They bottled and preserved the produce of the farm for winter use, and packed apples and potatoes in barrels to be transported to Cambridge. They read assiduously, and George wrote his articles and books. Boxford was only a short train ride from Boston so necessary academic business could be handled easily. Both Alice and George commuted to Boston when Wellesley, Harvard, or other responsibilities called.

But they also entertained. During the summer of 1897 twenty-five house guests were sheltered under their Boxford roof, one for three weeks, and fifteen people attended one dinner party.[69] Chicago friends, the Spragues, the Laughlins, the Hales, the Herricks, as well as family members, were often among their visitors.

Cambridge-Boxford was a kind of double sonata with the movements attuned to the seasons. Although the yearly patterns of their lives were tied to the academic calendar, they rang the changes in their rhythms in seasonal sequence, the first green buds of spring, July heat, autumn's colors, the black and whiteness of a Boxford December. Both Palmers were acutely aware of seasonal permutations at both their houses, a new shrub in bloom on Quincy Street, a shade of green in the Boxford woods. Every blossom, every horticultural triumph, every change of wind or temperature is documented in their letters to each other. Just as there had been a palpable physical passion between them early in their relationship, a sexuality that one hardly expected in staid middle-aged Victorians devoted to professional duties, their life together in the late 1890s had a visual and sensual element that revolved around place. They were conscious of where they were, be it Saginaw, Quincy Street, Boxford, or Venice. The Palmers were highly involved with people, but they were also involved with the flowers they saw, the water that moved past, and the air they breathed. They built themselves an expansive urban environment on Harvard Yard and a sylvan retreat at Boxford. It was a rich life.

The Palmers had young people living with them from the time

they acquired the Mason Street house, at least in part to help meet the expenses of a large establishment. Some were relatives, others were the children of friends, and all were treated as members of the family. Eric Palmer, the son of George's brother Fred, lived with them while at Harvard. Agatha Laughlin, daughter of one of the Palmers' Chicago academic friends, spent a year with them while she attended Miss Ingall's School. Lucy Sprague, whom Alice had known since she lived with the Spragues in Chicago for several weeks when Lucy was fourteen, spent her Radcliffe years with the Palmers. She came to Cambridge as a Radcliffe "special" in 1896 and in more than one way she became their surrogate daughter. She was with them in Paris when Alice died. When young Bobby Hale, whom they had known since their honeymoon journey in Italy, was ready for Harvard he also joined the family, and for awhile the Sprague's son Albert took his meals with them. There were others who lived on Quincy Street for shorter periods.[70]

The Palmers treated the more permanent residents among these young people as their children. They took them into their lives and in turn participated in the hopes, fears, and training of their young guests. They were nurturant parents, George perhaps more so than Alice because he was more often at home. While Alice was away at Chicago or on one lecture tour or another, he cherished their companionship, entertained their friends, and tried to instill a sense of order and discipline into their lives. He reported at length on his interactions with them to Alice. Lucy Sprague Mitchell wrote of the household that the Palmers "became a part of me and I became part of them," that she felt really free with them. They lived "a rich intellectual life and a rich human life and they took me into both."[71] The Palmers experienced the joys but also suffered the traumas of parenting. George's nephew Joe, always a problem, became Lucy's swain for awhile much to their discomfiture. Eventually he was expelled from Harvard for peddling pornography and was arrested. George was disgusted and upset, but he bailed him out and assisted him to skip bail and take off for Mexico.[72] References to this incident in George and Alice's correspondence are veiled. But George showed that he was no self-righteous martinet and that the expert on ethics was quite capable of dealing realistically with human problems, even if it meant bending the law.

It was a large and active household with many callers and many guests, professional and personal. Both Palmers did much of their professional work at home and many essentially business conferences were held at Quincy Street over luncheon or tea. Also George did some of his seminary teaching and conferred with students at home. The campus office for professors did not exist in the nineteenth century. Most teaching was done in classrooms or laboratories in or near the Yard, but all other academic chores were performed in professorial residences.

Answering the mail in the days before the telephone was a daily chore for a busy academic couple. Appointments were made, invitations given and accepted, recommendations requested and transmitted by letter, and these communications usually demanded immediate attention. Servants eased the Palmers' domestic chores considerably and spared them most of the drudgery, but there were no secretaries for busy professors. Those chores they performed themselves. It was not uncommon for them to report that the letter they at last found time to write to each other was the twentieth letter each had written that evening.[73]

5

Alice Freeman Palmer's established position in higher education made it possible for her to succumb to the richness of Cambridge life. Her role at the University of Chicago had provided her with an invincible redoubt and insured her continued importance in academia. She no longer needed an institutional platform. She now felt sure of her position in the professional world. She could enjoy her life as mistress of a varied household.

Women today easily fault Alice Palmer for abandoning her career at Chicago. If they find relinquishing her Chicago post acceptable, they wonder why she did not find another appointment. First of all, she was exhausted and unwell. Twice she turned her back on splendid professional opportunities because fully extending herself would have meant physical disaster. Secondly, George is partly responsible. He wanted Alice home and available. However, there is a third reason. Alice Palmer, like other highly trained women of the 1890s, found volunteer responsibilities that fit her professional qualifications deeply rewarding. She did not see the Wellesley trusteeship, for example, as busy work, something to occupy her time or to keep her from being bored. Nor did she view these tasks as making less than maximum use of her training and skills. Of course if she had lived in the 1970s she would have been president of a major university, but that is not when she lived. During the post-Chicago years Alice Palmer continued to play a major role in women's higher education. Many other married women working as unpaid volunteers saw themselves as using their training equally well. They were making crucial decisions that had profound effects on social policy.[74]

Alice Freeman Palmer's influence on women's higher education was multiplied by her marriage and the circles in which she moved. By the mid-1890s she and George probably knew personally everyone of importance in higher education in the United States. She knew the major English women educators, and he knew the British and German philosophers. She was intimate with the whole Chicago cultural and educational community. George knew most major college presidents in the United States and was consulted by them. Between them they were a veritable academic communications center, and one that was heavily used.

In January of 1902 while George Palmer was lecturing in Bangor, Maine, Alice gave a luncheon at their home on Quincy Street. Twelve women educators from the northeastern United States had been invited. All accepted. Carolyn Hazard, then president of Wellesley sat opposite Alice Palmer, but leaders from Smith, Pembroke, Vassar, and Ellen Richards, founder of the America Home Economics Association and active in Collegiate Alumnae, were all present. Palmer thought it "the pleasantest luncheon I have ever given." The last guests tarried until six o'clock discussing scholarships and opportunities for European graduate study for women.[75] This kind of informal influence made Alice Palmer's place in women's higher education unique. Had the dilemma at last been resolved? Had George Palmer's promise during their courtship days that by giving up the Wellesley presidency and joining forces with him at Cambridge she would "increase her powers," expand her influence, come true? Certainly it seemed an arguable proposition by the late 1890s. Nonetheless, if Alice Palmer had failed to insist on accepting the appointment at the University of Chicago, a choice George certainly resisted with all the arguments at his command, her position by 1900 as arbiter of women's higher education would have been much less secure.

Alice Palmer thought of her choice of marriage as positive. She constantly reassured herself that marriage was the way she wanted to live her life. She wrote George in 1897: "What a beautiful life we do have! I think of it more and more, especially when I am away from you and long to be there again. . . . No one else is like you dear."[76] She continually speaks in their correspondence of her joy in choosing marriage to such a worthy and stimulating partner. However, one cannot help but wonder at her need to constantly avow the wisdom of her choice.

Alice Palmer wrote a number of poems, many of which she gave to George as a birthday gift late in her life. Although this was a purely personal outpouring, and she expressly stipulated on her death bed that they be destroyed, in 1915 George Palmer published many of them in a slight volume, *A Marriage Cycle*. Whether the title was his or hers, I do not know. She may have attached it to the manuscript version when she presented it to him. As poems they leave much to be desired. The meter often falters; they almost never scan. The rhymes are often contrived. But she felt moved enough in thinking about their relationship to write them. Obviously she found a kind of catharsis in the act, as well as paying generous tribute to George as a husband, which she did in most of them. But perhaps her need indicates some kind of appeasement for second thoughts. And the second thoughts are there. In a poem called "The Last Anniversary" she writes:

> Fifteen years ago, dear
> Fifteen years today!
> Let us walk our fields together
> While we may.
>
> . . . .
>
> One third of my life, dear
> Since I heard you call,
> And put by my work and, rising,
> Gave you all.[77]

More revealing are verses she titled "Myself."

> Oh, to be alone!
> To escape from the work, the play,
> The talking every day!
> To escape from all I have done
> And all that remains to do!

To escape,—yes, even from you,
My only Love,—and be
Alone and free!

Could I only stand
Beneath pale moon and gray sky,
Where the winds and the sea-gulls cry,
And no man is at hand,
And feel the free air blow
On my rain-wet face, and know
I am free,—not yours, but my own,—
Free and alone!

. . . .

I am only you.
I am yours, part of you, your wife,
And I have no other life.
I cannot think, cannot do; I cannot breathe, cannot see;
There is "us," but there is not "me."
And worst, at your touch I grow
Contented so![78]

Certainly in these poems she expressed ambivalence about marriage and the course her life took. Did George see this? Probably not, or he would never have published them. George was a master at seeing only what he wanted to see in Alice's life.

However, George himself was not unwilling to test their marriage with second thoughts. He never quite gave up his first love. Did Alice not quite measure up? Was she less than tractable, and did he on some level resent this? He wrote Alice in 1901: "This is my original Wedding Day, and I should have been married thirty years had she lived.... Now we have had more than half that number, and nearly twice as many as poor Nell and I had. She was so exquisite. It is a loss you can never repair not to have known her."[79] One cannot help wonder how that letter made poor Alice feel. Perhaps she had worked through her feelings about Nell so well that it didn't matter, but I doubt it. No marriage is perfect, and certainly over the years the Palmers received in large measure love, strength, and understanding from each other, but Alice's ambivalence (and perhaps George's) remained.

One of the last portraits of Alice Freeman Palmer.
(Courtesy of Wellesley College Archives.)

6

On September 24, 1902, the Palmers again sailed for Europe. Lucy Sprague, who had lost her mother that year and who had once more fled to the Palmers for succor, was with them. This time their vessel was a cattle boat that rolled and tossed in early fall storms as the cattle bellowed their distress, but everyone seems to have had a good appetite and a rollicking time.[80] The trio spent a few days in the English Lake District following the haunts and allusions of George Herbert whose work George was then editing. They stayed briefly with the master of Balliol College at Oxford, and spent time researching Herbert at the British Museum and exploring the National Gallery and St. Paul's.[81]

The Palmers clearly enjoyed being accompanied by an energetic, young companion. Near the end of October they crossed the Channel to Paris where they found their old apartment unavailable, but they were able to establish themselves close by on the Avenue Marceau and again engaged Marie, their servant from previous visits. They easily resumed their usual routine, working on Herbert in the mornings (Lucy acted as George's research assistant) and excursions and museums in the afternoon.[82] On All Saint's Day, at Alice's request, they visited the cemetery at Père Lachaise where they had never been, hunting out the graves of the famous along with the thousands of other Parisians paying them honor. Alice bestowed a bunch of violets on the tomb of Héloise whom she had always admired. That night she said to George that although she believed the choice of disposal of the dead was for the living to make, "I hope I may be cremated."[83]

Before November was out Alice Palmer was ailing intermittently with abdominal pain, but between attacks she felt well. The attacks, however, did not disappear and became more severe. Her condition was diagnosed as intussusception of the intestine, in which the intestine telescopes on itself. She was told her illness was possibly congenital.[84] Eventually surgery was recommended. She understood its dangers and made her preparations. She canceled future engagements, counseled George how to best order his life for his first year of deep loss, and commissioned him to take care of Lucy who would be traumatized by two bereavements so close together. The surgery was at first seen as successful, but intestinal resection was invariably risky before antibiotics became available. Three days later, on December

6, 1902, she died in a small private Catholic hospital in Paris. She was forty-seven.[85]

Lucy braided Alice's chestnut hair in the crown she usually wore. There was a small simple service at the Foreign Chapel, and George had her body cremated as she had wished. Before the month was out, the bereft sixty-three-year-old man and the young woman forty years his junior made their way back across the Atlantic carrying a small wooden box containing Alice Freeman Palmer's ashes.[86] It was Lucy who made the sad journey to Saginaw to console the Freemans.

If George Palmer is an accurate reporter, Alice Palmer met death as she had lived—easily, pragmatically, making plans for her near and dear to ease the transition for them.[87] No one loved life more than Alice Palmer, but she also could accept death, as witnessed by the words she spoke at a friend's funeral: "We make too much of the circumstance we call death. All life is one. All service one, be it here or there. Death is only one little door from one room to another."[88] She may still have believed in heaven.

Alice Freeman Palmer had a short life, but a full one. She had pioneered at a coeducational university as one of its first woman students. She had been among the first women faculty at an early degree-granting college for women. She had presided directly and indirectly for nearly a quarter of a century over the development of Wellesley College into a first-rate college for women with a scholarly professional faculty. She had changed the patterns of coeducational universities through her connection with Chicago, not as much as she would have liked, but perhaps more than she knew. She had brought the New Woman to the twentieth century. She personally had traversed the course, from the emphasis on economic independence for single women in the 1880s through an independent career at Chicago as a married woman, to a kind of resolution through the creative volunteerism that marked many married professional women's efforts in the last decades of the nineteenth and first sixty years of the twentieth century. She had combined her volunteerism with her deeply felt need to contribute to the Palmers' financial support. She had experimented cautiously, as I have suggested earlier, with the 1920s New Woman's sexual liberties. Her life patterned the evolution of the New Woman.

Who knows what Alice Freeman Palmer would have had to contribute to the twentieth century. Very little, I think. She would have continued to be a positive force in promoting higher education for women, but others, like M. Carey Thomas, the new president of Bryn Mawr, would assume leadership. The Palmers' Cambridge salon would have gradually lost influence in the total academic picture as it did for aging George. As it was, Alice Freeman Palmer died to memorial accolades, Wellesley scholarships, a University of Michigan chair, a Chicago carillon, all named after her. She deserved them. She had done her work well for her time and place.

NOTES

1. George Herbert Palmer to Alice Freeman Palmer, January 7, 1895. Wellesley Typescripts.
2. Alice Freeman Palmer to Elizabeth Wallace, March 17, 1896.
3. Alice Freeman Palmer to Robert Herrick, July 30, 1895. Robert Herrick Papers, University of Chicago Archives. Alice Freeman Palmer to Anna McCoy, November 17, 1895.
4. George Herbert Palmer to Robert Herrick, September 7, 1895. Robert Herrick Papers, University of Chicago Archives.
5. Alice Freeman Palmer to Robert Herrick, September 23, 1895. Robert Herrick Papers, University of Chicago Archives.
6. Palmer, *Life*, 199.
7. Alice Freeman Palmer to Elizabeth Wallace, March 17, 1896.
8. Palmer, *Life*, 201–2.
9. Ibid., 202.
10. Alice Freeman Palmer to Robert Herrick, December 1, 1896. Robert Herrick Papers, University of Chicago Archives.
11. Minutes of the Board of Trustees, March 27, 1895; Minutes of the Executive Committee, April 23, 1897. Wellesley College Archives.
12. Alice Freeman Palmer to George Herbert Palmer, [January] 1897. George Herbert Palmer Papers, Houghton Library, Harvard University.
13. *Wellesley College Catalog*, 1896–97, 19; Palmieri, "Adamless Eden," 163–71.
14. Minutes of the Board of Trustees, June 3, 21; October 6, 1897. Wellesley College Archives.
15. Alice Freeman Palmer to George Herbert Palmer, May 5, 1898. George Herbert Palmer Papers, Houghton Library, Harvard University.
16. Minutes of the Executive Committee, May 4, 25; September 21; Minutes of the Board of Trustees June 2, 20, 1898; February 2, 1899. Wellesley College Archives.
17. Alice Freeman Palmer to George Herbert Palmer, May 5, 1898. George Herbert Palmer Papers, Houghton Library, Harvard University. Minutes of the Board of Trustees, February 1, 1900. Wellesley College Archives.

18. President's Reports 1896, 40–41; Ibid., 1898, 35. Wellesley College Archives.

19. Minutes of the Executive Committee, February 23, 1898. Wellesley College Archives.

20. Wells, *Marks and Woolley*, 53–54.

21. Minutes of the Board of Trustees, March 7, 1899. Wellesley College Archives.

22. See Margaret Clapp, "Caroline Hazard" in *Notable American Women*, 2:169–70; Glasscock, *Wellesley*, 60– 63.

23. This assessment is based on the minutes of the Trustees and Executive Committee for those years.

24. Minutes of the Board of Trustees, June 7, 1900. Wellesley College Archives.

25. Alice Freeman Palmer to Vida Scudder, June 6, 1900.

26. Ibid.

27. Alice Freeman Palmer to Anna McCoy, March 27, 1900.

28. Diary, 1899.

29. Alice Freeman Palmer to George Herbert Palmer, undated [ca. March or April 1902]. Wellesley Typescripts.

30. Diary enclosed in letter, Alice Freeman Palmer to George Herbert Palmer, January 30, 1902. Wellesley Typescripts. Palmer, *Life*, 252–54.

31. Regina Markell Morantz-Sanchez, *Sympathy and Science: Women Physicians in American Medicine* (New York: Oxford University Press, 1985), 244, 399n.

32. Diary enclosed in letter, Alice Freeman Palmer to George Herbert Palmer, January 30, 1902. Wellesley Typescripts.

33. A. F. Palmer, *Why Go to College*.

34. Ibid., 33. A. F. Palmer, "Higher Education of Women" in Brackett, *Woman and the Higher Education*, 117–22.

35. A. F. Palmer, *Why Go to College*, 34.

36. Ibid., 34–35.

37. A. F. Palmer, "Higher Education of Women," 117–18.

38. Ibid., 38.

39. Annie Nathan Meyer, *Barnard Beginnings* (Boston: Houghton Mifflin Co., 1935), 43–45; Annie Nathan Meyer, *It's Been Fun: An Autobiography* (New York: Henry Schuman, 1951), 176.

40. I disagree, especially in emphasis, with the analysis in Roberta Frankfort's *Collegiate Women*.

41. George Herbert Palmer to Robert Herrick, May 23, 1897. Robert Herrick Papers, University of Chicago Archives.

42. Alice Freeman Palmer to George Herbert Palmer, June 17, 1898. George Herbert Palmer Papers, Houghton Library, Harvard University.

43. Alice Freeman Palmer to George Herbert Palmer, November 3, 1897. George Herbert Palmer Papers, Houghton Library, Harvard University.

44. Alice Freeman Palmer to George Herbert Palmer, April 26, 1898. George Herbert Palmer Papers, Houghton Library, Harvard University.

45. Diary, November 9, 1898.

46. Alice Freeman Palmer to George Herbert Palmer, August 26, 1901. Wellesley Typescripts.

47. Correspondence of Alice Freeman Palmer and George Herbert Palmer, August 1901. Wellesley Typescripts. Verbrugge, *Able-Bodied Womanhood,* 174.

48. Diary, 1898, 1899, 1900, 1901.

49. Alice Freeman Palmer to George Herbert Palmer, June 22, 1901. Wellesley Typescripts.

50. Alice Freeman Palmer to George Herbert Palmer, December 14, 1901. Wellesley Typescripts.

51. Alice Freeman Palmer to George Herbert Palmer, July 15, 7, 1899. George Herbert Palmer Papers, Houghton Library, Harvard University; Diary, 1899.

52. Alice Freeman Palmer to George Herbert Palmer, August 7, 1900. George Herbert Palmer Papers, Houghton Library, Harvard University.

53. Alice Freeman Palmer to George Herbert Palmer, April 13, 1902. Wellesley Typescripts.

54. Diary, 1893.

55. Diary, 1897–99.

56. George Herbert Palmer to Robert Herrick, January 16, 1901. Robert Herrick Papers, University of Chicago Archives.

57. Diary, 1899.

58. See the *Women's Missionary Magazine,* August 1930, 12, in the Charlotte Hawkins Brown Papers, Schlesinger Library, Radcliffe College.

59. Alice Freeman Palmer to George Herbert Palmer, February 15, 1900, undated. George Herbert Palmer Papers, Houghton Library, Harvard University.

60. Morris, "Alice Freeman Palmer," 170; Diary, 1900.

61. Alice Freeman Palmer to George Herbert Palmer, May 21, 22, 1890. Wellesley Typescripts.

62. George Herbert Palmer to Alice Freeman Palmer, May 28, 1890; Alice Freeman Palmer to George Herbert Palmer, May 29, 1890. Wellesley Typescripts.

63. Diary, 1890.

64. George Herbert Palmer to Alice Freeman Palmer, January 2, 1894. Wellesley Typescripts.

65. Correspondence of Alice Freeman Palmer and George Herbert Palmer, January-April 1894. Wellesley Typescripts. Diary, January 1894; Mitchell, *Two Lives,* 117.

66. Mitchell, *Two Lives,* 119–22.

67. Diary, 22–26 September 1896.

68. Diary, 1891.

69. Diary, 1897.

70. The diary in Alice Freeman Palmer Papers records who is living with

them each year, and of course, these household members are frequently mentioned in the correspondence (Diary, 1890–1902).

71. Mitchell, *Two Lives*, 121.

72. Ibid., 126.

73. Alice had a secretary, Anna McCoy, when she was president of Wellesley and also used stenographic help on occasion. Frances Willard employed multiple typists by the 1890s. Perhaps women were quicker than men to use stenographic assistance. President Angell of the University of Michigan never employed clerical help, even in the twentieth century. George took up the typewriter briefly in the early 1890s but seemed to abandon it after a brief experiment. A few typewritten letters of Alice exist for the late 1890s, but whether she typed them herself, used a professional typist, or perhaps the services of one of the young people in the house, is not clear. The typewriter, which began to catch on in the 1880s, quickly changed office practice in the business world and made professional stenographers essential, but academicians were slower to adopt the new technology. See JoAnne Yates, *Control through Communication: The Rise of System in American Management* (Baltimore: Johns Hopkins University Press, 1989), chap. 2.

74. Although Anne Firor Scott in *Natural Allies: Women's Associations in American History* (Urbana: University of Illinois Press, 1992), is principally concerned with the associations and not the continuance of a career as a volunteer, much of what she says about women's satisfactions and opportunities in voluntary organizations applies to Alice Palmer's life after 1895. (See especially page 24 and chapter 8.) Scott discusses the ease with which women combined volunteer responsibilities with paid work (155–57).

75. Alice Freeman Palmer to George Herbert Palmer, January 30, 1902. Wellesley Typescripts.

76. Alice Freeman Palmer to George Herbert Palmer, November 2, 1897. George Herbert Palmer Papers, Houghton Library, Harvard University.

77. A. F. Palmer, *A Marriage Cycle*, 67.

78. Ibid., 36–37.

79. George Herbert Palmer to Alice Freeman Palmer, June 15, 1901. Wellesley Typescripts. Helen Magill White, Andrew Dickson White's second wife, felt keenly that her husband treasured his first wife above her, since he arranged to be buried next to her, had her picture in every room of their house, and permitted his first wife's mother and sister to go on living with them after their marriage (Altschuler, *Better than Second Best*, chap. 5). George was not quite so insensitive, but he never forgot or let Alice forget his Ellen.

80. Mitchell, *Two Lives*, 129–30; Diary, 1902.

81. Mitchell, *Two Lives*, 130; Palmer, *Life*, chap. 14.

82. Mitchell, *Two Lives*, 130; Palmer, *Life*, chap. 14.

83. Palmer, *Life*, 323.

84. Alice's brother Fred was later to specialize in this kinds of surgery and according to Alice's niece, Fred's daughter Stella Novy, he never lost a case. Interview with Stella Novy, October 1988, by Ruth Bordin.

Bibliography

Primary Sources

Bryn Mawr College, Bryn Mawr, Pennsylvania
    Bryn Mawr College Archives
        M. Carey Thomas Papers

Carleton College, Northfield, Minnesota
    Carleton College Archives
        Margaret Evans Papers

Harvard University, Cambridge, Massachusetts
    Harvard University Archives
        Charles W. Eliot Papers
        Overseers Reports
    Houghton Library
        George Herbert Palmer Papers
        Horace Scudder Papers
    Schlesinger Library of Women's History, Radcliffe College
        Elizabeth Cabot Cary Agassiz Papers
        Charlotte Hawkins Brown Papers
        Saturday Morning Club Papers
        Anna Boynton Thompson Papers
        Woman's Education Association Papers

Massachusetts State Archives, Boston, Massachusetts
    Minutes of the State Board of Education

University of Chicago, Chicago, Illinois
    University of Chicago Archives
        Sophonisba Breckenridge, Manuscript Autobiography
        William Rainey Harper Papers
        Robert Herrick Papers
        Harry Pratt Judson Papers
        Harriet Monroe Papers
        Marion Talbot Papers
        Madelin Wallin Papers

University of Michigan, Ann Arbor
  Alumni Office, Alumni Records, Lucy Andrews File
  Bentley Historical Library
    University of Michigan Archives
      Announcements, 1872–76
      Annual Calendar, 1872–82
      Chronicle
      Palladium
      President's Report, 1872–73
    James B. Angell Papers
    Edward Barry Scrapbooks
    Colman Hutson Papers
    Levi Lockwood Papers
    Mary Olive Marston Papers
    Eliza Mosher Papers
    Alice Freeman Palmer Papers
    Calvin Thomas Diary
    Mary Alice Williams Papers

Wellesley College, Wellesley, Massachusetts
  Wellesley College Archives
    Class of 1883 Papers
    Class of 1887 Papers
    Emma Emerson Dyer Papers
    Lucy Friday Scrapbooks
    Helen B. Hart Papers
    Horsford Papers
    Carrie Huntington Papers
    Minutes of the Board of Trustees
    Minutes of the Executive Committee
    Alice Freeman Palmer Papers
    President's Reports
    Cathy Roberts-Gersh Manuscript
    Helen Shafer Papers
    Trustees Ledgers
    Wellesley Annals
    Wellesley College Catalogs
    Wellesley Typescripts, Correspondence of Alice
      Freeman Palmer and George Herbert Palmer

Published Materials

Abbott, Edward. "Wellesley College." *Harper's New Monthly Magazine* 53 (August 1876): 322–32.
Abbott, Lyman. "Alice Freeman Palmer—A Sketch." *Outlook* 112 (January 12, 1916).

————. Reminiscences. Boston: Houghton Mifflin Co., 1915.

————. *Silhouettes of My Contemporaries*. London: George Allen and Unwin, 1922.

Abrams, Ann Uhry. "Frozen Goddess: The Image of Woman in Turn of the Century American Art." In *Women's Being, Women's Place: Female Identity and Vocation in American History*, ed. Mary Kelley. Boston: G. K. Hall and Co., 1979.

Addams, Jane. *Twenty Years at Hull House*. New York: New American Library, 1961.

Albisetti, James G. *Schooling German Girls and Women: Secondary and Higher Education in the Nineteenth Century*. Princeton: Princeton University Press, 1988.

Alir-am, Pnina, and Dorinda Outram, eds. *Uneasy Careers and Intimate Lives: Women in Science, 1789–1979*. New Brunswick, N.J.: Rutgers University Press, 1987.

Allmendinger, David F., Jr. *Paupers and Scholars: The Transformation of Student Life in Nineteenth Century New England*. New York: St. Martin's Press, 1975.

Altschuler, Glenn C. *Better than Second Best: Love and Work in the Life of Helen Magill*. Urbana, Ill.: University of Illinois Press, 1990.

Anderson, Olive San Louie. *An American Girl and Her Four Years in a Boys' College*. New York: Appleton and Co., 1878.

Anderson, R. *History of the Sandwich Islands Mission*. Boston: Congregational Publishing Society, 1890.

Angell, James Burrill. "The Life of Alice Freeman Palmer." *Michigan Alumnus* 14 (June 1908): 402–10.

————. *The Reminiscences of James Burrill Angell*. New York: Longmans, Green, and Co., 1912.

Antler, Joyce. "After College, What? New Graduates and the Family Claim." *American Quarterly* 32, no. 4 (Fall 1980): 409–34.

————. *The Educated Woman and Professionalization: The Struggle for a New Feminine Identity*. New York: Garland Press, 1987.

————. *Lucy Sprague Mitchell: The Making of a Modern Woman*. New Haven: Yale University Press, 1987.

————. "Was She a Good Mother: Some Thoughts on a New Issue for Feminist Biography." In *Women and the Structure of Society: Selected Research from the Fifth Berkshire Conference on the History of Women*, ed. Barbara Harris and Jo Ann McNamara. Durham: Duke University Press, 1984.

————, and Sari Knopp Biklen. *Changing Education: Women as Radicals and Conservators*. Albany: State University of New York Press, 1990.

Astin, Helen. *The Woman Doctorate in America*. New York: Russell Sage Publications, 1969.

Banta, Martha. *Imaging American Women: Idea and Ideals in Cultural History*. New York: Columbia University Press, 1987.

Barry, Kathleen. *Susan B. Anthony: A Biography of a Singular Feminist*. New York: New York University Press, 1988.

Bateson, Catherine. *Composing a Life.* New York: Atlantic Monthly Press, 1989.

Bernard, Jessie. *Academic Women.* University Park: Pennsylvania State University Press, 1964.

Bishop, Morris L. *History of Cornell.* Ithaca: Cornell University Press, 1962.

Black, Naomi. *Social Feminism.* Ithaca: Cornell University Press, 1989.

Bland, Lucy. "Marriage Laid Bare." In *Labour and Love: Women's Experience of Home and Family, 1850–1940,* ed. Jane Lewis. Oxford: Basil Blackwell, 1986.

———. "The Married Woman, the 'New Woman,' and the Feminist: Sexual Politics of the 1890s." In *Equal or Different: Women's Politics, 1800–1914,* ed. Jane Rendall. Oxford: Basil Blackwell, 1987.

Bledstein, Burton. *The Culture of Professionalism: The Middle Class and the Development of Higher Education in America.* New York: W. W. Norton, 1976.

Blitz, Rudolph C. "Women in the Professions, 1870–1970." *Monthly Labor Review,* May 1974, 34–39.

Bolton, Sarah K. *Successful Women.* Boston: D. Lothrop and Company, 1888.

Bordin, Ruth. *Andrew Dickson White: Teacher of History.* Bulletin no. 8. Ann Arbor: Michigan Historical Collections, 1958.

———. *Frances Willard: A Biography.* Chapel Hill: University of North Carolina Press, 1986.

———. *The University of Michigan: A Pictorial History.* Ann Arbor: University of Michigan Press, 1967.

Boydston, Jean, Mary Kelley, and Anne Margolis. *The Limits of Sisterhood: The Beecher Sisters on Women's Rights and Woman's Sphere.* Chapel Hill: University of North Carolina Press, 1988.

Boyer, Ernest L. *College: The Undergraduate Experience in America.* New York: Harper and Row, 1987.

Boylan, Anne M. *Sunday School: The Formation of an American Institution, 1790–1880.* New Haven: Yale University Press, 1988.

Brackett, Anna C., ed. *Woman and the Higher Education.* New York: Harper Bros., 1893.

Braude, Ann. *Radical Spirits: Spiritualism and Women's Rights in Nineteenth Century America.* Boston: Beacon Press, 1989.

Breckenridge, Sophonisba. *Women in the Twentieth Century.* New York: McGraw, Hill, 1933.

Brown, Dorothy. *Setting a Course: American Women in the 1920s.* Boston: Twayne, 1987.

Brown, Louise Fargo. *Apostle of Democracy: The Life of Lucy Maynard Salmon.* New York: Harper Bros., 1943.

Buechler, Steven M. *The Transformation of the Woman Suffrage Movement: The Case of Illinois, 1850–1920.* New Brunswick, N.J.: Rutgers University Press, 1986.

———. *Women's Movements in the United States.* New Brunswick, N.J.: Rutgers University Press, 1990.

Buhle, Mary Jo. *Women and American Socialism, 1870–1920*. Urbana: University of Illinois Press, 1981.

Burg, David F. *Chicago's White City of 1893*. Lexington: University Press of Kentucky, 1976.

Burgess, Dorothy. *Dream and Deed: The Story of Katharine Lee Bates*. Norman: University of Oklahoma Press, 1952.

Burke, Colin B. *American Collegiate Populations: A Test of the Traditional View*. New York: New York University Press, 1982.

Burstyn, Joan. *Victorian Education and the Ideal of Womanhood*. London: Croom Helm, 1980.

Campbell, Barbara Kuhn. *The "Liberated" Woman of 1914: Prominent Women in the Progressive Era*. Ann Arbor, Mich.: UMI Research Press, 1979.

Carson, Mina. *Settlement Folk: Social Thought and the American Settlement Movement, 1855–1930*. Chicago: University of Chicago Press, 1990.

Carter, Susan. "Academic Women Revisited: An Empirical Study of Changing Patterns in Women's Employment in College and University Faculty, 1890–1963." *Journal of Social History* 14 (Summer 1981).

Chafe, William H. *The Paradox of Change: American Women in the Twentieth Century*. New York: Oxford University Press, 1991.

Chamberlain, Meriam K. *Women in Academe*. New York: Russell Sage, 1988.

Clapp, Margaret. "Caroline Hazard." In *Notable American Women,*. ed. Edward T. James and Janet Janes. Cambridge, Mass.: Harvard University Press, 1971.

Clarke, Edward H. *Sex in Education: A Fair Chance for the Girls*. Boston: Osgood, 1873.

Clifford, Geraldine Joncich. *Lone Voyagers: Academic Women in Coeducational Universities, 1870–1937*. New York: Feminist Press, 1989.

———. "'Shaking Dangerous Questions from the Crease': Gender and American Higher Education." *Feminist Issues* 3, no. 2 (1983): 3–62.

Clinton, Catherine. *The Other Civil War: American Women in the Nineteenth Century*. New York: Hill and Wang, 1984.

Cogan, Frances B. *The All–American Girl: The Ideal of Real Womanhood*. Athens: University of Georgia Press, 1989.

Conable, Charlotte Williams. *Women at Cornell: The Myth of Equal Education*. Ithaca: Cornell University Press, 1967.

Conant, Martha Pike. *A Girl of the Eighties*. Boston: Houghton Mifflin Co., 1931.

Converse, Florence. *Wellesley College: A Chronicle of the Years 1875–1938*. Wellesley, Mass.: Hathaway House Bookshop, 1939.

Conway, Jill K. *The First Generation of American Women Graduates*. New York: Garland Press, 1987.

———. "Perspectives on the History of Women's Education in the United States." *History of Education Quarterly* 14 (Spring 1974): 1–30.

Cook, Blanche Weisen. "Female Support Networks and Political Activism: Lillian Wald, Crystal Eastman, Emma Goldman." *Chrysalis* 3 (1977).

Cookingham, Mary E. "Blue Stockings, Spinsters, and Pedagogues: Women College Graduates, 1865–1919." *Population Studies* 38 (1984): 349–64.

Cott, Nancy F. *The Grounding of Modern Feminism.* New Haven: Yale University Press, 1987.

———, ed. *A Woman Making History: Mary Ritter Beard Through Her Letters.* New Haven: Yale University Press, 1990.

Cross, Barbara M. *The Educated Woman in America: Selected Writings of Catharine Beecher, Margaret Fuller, and M. Carey Thomas.* New York: Teacher's College Press, 1965.

Cunningham, Gail. *The New Woman and the Victorian Novel.* London: Macmillan, 1978.

Deegan, Mary Jo. *Jane Addams and the Men of the Chicago School.* New Brunswick, N.J.: Rutgers University Press, 1988.

Diner, Steven J. *A City and Its Universities: Public Policy in Chicago, 1892–1919.* Chapel Hill: University of North Carolina Press, 1980.

Dobkin, Marjorie Housepian, ed. *The Making of a Feminist: Early Letters and Journals of M. Carey Thomas.* Kent, Ohio: Kent State University Press, 1979.

Donnan, Elizabeth. "Henry Fowle Durant." *Dictionary of American Biography.* 3:541–42.

Drachman, Virginia G. "Female Solidarity and Professional Success: The Dilemma of Woman Doctors in Late Nineteenth Century America." *Journal of Social History* 15 (Summer 1982): 607–19.

DuBois, Ellen, et al. *Feminist Scholarship: Kindling the Groves of Academe.* Urbana: University of Illinois Press, 1987.

Ehrenreich, John H. *The Altruistic Profession: A History of Social Work and Social Policy in the United States.* Ithaca: Cornell University Press, 1985.

Elliott, Orrin L. *Stanford University: The First Twenty-Five Years.* Stanford: Stanford University Press, 1937.

Faderman, Lillian. *Surpassing the Love of Men: Romantic Friendship and Love between Women from the Renaissance to the Present.* New York: William Morrow Co., 1982.

Faragher, John Mack, and Florence Howe, eds. *Women and Higher Education in American History: Essays from the Mount Holyoke College Sesquicentennial Symposia.* New York: W. W. Norton and Co., 1988.

Ferrier, William W. *Origin and Development of the University of California.* Berkeley: Sather Gate Book Shop, 1930.

Fish, Virginia Kemp. "'More than Lore': Marion Talbot and Her Role in the Founding Years of the University of Chicago." *International Journal of Women's Studies* 8 (May/June 1985), 228–49.

Fitzpatrick, Ellen. *Endless Crusade: Women Social Scientists and Progressive Reform.* New York: Oxford University Press, 1990.

Fowler, Robert Booth. *Carrie Catt: Feminist Politician.* Boston, Mass.: Northeastern University Press, 1986.

Frankfort, Roberta Wein. *Collegiate Women: Domesticity and Career in Turn of the Century America.* New York: New York University Press, 1977.

———. "Women's College and Domesticity." *History of Education Quarterly* (Spring 1974): 31–47.

Freedman, Estelle B. "The New Woman: Changing Views of Women in the 1920s." *Journal of American History* 61 (September 1974): 372–93.

Fryer, Sarah Beebe. *Fitzgerald's New Women: Harbingers of Change.* Ann Arbor, Mich.: UMI Research Press, 1988.

Glasscock, Jean, ed. *Wellesley College 1875–1975: A Century of Women.* Wellesley, Mass.: Wellesley College, 1975.

Glazer, Penina Migdal, and Miriam Slater. *Unequal Colleagues: The Entrance of Women into the Professions, 1890–1940.* New Brunswick, N.J.: Rutgers University Press, 1987.

Goodspeed, Thomas Wakefield. *A History of the University of Chicago: The First Quarter Century.* Chicago: University of Chicago Press, 1972.

Gordon, Lynn D. "Coeducation on Two Campuses: Berkeley and Chicago, 1890–1912." In *Woman's Being, Woman's Place: Female Identity and Vocation in American History.* Edited by Mary Kelley. Boston: G. K. Hall, 1979.

———. *Gender and Higher Education in the Progressive Era.* New Haven: Yale University Press, 1990.

———. "The Gibson Girl Goes to College: Popular Culture and Women's Higher Education in the Progressive Era." *American Quarterly* 39 (Summer 1987): 211–30.

Graham, Patricia Albjerg. "Expansion and Exclusion: A History of Women in Higher Education." *Signs* 3 (Summer 1978): 759–73.

Green, Elizabeth. *Mary Lyon and Mount Holyoke: Opening the Gates.* Hanover, N.H.: University Press of New England, 1979.

Grimshaw, Patricia. *Paths of Duty: American Missionary Wives in Nineteenth Century Hawaii.* Honolulu: University of Hawaii Press, 1989.

Groneman, Carol, and Mary Beth Norton. *"To Toil the Livelong Day": American Women at Work, 1780–1980.* Chapel Hill: University of North Carolina Press, 1987.

Gunson, Neil. *Messengers of Grace: Evangelical Missionaries in the South Seas.* Melbourne: Oxford University Press, 1978.

Hackett, Alice Payne. *Wellesley: Part of the American Story.* New York: E. P. Dutton, 1949.

Hague, Amy. "Give Us a Little Time to Find Our Places: Women Students at the University of Wisconsin, 1875–1900." Master's thesis, University of Wisconsin, 1983.

———. "What If the Power Does Lie Within Me?!": Women Students at the University of Wisconsin, 1875–1900." *History of Higher Education Annual* 1984, 78–100.

Handlin, Oscar and Mary. *The American College and American Culture: Socialization as a Function of Higher Education.* New York: McGraw Hill, 1970.

Harris, Barbara J. *Beyond Her Sphere: Women and the Professions in American History.* Westport, Conn.: Greenwood Press, 1978.

———, and Jo Ann McNamara, eds. *Women and the Structure of Society: Selected*

Research from the Fifth Berkshire Conference on the History of Women. Durham, N. C.: Duke University Press, 1984.

Hazard, Caroline, ed. *An Academic Courtship: Letters of Alice Freeman Palmer and George Herbert Palmer.* Cambridge: Harvard University Press, 1940.

————. *From College Gates.* Boston: Houghton Mifflin Co., 1925.

Heilbrun, Carolyn. *Writing a Woman's Life.* New York: W. W. Norton, 1988.

Herbst, Jurgen. *And Sadly Teach: Teacher Education and Professionalism in American Culture.* Madison: University of Wisconsin Press, 1989.

Herrick, Robert. *Chimes.* New York: Macmillan, 1925.

————. *The Gospel of Freedom.* New York: Macmillan Co., 1898.

————. *The Web of Life.* New York: Macmillan Co., 1900.

Higginson, Thomas Wentworth. "The Founder of Wellesley College." *Woman's Journal* 12 (October 15, 1881).

Hinman, Marjorie B., and Bernard Osborn. *Historical Essays of Windsor, Township and Village.* Windsor, N. Y.: Broome County, 1976.

Hocking, William Ernest. "George Herbert Palmer." In the *Dictionary of American Biography* 7:180–83.

Horowitz, Helen Lefkowitz. *Alma Mater: Design and Experience in the Women's Colleges from Their Nineteenth Century Beginnings to the 1930s.* New York: Alfred Knopf, 1984.

————. *Campus Life: Undergraduate Cultures from the End of the Eighteenth Century to the Present.* Chicago: University of Chicago Press, 1987.

————. *Culture and the City: Cultural Philanthropy in Chicago From the 1880s to 1917.* Lexington: University Press of Kentucky, 1976.

Howe, Florence. *Myths of Coeducation: Selected Essays, 1964–1983.* Bloomington: University of Indiana Press, 1984.

Howe, Julia Ward. *Sex and Education: A Reply to Clarke.* Cambridge, Mass.: Roberts Bros., 1874.

Howells, Dorothy Elia. *A Century to Celebrate.* Cambridge, Mass.: Radcliffe College, 1978.

Hughes, Judith M. "Yet Another New Woman?" *Psychohistory Review* 17 (Fall 1988): 65–83.

Hummer, Patricia M. *The Decade of Elusive Promise: Proper Women in the United States, 1920–1930.* Ann Arbor, Mich.: UMI Research Press, 1979.

James, Edward T., and Janet James, eds. *Notable American Women, 1607–1950.* 3 vols. Cambridge, Mass.: Harvard University Press, 1971.

James, Henry. *Daisy Miller.* London: Martin Secker, 1915.

James, Henry Thomas. *Charles W. Eliot: President of Harvard.* 2 Vols. Boston: Houghton Mifflin Co., 1930.

Jenkins, William D. "Housewifery and Motherhood: The Question of Role Change in the Progressive Era." In *Woman's Being, Woman's Place: Female Identity and Vocation in American History,* ed. Mary Kelley. Boston: G. K. Hall, 1979.

Kammen, Michael. *Selvedges and Biases: The Fabric of History in American Culture.* Ithaca: Cornell University Press, 1987.

Katz, Esther and Anita Rapone, eds. *Women's Experience in America: An Historical Anthology.* New Brunswick, N.J.: Transaction Books, 1980.

Katz, Michael B. *Reconstructing American Education.* Cambridge: Harvard University Press, 1987.

Kelley, Mary, ed. *Woman's Being, Woman's Place: Female Identity and Vocation in American History.* Boston: G. K. Hall, 1979.

Keohane, Robert E. "Mary Sheldon Barnes." In *Notable American Women, 1607–1950,* ed. Edward T. James and Janet James, 1:92–93. Cambridge, Mass.: Harvard University Press, 1971.

Kerber, Linda. "Separate Spheres, Female Worlds, Woman's Place: The Rhetoric of Women's History." *Journal of American History* 75 (June 1988): 9–39.

Kerns, Kathryn M. "'Farmer's Daughters': Women at Alfred Academy and University Before the Civil War." *History of Higher Education Annual* 6 (1986): 11–28.

Kingsley, Florence Morse. *The Life of Henry Fowle Durant: Founder of Wellesley College.* New York: Century Co., 1924.

Krug, Edward. *The Shaping of the American High School, 1880–1920.* New York: Harper and Row, 1964.

Lageman, Ellen Condliffe. *A Generation of Women: Education in the Lives of Progressive Reformers.* Cambridge: Harvard University Press, 1979.

Larson, Magali Sarfatti. *The Rise of Professionalism: A Sociological Analysis.* Berkeley: University of California Press, 1977.

Lasser, Carol, ed. *Educating Men and Women Together: Coeducation in a Changing World.* Urbana: University of Illinois Press, 1987.

Ludmere, Kenneth. *Learning to Heal: The Development of American Medical Education.* New York: Basic Books, 1985.

Lystra, Karen. *Searching the Heart: Women, Men, and Romantic Love in Nineteenth Century America.* New York: Oxford University Press, 1989.

Mann, Arthur. *Yankee Reformers in the Urban Age: Social Reform in Boston, 1880–1890.* Cambridge, Mass.: Belknap Press, 1954.

Marks, Patricia. *Bicycles, Bangs, and Bloomers: The New Woman in the Popular Press.* Lexington: University Press of Kentucky, 1990.

McCarthy, Kathleen D. *Noblesse Oblige: Charity and Cultural Philanthropy in Chicago, 1849–1929.* Chicago: University of Chicago Press, 1982.

McClellan, Edward, and William J. Reese. *The Social History of American Education.* Urbana: University of Illinois Press, 1988.

McGuigan, Dorothy Gies. *A Dangerous Experiment: One Hundred Years of Women at the University of Michigan.* Ann Arbor: University of Michigan Center for Continuing Education of Women, 1970.

Meyer, Annie Nathan. *Barnard Beginnings.* Boston: Houghton Mifflin Co., 1935.

———. *It's Been Fun: An Autobiography.* New York: Henry Schuman, 1951.

Miller, Alice Duer, and Susan Myers. *Barnard College: The First Fifty Years.* New York: Columbia University Press, 1939.

Mitchell, John Pearce. *Stanford University, 1916–1948.* Stanford: Board of Trustees, 1958.

Mitchell, Lucy Sprague. *Two Lives: The Story of Wesley Clair Mitchell and Myself.* New York: Simon and Schuster, 1953.

Moldow, Gloria. *Women Doctors in Gilded Age Washington: Race, Gender, and Professionalization.* Urbana: University of Illinois Press, 1987.

Morantz-Sanchez, Regina Markell. *Sympathy and Science: Women Physicians in American Medicine.* New York: Oxford University Press, 1985.

Morris, George Perry. "Alice Freeman Palmer." *American Monthly Review of Reviews* (February 1903): 167–71.

Mueller, Margarethe. *Carla Wenckebach: Pioneer.* Boston: Merrymount Press, 1908.

Muncy, Robyn. *Creating a Female Dominion in American Reform, 1890–1935.* New York: Oxford University Press, 1991.

Newcomer, Mabel. *A Century of Higher Education for Women.* New York: Harper Bros., 1959.

Olin, Helen M. *The Women of a State University.* New York: G. P. Putnam and Sons, 1909.

Palmer, Alice Freeman. *A Marriage Cycle.* Boston: Houghton Mifflin Co., 1915.

———. *Why Go to College.* New York: Thomas Y. Crowell and Co., 1897.

———, and George Herbert Palmer. *The Teacher: Essays and Addresses on Education.* Boston: Houghton Mifflin Co., 1908.

Palmer, George Herbert. *The Life of Alice Freeman Palmer.* Boston: Houghton Mifflin Co., 1908.

———. *The Autobiography of a Philosopher.* Boston: Houghton Mifflin Co., 1930.

———. *A Service in Memory of Alice Freeman Palmer.* Boston: Houghton Mifflin Co., 1903.

Palmieri, Patricia Ann. "Here Was Fellowship: A Social Portrait of Academic Women At Wellesley College, 1880–1920." *History of Education Quarterly* 23 (Summer 1983).

———. "In Adamless Eden: A Social Portrait of the Academic Community at Wellesley College, 1875–1920." Ph.D. Diss., Harvard University, 1981.

———. "Patterns of Achievement of Single Academic Women at Wellesley College." *Frontiers* 5 (Spring 1985).

Patai, Daphne, ed. *Looking Backward, 1988–1888: Essays on Edward Bellamy.* Amherst: University of Massachusetts Press, 1988.

Peckham, Howard H. *The Making of the University of Michigan.* Ann Arbor: University of Michigan Press, 1967.

Personal Narratives Group, eds. *Interpreting Women's Lives: Feminist Theory and Personal Narratives.* Bloomington: University of Indiana Press, 1989.

Polacheck, Hilda Satt. *I Came a Stranger: The Story of a Hull House Girl.* Edited by Dena Polacheck Epstein. Urbana: University of Illinois Press, 1989.

Quilligan, Maureen. "Rewriting History: The Difference of Feminist Biography." *Yale Review* 77 (March 1988): 259–86.

Rendall, Jane, ed. *Equal or Different: Women's Politics, 1800–1914*. Oxford: Basil Blackwell, 1987.

Rosenberg, Rosalind. *Beyond Separate Spheres: Intellectual Roots of Modern Feminism*. New Haven: Yale University Press, 1982.

————. "The Academic Prism: The New View of American Women." In *Women of America: A History*, edited by Carol Ruth Berkin and Mary Beth Norton. Boston: Houghton Mifflin Co., 1979.

Rossiter, Margaret. *Women Scientists in America*. Baltimore: Johns Hopkins University Press, 1982.

Rota, Tiziana F. "Between 'True Women' and 'New Women': Mount Holyoke Students, 1837–1908." Ph.D. Diss., University of Massachusetts, 1983.

Rothman, Ellen K. *Hands and Hearts: A History of Courtship in America*. New York: Basic Books, 1984.

Rothstein, William G. *American Physicians in the Nineteenth Century*. Baltimore: Johns Hopkins University Press, 1972.

————. *American Medical Schools and the Practice of Medicine*. New York: Oxford University Press, 1987.

Rousmaniere, John P. "Cultural Hybrid in the Slums: The College Woman and the Settlement House, 1889–1894." *American Quarterly* 22 (Spring 1970): 45–66.

Rucker, Darnell. *The Chicago Pragmatists*. Minneapolis: University of Minnesota Press, 1969.

Ruegamer, Lena. "Chicago Women Reformers, 1863–1893: The Development of an Elite Network." Paper presented at the Conference on Female Spheres, New Harmony, Indiana, October 1981.

Rury, John L. "Vocationalism For Home and Work: Women's Education in the United States, 1880–1930." In *The Social History of American Education*. ed. Bernard McClellan and William J. Reese. Urbana: University of Illinois Press, 1988.

Ryan, W. Carson. *Studies in Early Graduate Education*. New York: Arno Press, 1971.

Sahli, Nancy. "Smashing: Women's Relationships Before the Fall." Chrysalis 8 (1979): 17–27.

Schiebinger, Londa. *The Mind Has No Sex: Women in the Origins of Modern Science*. Cambridge: Harvard University Press, 1989.

Schuyler, Montgomery. "Architecture of American Colleges: Three Women's Colleges, Vassar, Wellesley, and Smith." *Architectural Record* 31 (1912): 512–37.

Schwager, Sally. "Educating Women in America." *Signs* 12 (Winter 1987): 333–72.

————. "Harvard Women." Ph.D. Diss., Harvard School of Education, 1982.

Schwarz, Judith. "Yellow Clover: Katharine Lee Bates and Katharine Coman." *Frontiers* 4 (1979).

Scott, Anne Firor. "The Ever-Widening Circle: The Diffusion of Feminist Values from the Troy Seminary 1822–1872." *History of Education Quarterly* 19 (Spring 1979): 3–25.

————. *Natural Allies: Women's Associations in American History.* Urbana: University of Illinois Press, 1992.

————. "What, Then, Is This New Woman?" *Journal of American History* 65 (December 1978): 679–703.

————, and Andrew M. Scott. *One Half the People: The Fight For Woman Suffrage.* Philadelphia: Lippincott, 1975.

Scudder, Vida. *On Journey.* New York: Dutton, 1937.

————. *A Listener in Babel.* Boston: Houghton Mifflin Co., 1903.

Seller, Maxine Schwartz. "A History of Women's Education in the United States: Thomas Woody's Classic Sixty Years Later." *History of Education Quarterly* 29 (Spring 1989): 95–107.

Shaw, Wilfred B., ed. *The University of Michigan: An Encyclopedic Survey.* Ann Arbor: University of Michigan, 1941–58. 4 vols.

Showalter, Elaine. *Sexual Anarchy: Gender and Culture at the Fin de Siècle.* New York: Viking Press, 1990.

Sicherman, Barbara. "Colleges and Careers: Historical Perspectives on the Life and Work Patterns of Women College Graduates." Manuscript, 1987.

————. *Alice Hamilton: A Life in Letters.* Cambridge: Harvard University Press, 1984.

Simeone, Angela. *Academic Women: Working Toward Equality.* New York: Burgin and Garvey, 1987.

Sklar, Kathryn Kish. *Catharine Beecher: A Study in Domesticity.* New Haven: Yale University Press, 1973.

Smith, H. P. *A History of Broome County, New York.* Syracuse: D. Mason and Co., 1885.

Smith-Rosenberg, Carroll. *Disorderly Conduct: Visions of Gender in Victorian America.* New York: Oxford University Press, 1985.

————. "The Female World of Love and Ritual: Relations Between Women in Nineteenth Century America." *Signs* 1 (Autumn 1975): 1–30.

————. "The New Woman and the New History." *Feminist Studies* 3 (1975): 185–98.

Sochen, June. *The New Woman: Feminism in Greenwich Village, 1910–1920.* New York: Quadrangle Books, 1972.

Solomon, Barbara Miller. *In the Company of Educated Women: A History of Women and Higher Education in America.* New Haven: Yale University Press, 1985.

Storr, Richard J. *Harper's University: The Beginnings.* Chicago: University of Chicago Press, 1966.

Talbot, Marion. "The Challenge of a Retrospect." *University Record* [Chicago] 87 (April 1925).

————. *The Education of Women.* Chicago: University of Chicago Press, 1910.

————. *More than Lore: The Reminiscences of Marion Talbot.* Chicago: University of Chicago Press, 1936.

————, and Lois Kimball Mathews Rosenberry. *The History of the American Association of University Women.* New York: Houghton Mifflin Co., 1931.

Thomas, Mary Martha. "The New Woman in Alabama, 1890–1920." *Alabama Review* 43 (July 1990): 163–80.

Thwing, Charles F. *The College Woman.* New York: Baker and Taylor, 1894.

Treichler, Paula A., Cheris Kramarae, and Beth Stafford, eds. *For Alma Mater: Theory and Practice in Feminist Scholarship.* Urbana: University of Illinois Press, 1985.

Ueda, Reed. *Avenue to Adulthood: The Origins of the High School and Social Mobility in an American Suburb.* New York: Cambridge University Press, 1987.

Vellis, Kenneth A. "Prosperity's Child: Some Thoughts on the Flapper." In *Women's Experience in America,* eds. Esther Katz and Anita Rapone. New Brunswick, N.J.: Transaction Books, 1980.

Verbrugge, Martha H. *Able-Bodied Womanhood: Personal Health and Social Change in Nineteenth Century Boston.* New York: Oxford University Press, 1988.

Vesey, Laurence R. *The Emergence of the American University.* Chicago: University of Chicago Press, 1965.

Vicinus, Martha. *Independent Women: Work and Community For Single Women, 1850–1920.* Chicago: University of Chicago Press, 1985.

Wade, Louise C. *Graham Taylor: Pioneer for Social Justice, 1851–1930.* Chicago: University of Chicago Press, 1964.

Wallace, Elizabeth. *The Unending Journey.* Minneapolis: University of Minnesota Press, 1952.

Ware, Susan. *Partner and I: Molly Dewson, Feminism, and New Deal Politics.* New Haven: Yale University Press, 1987.

Welch, Lynne B. *Women in Higher Education.* New York: Praeger Publishers, 1990.

Wells, Anna Mary. *Miss Marks and Miss Woolley.* Boston: Houghton Mifflin Co., 1978.

Wendell, Barrett. "The Relations of Radcliffe College with Harvard." *Harvard Monthly* 29 (October 1899): 1–9.

Wheeler, Emma F. "Households of Women." *Critic* 15 (August 24, 1889).

White, Marian Churchill. *A History of Barnard College.* New York: Columbia University Press, 1954.

Willis, Annie Isabel. "A Noted Woman Educator." *Education* 10 (April 1890): 469–72.

Wilson, Elizabeth. *Fifty Years of Association Work Among Young Women, 1866–1916.* New York: New York Young Women's Christian Association, 1916.

Woody, Thomas. *A History of Women's Education in the United States.* 2 vols. New York: Science Press, 1929.

Yates, JoAnne. *Control through Communication: The Rise of System in American Management.* Baltimore: Johns Hopkins University Press, 1989.

Index

Hearst, Phoebe, 241
Heath, Lena, 124
Herrick, Robert, x, 249, 252, 269, 270, 276, 278, 281
Higher education of women, 33–37; English colleges, 35; in Germany, 35; in the United States, 120
Hill, Junius, W., 132
Hodgkins, Louise, 124, 130
Holmes, Oliver Wendell, 180
Home Missionary Association, 208
Horowitz, Helen Lefkowitz, 45–46, 61 (n.58)
Horsford, Eben, ix, 95–96, 116, 128, 129, 132–34, 142, 155, 167, 201, 207, 208, 253, 279
Horsford, Lillian, 166, 167, 168
Horton, Mary, 99
Hostetter, Abram, 76
Hotel Beatrice, 235, 240
Houghton, Sarah, 167
Howard, Ada, 99, 107, 116, 117, 118
Hull House, 236

Illinois Woman's Alliance, 236
International Conference on Education, 144
International Institute for Girls, 208
Irvine, Julia, 253, 271, 272

James, Henry, 2, 3
James, William, 230, 280
Johns Hopkins University, 224, 237, 273–74
Jordan, David Starr, 214, 223
Judson, Henry Pratt, 227, 232, 249, 251, 256

Kingsley, Florence, 99
Kirk, Edward N., 98
Kittridge, George Lyman, 250
Knapp, William I., 224
Knox, James, 15
Knox College, 99

Lake Geneva Seminary, 67–68
Laughlin, Agatha, 282
Laughlin, Lawrence, x, 249, 250, 252, 256, 281
Lexington, Massachusetts, 103
Liliuokani (Queen of Hawaii), 140–41
Lord, Frances, 99, 129, 130, 271
Lovell, Ellen Louise, 260 (n.8)
Lovett, Robert Morss, 249–50, 251
Lyon, Mary, 29, 90

Mabie, Hamilton, 114
McCoy, Anna, 132, 144, 273, 293 (n.73)
Marsh, George, 232
Marston, Olive Mary, 2, 8, 66, 83–84, 99, 102
Massachusetts Institute of Technology, 234
Massachusetts State Board of Education, 1, 208, 214–16, 273
Meyer, Annie Nathan, 275
Microscopical Society, 123
Mitchell, Lucy Sprague, 10, 159, 172, 192, 207, 282, 287–89
Monroe, Harriet, 242
Moody, Dwight, 167, 271
Morgan, Anne, 271
Morrill Act, 34
Mosher, Eliza, 2, 46, 57, 128, 207, 254
Mount Holyoke College, 8, 34, 37, 88–89, 90, 114
Munserberg, Hugo, 280

Nelson, Jenny, 99
Networking, 58, 83–84
New England Hospital for Women, 276
Newnham College, 144
New Woman, viii, 2–5, 289
New York Belting Company, 117
Norumbega cottage, 134

Oberlin College, 8, 34, 72
Otego, New York, 52, 66